"A loving account of the two faces of Chile. A necessary reading, for those interested in social processes from the view of a 'foreigner,' who adopted the country as her own. "   **Juani Funez Gonzalez**
School of Social Sciences
U. of California, Irvine, CA

"Eva Krutein's personal experiences provide a compelling and fascinating foundation from which to view Chilean culture in the broad sense. The impact of providing humanized images of people, many of whom later became victims, prevents them from ever being reduced to statistics. The author's dedicated humanism shines through, but the ideological dichotomies and political divisions are also humanized and made immediate in their expression by friends, who were also divided, even within families. The reader is carried along and shares the emotions of the author as the story unfolds, unveiling the tragic savagery of **machismo** and of oppressive poverty, of the class conflict it engendered, and of the consequences. "
Roger Dittman
California State University, Fullerton, CA
National Coordinator, Federation of Scholars & Scientists

"The author's abundant love for people provides the source of her political understanding. "   **Cecelia Pollock**
Chair, Latin Affairs Committee
Concerned Citizens for Peace, Laguna Hills, CA

"A truly riveting story of suspense, drama and courage. "   **Bea Foster**
President & Executive Director
California Peace Academy

PARADISE FOUND,

AND LOST

Odyssey in Chile

Eva Krutein

copyright © 1994 by Eva Krutein

Printed in the United States of America
First Printing, 1994
ISBN: 0-938513-16-8
Library of Congress Catalog Number: 94-70696

AMADOR PUBLISHERS
P. O. Box 12335
Albuquerque, NM 87195 USA

For Manfred,

who took me through
the wonders of the world

Publisher's Preface

Every independent publishing company must seek its special niche, we are told. Ours is "stories." But all our stories do more than entertain — they refresh and nurture, they liberate, they reveal truth. The fiction that we publish is "true," in this deeper metaphorical sense.

The stories that Eva Krutein shares with us, which we are glad to share with the world, are also true in the more literal sense. These things really happened, to her and Manfred, and their children and all the people she tells about. We are impressed with the way readers, and even critics, respond: "This reads like a novel!"

In EVA'S WAR we went through the end of World War II, seeing it from a perspective that was new to most of us. It is a rip-roaring adventure story, with serious philosophical implications. It does more than entertain — it challenges us to rethink attitudes and values we've been assuming were fixed.

Now in PARADISE FOUND, AND LOST we go to an exotic, faraway country. Yes, we remember hearing about Chile in the news, and some of the news was a frightful horror story. Eva introduces us to real people. We encounter poverty, racism and injustice, as experienced by people we have learned to care about. We see political involvement in social change, from a new perspective.

The oppression of women comes up constantly in both books. I recall a Latin teacher in high school many decades ago, showing us how Roman authors were impressed, not to say puzzled, by the way "the Germanic tribes" consistently honored and respected their women. *Machismo* is not a universal given, for which we can all be thankful.

Amador Publishers is very proud to present this sequel to EVA'S WAR. Eva's life has been quite remarkable, to say the least, and her ability and willingness to share it with us are gifts we value highly.

Harry Willson

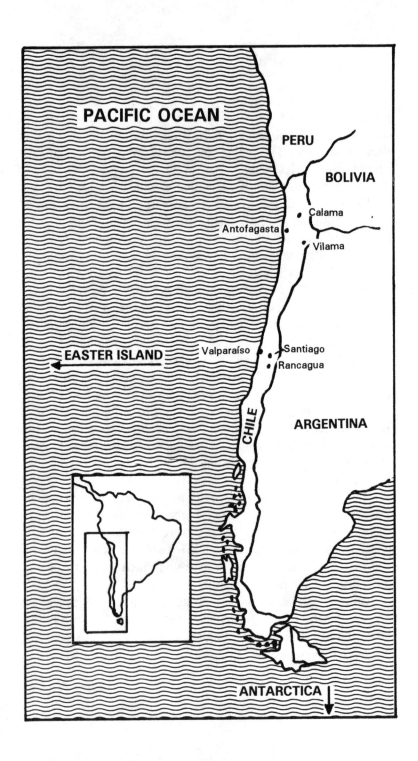

CONTENTS

BOOK ONE

BOOK TWO

BOOK ONE

1. FIRST STEPS

Santiago, Chile, 1951

I fell in love with our adopted country, Chile, on the very first day. Manfred, I and our three daughters viewed Santiago from Santa Lucía hill which jutted skyward above the sprawling capital. At the city's edge, the snow-capped Andes lifted their stately peaks as if to protect the country — and us — from the rest of the world. The war-torn Europe we had known lay across the Atlantic. I felt only gratefulness and commitment to the nation that showed generosity and tolerance to immigrants, now and in past centuries. We climbed down the hill, amused by the numerous intertwined lovers on the park's benches. Suddenly we heard a woman cry out in anguish and despair. At the street level, we stood in shock. A young, black-haired man in faded clothes was beating a visibly pregnant woman, who clutched a baby in her arms. He slapped her face, pulled her ears and shook her shoulders. The baby fell to the ground and began to cry.

I took a step toward her — only to be held back by my husband's hand. "The guy is drunk. Stay here!"

In vain I tried to break away from his grip. A woman a victim of man's brutality — I had to help this mother!

Manfred still had a strong grip on my shoulder; moreover I felt my children clinging to my body. No one else seemed to be around.

The battered mother picked up her crying baby from the ground, cradling, soothing it while she herself sobbed, black hair disheveled, tears running down her brown cheeks.

The man's dark face distorted with anger. He yanked a bottle from his worn-out jacket, uncorked it and drank it in one gulp

1

as though to put an end to his fury. Putting the bottle away, he grabbed the woman's hand and dragged her and the toddler away.

I stood there, bewildered, mechanically stroking my three girls' hair. "Is that -- Chile?" I asked in shock.

"We can't judge the whole nation from this scene," Manfred said. "Let's not have this spoil our first day here. Remember the fantastic view we had from the hill. Chile is as beautiful as I always imagined."

The image of the snow-crowned Andes brushed the miserable scene aside. "Oh yes, the mountains are splendid."

"Let's go see what the people downtown look like." He picked up 15-month-old Renate.

I followed him down the mildly sloping street, hand in hand with my four-year-old Little Bear, who had inherited my former nickname, and seven-year-old Lilo, who had updated her name from Lili.

"We'll see much more beauty in the future," Manfred said.

Within minutes we were immersed in the bustle of Chile's capital. Large crowds swarmed on Estado Street's sidewalks.

"As if half of Santiago's two million people are on the road," Manfred said.

We sauntered along, wide-eyed with curiosity, lost in amazement at the new throng, so different from the Germans.

At five-foot-three, I was used to looking up at most people in Germany, but here I found myself at eye level with the majority. Half the men, in dark business suits, a white handkerchief protruding from their breast pocket, with black ties and gray felt hats, were as short as I. Dark-eyed and deeply tanned, they strolled along without haste. They seemed ready to flirt anytime. Yet after a quick glance at me and then Manfred they averted their eyes; with a man at my side, I seemed protected from their flirtation.

"They all look alike to me," I complained.

"It will take a while until we can tell them apart."

"There are so many people on the sidewalks, but we never

bump into anyone."

"Latins are more agile than Germans." He put Renate down. "Look at the women!"

Jealousy overcame me as I stared at my well-coiffed and artfully made-up counterparts. They wore high heels and dangling earrings at high noon. In the latest style, waists wasp-like, breasts swelling, they proceeded by slow, gliding steps, swinging their hips as if to flirt with every man they passed. A constant cooing filled the air. How badly must I, unobtrusively dressed and without make-up and glittering accessories, compare with these sirens! How long would Manfred, blond, blue-eyed and handsome as a movie star, be able to withstand this enticement?

Two of the well-groomed, dark-haired ladies stopped in front of our children.

"*¡Qué lindo!* How cute!" one said, extending the "eee" in exaggeration. She bent down, gently stroked Renate's brown hair and then kissed the child whose brown eyes widened in astonishment.

The lady looked at our two oldest girls. "*Mire, qué rubia,* look how blond!" she said, gently touching their hair. Then the two went on their way.

"Chileans are nice!" Lilo said. The children may not have understood the lady's words, but they sensed her admiration.

Touched by the woman's warmth and proud of my daughters' public appeal, I pulled the family to the shop windows, which displayed chic clothes for every age. In front, shoe shiners polished men's leather shoes as if their salvation depended on the brilliance. From the open door of a restaurant smells of fried oil penetrated my nose.

"I'm hungry," Little Bear announced, although she'd just had a huge breakfast.

"We'll eat later," I said.

Street vendors bawled out to the passers-by the quality of their safety pins, earrings and rosaries, spread out on cloth. "*¡Mire, Señora! ¡Mire, Señorita! Muy barato,* very cheap..."

An organ grinder's waltz supplied the background to the hustle — "one, two-three, one two-three." I smiled. How the spectacle resembled the street scenes in Italian operas! And I was in the middle of this stage!

Rising above the tumult, the private Fords, Chevies and Opels honked their way through the dense traffic, chasing their rivals aside. Passengers hung from the doors of buses as though saving their lives from the street chaos. Horse-drawn and hand-pushed carts, loaded with boxes and bags, threaded their way through the frenetic traffic. The turmoil was breath-taking and — exhilarating.

I stepped back from the street traffic and almost stumbled over a woman who sat on the sidewalk. A scarf covered her hair. From her lined face her dark eyes shot flashes toward me. A gypsy! More opera!

"*¡Su mano!* Your hand!" she demanded, stretching her own out to me. With reluctance I extended mine to her.

She didn't look at my palm, just kept holding my hand as if to remain in physical contact. In contrast to her loud demand for my hand, she now whispered to me. "*Chile está perdido. Chile está perdido. ¡Váyase! ¡Váyase!*"

An icy hand pressed my heart together. I understood her message. "Chile is doomed. Get out of here!" I straightened up and took a deep breath. What nonsense! We'd left Germany because we thought Europe was doomed and we were going to rescue Western culture and modern technology and enrich Chile with them. The gypsy was a fraud! She probably hated foreigners. Or she just liked to scare people.

Lilo's hand pulled at mine. "Mommy, come on!"

Manfred and the two other girls were ahead of us and I hurried to join them with Lilo.

Weaving through the crowds we turned to Agustinas Street and its high-rise buildings. Inside one we took the elevator to the office of our travel agent, Vera Hermann, whose immigration skills had brought us from Hamburg, West Germany to Chile, our adopted country.

When Vera saw us enter, she took her cigarette from her mouth and snuffed it out in the ashtray. Briefly touching her gray, braided hair, pinned-up in a bun, she rose from her typewriter. "You must be the Kruteins! Well, how are my newcomers doing?"

Shaking hands with her, I looked around the cramped space, sparsely furnished with a typewriter desk, a small round table and three chairs for visitors. On a wall hung a huge, colorful map of South America with the vertical shoe-string of Chile on its west coast.

Vera asked us to sit down and offered us cigarettes. Manfred took one and lit it. She handed colorful travel pamphlets to the children.

The wife-beating scene on my mind, I told Vera what we had witnessed.

"You plunged right into one of Latin America's great problems," she said. "Women's lack of rights."

"Does it mean wife-beating is taken for granted here — in 1951?"

"Many women have a hard time."

"I've also seen the ladies downtown dance attendance on the men."

"You've discovered Chile's class differences. A poor woman's humiliation and middle-class women's seductiveness."

"What class will we belong to?"

"You'll be *gringos* — inexperienced foreigners. You are thirty and a pianist. Young and talented. Make the most of it!" She picked up a newspaper from the desk. "Here's something for you: the CONDOR, our German-language newspaper." She pointed to a column. "In the Purísima church there's a German mass."

"I thought we should seek out Spanish-speaking people to get used to the language," Manfred said.

"You'll learn Spanish from your children, as soon as they go to school," she said. "But I urge you to go to the Purísima and make contacts with German-speaking people. You'll need them

for quite a while. There are too many new things here.
Fortunately, Chileans adore everything German. You'll find
many open arms."

She turned to Lilo who had discovered the big Chile map on
the wall. "This is your new homeland, Lilo." She drew out the
vowels: Leeloh. "Chile is a long rope almost from the equator
all the way down to the South Pole. It's the most beautiful
country in the world. And here in the southern hemisphere we
have winter when the Germans have summer."

She reached for a jar and put candies in the children's hands
while Manfred and I attended to the immigration papers.

"We have to go to the bank," Manfred said at last. "To
exchange our deutschmark for Chilean pesos."

"The Banco de Chile is right across the street."

We thanked her and said goodbye.

Vera turned to me. "If you need help, I'm always here."

"What a nice lady," Lilo said in the elevator which took us
down to the street level. I agreed with her. Vera — the first
anchor in the uncertainty of our new life!

Back on the street people mostly ignored the signal lights, so
we too threaded our way through the dense traffic to the other
side. While Manfred took the children into the bank I stayed
outside to suck in the exoticism of the street scene.

Blinded by the glaring sun, I pulled dark glasses from my
handbag and accidentally knocked my coin purse onto the
sidewalk. Immediately, one of the well-dressed passers-by
stooped to pick it up and handed it over to me. I stared at the
dark-eyed, smiling gentleman. *"Muchas gracias,"* I said.

He said, *"De nada,* it's nothing," with his charming smile.
He raised his hat gallantly, uncovering pitch-black hair, which
gleamed with perfumed oil, and bowed slightly. "I can hear your
accent. You are European, aren't you?"

"Alemana, German," I said.

"¡Maravilloso! Wonderful!" he exclaimed as if he just had
won a big prize. "May I invite you for a café expresso,
señorita?"

I should have stopped this street conversation long ago, but a feeling of warmth and being welcome, bestowed on me even by a stranger, held me back.

At this moment, Manfred and the children emerged from the bank and joined me. I'd never forget the disappointed look on the cavalier's swarthy face as he realized I was already engaged. He raised his hat, bowed slightly and left.

"Who was that?" Manfred asked.

I told him.

"You see, men here are ready anytime." A roguish smile appeared on his face. "The teller flirted with me, too."

Jealousy swept through me when I saw the delight in his face as he looked at the passing women, who swayed their hips in serpent-like motion as if only flirting and love mattered in the world.

Was this the Land of Beauty and Promise? Or a world of sorrow and cruelty?

2. REAL FRIENDS

On a sunny afternoon, two weeks after our arrival in Santiago, the five of us took the packed bus along the wide Irarrázaval Boulevard to the house of Ricardo and Gloria Toro, whom we had met after Sunday mass. Smart Vera, to send us to meet German-speaking people who could watch our first steps in Chile!

The Toros told us they were looking for people of their own age with whom they could practice their German and we soon realized we'd come in handy for each other.

Now, excited and grateful, we were on our way to them, squeezed into an ancient bus.

"I'm suffocating!" cried Lilo, who with Manfred and me stood impacted among passengers behind the driver. Heat and stench from the exhaust gases were unbearable. Fortunately, two friendly ladies had placed Little Bear and Renate on their laps.

"Look at the rearview mirror," I told Lilo. "There's the Virgin Mary glued on, complete with a bleeding heart."

"There's also a bunch of saints," Manfred said, "the Pope, a soccer team and dangling rosary beads."

The driver, sweating in his wrinkled, formerly white shirt, juggled his archaic vehicle through the seething traffic. "He uses his horn instead of his brakes," Manfred said. "Besides selling tickets and returning change."

I shook my head. "He must have nerves of steel." Busses came from the side toward us like cannonballs, but neither vehicle reduced speed nor rammed the other.

At last the bus dropped us at an intersection. I gazed down the tree-lined street to the Toros. It appeared calm, even sleepy, on one side the great wall of the Andes and on the other white

8

adobe bungalows, shielded by walls or fences and wrought-iron gates — charmed ghost houses with no living humans visible. But as we passed by the first house, a German shepherd behind its fence jumped up, snarling and barking so fiercely that Renate began to cry. Since each house was guarded by such an attack dog raging against us, we began to walk in the middle of the street, holding tight to the children's hands to reassure them.

Graffiti in huge black letters shouted from walls: AFUERA LOS YANKIS. "Yankees go home?" I asked. "Why? And where are the Americans? I haven't seen any."

Another block farther on the walls bore NERUDA and ALLENDE. "What does Neruda mean? And Allende?" I asked.

"Let's ask Ricardo," Manfred said.

We arrived at the Toros' modern white one-story house, surrounded by poplar trees and weeping willows, splashed by red bougainvillea. And no attack dog in sight.

At three o'clock sharp we rang the bell at the iron gate. A petite maid arrived, complete with black dress and white apron.

"¿Los Toros?" I asked.

"Sí, Señora." She took the chain off the gate, admitted us and locked up behind us.

The small living room was shrouded in darkness because of the closed blinds which provided coolness and comfort. Neither Dr. Toro nor his wife appeared. We sat on leather armchairs, surveying one wall, which was completely covered by a huge bookcase, and another by prints of world-known paintings.

After a while the maid brought cold papaya juice for all of us. I seized the opportunity to practice my Spanish with her. "What's your name?"

"Filomena."

"Where is Señora Toro?" Filomena patiently repeated the answer, and finally I figured out that our hostess had taken three of her children to get haircuts. "When will she be back?"

"No sé, señora, I don't know."

"What time is it now?" I asked.

"I can't read the time, señora."

My spirits went down. "They forgot the invitation," I said to Manfred, who was absorbed in a newspaper.

As if to make up for our disappointment, Filomena gestured vividly, urging our children and me to come with her to the backyard. Two black-haired, dark-eyed and deeply tanned girls fought for the swing, spraying each other with the garden hose. I led my three hesitant girls to them, who immediately were included in their activities.

"How many children do the Toros have?" I asked.

"Cinco." Filomena showed five fingers.

At about four o'clock, the tiny lady of the house, dressed in a blue silk blouse and narrow skirt, appeared with two boys, whose short black hair gleamed with hair-oil. "Oh, you are already here?" she asked, her brown eyes big with surprise. She hugged me and I enjoyed her warmth flooding over me.

"Didn't you say three o'clock?" I asked.

"Maybe. But time by the clock is not strictly observed here. You have to get used to it." She looked strong and energetic. Tight brown curls sat decoratively above her slightly bulging forehead. Her fair skin showed her European origin. Born and raised in Germany, she already was so Chileanized that she didn't think of showing up on time. And, as she'd told us after church, she was on the brink of forgetting her native language. "Didn't you bring your children along?" she asked.

"They're playing with yours in the backyard."

"Good." She sent the boys out too and sat down on the sofa.

I still was confused. "When is one supposed to show up when invited at a certain time?"

"Hardly any 'time' is certain here. For the afternoon at about five. For dinner at nine-thirty or ten."

A moment later we heard light, fast steps approaching. The door opened and our host, Dr. Ricardo Toro, rushed in — with flashing eyes and a radiant smile. As short as myself, in black trousers and an open-collared white shirt without a tie, he resembled more a tennis coach than a physician. He looked very Spanish with his shiny black hair and a deep tan. Most impressive were his fiery, dark, almond-shaped eyes which seemed never to rest. He greeted us in fluent, Spanish-accented German, "Hallo, my favorite Germans," and with Chilean warmth he kissed me on both cheeks and hugged Manfred. I felt at home. Ricardo offered a cigarette to Manfred — not to me. I already knew: women weren't expected to smoke. Fine with me, I was a non-smoker. Ricardo lit a pipe and snuggled into his armchair in obvious contentment.

"Don't you have a dog in the garden?" I asked. "In every front yard we passed there was a dog, barking at us ferociously."

"We don't need one," Ricardo said. "There are no valuables in this house. It's enough that doors and windows are locked." I wondered where he was hiding his expensive things, which he as a physician certainly owned. As if searching for an answer I looked at Gloria and saw two vertical lines growing between her brows. There seemed to be a disparity of views between them and I wondered what caused it.

"Tell us why you left Germany," Gloria said.

Manfred took a long drag from his cigarette. "It may sound unbelievable, but I gave up my own shipyard with 350 workers."

Ricardo sat up from his comfortable position. "You owned a shipyard? You are thirty-four, aren't you?" Manfred nodded. "Pretty young for a shipyard director. But why did you give it up? Because of bad business?"

Manfred shook his head. "Business was going very well." He looked out the window as if picturing Hamburg. "There were many reasons. First: The potential Soviet invasion of Western Europe. At the end of the war Eva and Lilo barely escaped from the Russians and their marauding and their mass rapes. Her parents did not make it. This time we were going to leave before the storm."

"I've heard about those atrocities," Ricardo said. "So Eva and Lilo fled the Russians and ran from East to West Germany?"

"Yes. In 1945. Reason number two: I had too many responsibilities at the shipyard. And those never-ending negotiations with the German government! At the same time we were controlled by the British government."

"The British probably feared the German competition in the ship-building world, right?"

Manfred nodded. "Very much so. And that all gave me ulcers. My doctor said I had to change my lifestyle to avoid a sure heart attack. Finally, a disagreement with my partner cleared it up. I saw the need to expand the shipyard, but he didn't. So to keep my mental and physical health I took a radical cut and went far away."

I sighed. In a few sentences Manfred had summarized his years of excruciating struggle. I wondered how much any outsider could really understand. What we hadn't said was that we were proud to bring Germany's modern technology and its music and literature to Chile.

Ricardo showed his understanding. "Obviously you didn't flee from poverty. Our immigration visas are very expensive."

"Twice the travel costs," Manfred said.

"In a way I feel sorry that Germany lost you," Ricardo said pensively. "I studied in Berlin for five years and I know the Germans well. They are immensely industrious."

Manfred shrugged. "Germany was too strait-laced for us. And we yearn to experience something new."

"And why Chile, this last corner of the world?"

"Because it seems to be the only country that likes Germans."

"That's because the Germans cleared the land in the south a hundred years ago," Ricardo said. "They intermarried with us and lightened up the race."

In a flash I understood that by having his family with a German he intended to improve the Chilean race.

He turned to me. "I understand you are a pianist and an opera coach. You'll find more open doors than you need." He faced Manfred. "You should be able to relax here, Manfredo," Ricardo continued. "Chile is a live-and-let-live society."

"Good to hear." Manfred crossed his legs. "As an engineer I thought about going to the United States. But we had no sponsors and couldn't get a visa, so we decided on Chile."

"Immigration laws can change," Ricardo said.

Manfred chuckled. "Then Chile is only a detour to the United States."

"I hope not," Gloria said emphatically.

"I don't take his wisecrack about the detour seriously," I said. "His goal is Chile as much as mine."

The maid brought in coffee and cake. "Let's sit down at the table," Gloria said. "Filomena will feed the children at the garden table."

We moved to the dining room and sat at a long table big enough for a large family. I sat close to Ricardo and realized that his skin wasn't sun-tanned but had an olive color. His dark eyes were vivid and intelligent, it seemed nothing could be hidden from them. There was no sign of flirting with me and I liked him even more because of that.

Gloria passed the vanilla-smelling cake to me. "It's *torta de mil hojas,* cake of a thousand leaves."

"It's super sweet. Delicious." I took a second bite. "By the way, we saw graffiti on the walls. AFUERA LOS YANKIS. Do they hate Americans here?"

Ricardo's eyes flashed with rage. "Americans exploit our country. They get an enormous profit from the copper mines in the north and take it out of the country!"

It was my first exposure to an international economic problem. "Who owns the mines?"

"The Americans!"

"Can't they take what they own?"

Gloria shot an angry look at him. "That's what I believe too."

With his voice raised Ricardo said, "What Chile needs is to get its mines back from the exploiters!"

The tension in the room was almost tactile. I hastened to dispel it. "Other graffiti said NERUDA. What's that?"

With pride in his voice Ricardo replied, "Pablo Neruda is our greatest poet."

"Why do they smear his name on the walls?"

He avoided my eyes. "It's political."

"And what is ALLENDE?" Manfred asked.

A mocking smile appeared on Gloria's face. "Ricardo's colleague."

"A medical doctor?" Manfred asked, astonished. "How did his name get on the walls?"

Ricardo took a sip from his coffee. "He's a physician. He was the minister of health, and now he's a politician."

Gloria's eyebrows knit. An icy silence spread out. She got up. "Finally it's cooling off." She opened the shutters to let the last rays of sun filter through the orange trees into the room. "You'll like our climate. It's September, spring begins and the trees will be in bloom. You've probably never seen such splendor."

"I can hardly wait," I said. "We come from an area where it rained 375 days a year."

Ricardo grinned. "You're exaggerating like a Chilean. You'll fit right in here."

Gloria bent forward to me. "How long do you folks want to stay in the boarding-house?"

"Until our furniture arrives from Germany."

"That can take months," Ricardo said. "You should rent a house."

"With no furniture?"

"We can lend you some," he said. "I really mean it."

Gloria sided with him. "Lilo should go to school as soon as possible. We'd like to help."

After an intensive discussion about house, furniture and school I glanced outside at the beginning of twilight. "Time to go home. Apparently the children are having a good time. We didn't hear them at all."

Gloria got up. "I'll call your girls."

They appeared with glowing cheeks and radiant eyes. "It was so much fun!" Lilo said.

"We got lots of cake!" Little Bear shouted.

Gloria bent down to Little Bear and stroked her blond hair. "You look exactly like your Papi." She picked up Renate. "And

you already look a bit Chilean. Soon you'll be a señorita."
We thanked the Toros for their hospitality and friendship and
left our new friends' home.

Out on the street we stood spellbound. Around us, the
mountains, the street, the trees and the bungalows appeared as
if they were covered with purple chiffon veils, gently waving
through the air. "Oh my God," I whispered. "This is incredible."
"A sunset miracle," Manfred said, lost in wonder. He and the
children were covered with the eerie hue. We strode through the
violet wonder as it gradually darkened. The cool evening wind
rose to greet us and we pulled our sweaters over our heads. We
became aware of the snarling dogs, outdoing each other in fury.
We watched out for a bus and soon were lucky to get one where
passengers weren't hanging from the doors. We squeezed
ourselves in and even got two seats. We took Little Bear and
Renate on our laps while Lilo stood next to us.

Suddenly a black-haired boy of about ten jumped from the
dark street onto the moving bus. The newcomer, instead of
paying the driver, began to sing with a clear voice. To my
delight, he was right on pitch.

"Mi corazón, mi amor," he sang — My heart, my love.
While he sang, his quick eyes scanned the audience for a
movement toward a wallet. Never stopping his song, he collected
one coin after the other.

I gave Lilo a peso coin which she held out. He took it from
her and — wonder of wonder — he interrupted his serenade.
Saying, *"¡Gracias, rubia!* Thanks, blondie," he kissed her on her
cheek and rushed to the door.

"Early practice makes a master," Manfred said.
"Of kissing or of music?" I asked.
"This is a land of lovers." In a flash the thought entered my
mind that we some day might have Chilean son-in-laws.

Darkness had fallen over the city as we left the bus. Before
a butcher's store a woman crouched on the cement floor.
Holding a small bundled baby in one arm, she stretched out a
hand toward the passers-by with an imploring glance. When I

opened my handbag for a coin or two, a policeman with a snarling German shepherd appeared from nowhere, shouting and directing his dog against her.

I clutched Manfred's arm. "God, the dog will get her!" The beast reached the woman and pulled at her faded skirt. She cried out aloud, jumped and, tightly clutching her baby, managed to tear the skirt out of the dog's snout. Under the policeman's curses she fled from the scene. The dog spat out the shred.

"Why was the lady sitting on the street?" Lilo asked, who had never seen a beggar.

"She's poor and needed money for her baby," I said.

"Why then was the policeman chasing her away?"

The shouting of two men distracted us from an answer. A shabbily dressed youngster hurled insults at a well-dressed middle-aged man. A third one knocked down the youth. Within minutes a whole bunch of rowdies hit and kicked whoever was reachable, pushing us bystanders backwards.

"¡Carabineros! Police!" people yelled. Manfred and I grabbed the children and ran away with the crowd.

A shock made me turn back to Manfred. "Where's Renate?"

"Didn't you pull her along?" Manfred asked.

"No, you did!" I shouted in despair. Yelling and whistling, the mob dispersed into different directions.

Manfred's eyes flashed. "Back to the bus station!"

Oh God, would I ever see my little girl again? As we arrived at the bus stop only a few people were waiting for transportation. Under a street light on a bench sat a portly matron, holding Renate on her lap, rocking her gently and saying soothing words to her. I dashed forward. "Renate! My treasure!"

She looked up and smiled. I took her from the woman's lap, hugged and kissed her. The matron's face radiated. "¡Mamita volvió! Mommie's back," she said to Renate, got up, waved at her, turned and went her way as if her job was now completed. All I could do was send up a prayer for the friendly protector.

3. WOMEN'S TORMENT

On the first night at our newly-rented bungalow on the outskirts of Santiago I lay in one bed together with Little Bear at my side and Renate across our feet. With wide-open eyes I listened to Manfred snoring in the other bed, hoping he wouldn't wake Lilo at his side. Yet despite the crowdedness of our beds my children were warm and safe.

How blessed we were to live under Chile's sun instead of Hamburg's eternal rain! At every moment to gaze in reverence at the gigantic, snow-covered Andes, at whose feet we lived now! Surely, this was as close to paradise as we could ever come.

Suddenly I felt my bed sway. A hard jolt struck. Another, even stronger shake followed. "Earthquake!" Manfred shouted in the dark. "Run to the backyard!"

I jumped out of bed, snatched up Renate and dragged Little Bear. She lost my hand. "Mami! Mami!" she cried. I turned and grabbed her hand. We ran through the door into the garden.

"Sit down," Manfred said, his arm around Lilo's shoulder. "Nothing can fall on us here. It can't last very long."

Trembling with fear and cold, we crouched on the grass. The only light was a full moon. An aftershock jolted us. Nowhere to turn, we huddled together for mutual support. Gradually, the swaying of the ground began to lessen. The children still whimpered and I put my arms around whomever I could reach and tried to calm them, although I was trembling. My adored Chile didn't even have firm ground!

Finally the terrible shaking of the earth stopped. "Nowhere in the world is safe," I moaned. "That was like an air raid. The same mortal terror."

"There's a difference. In the war we learned to hate the people who launched the bombs. But an earthquake isn't human. It has no malice. You can't hate nature."

"I was as scared as during the bombings."

"We have to get used to it. This probably won't be the last earthquake." As if on call, the earth hit again. A loud crash reverberated from the direction of the house. The children screamed, clinging to us like climbers to rocks. I trembled like a leaf on an aspen. I turned around. Our free-standing kitchen had collapsed. We sat in shock.

After a while I realized that the earth had been still for a long time. The full moon shone undisturbed, stars glowed and snow shimmered on the mountains.

Manfred got up first. We approached our caved-in kitchen, which Manfred called a "fox hole," because it had no window. Now it looked like a ruin in a ghost town. The corrugated iron roof had fallen onto the sink, but the walls stood intact. The two-burner gas stove still stood on top of the three suitcases we used as a base. Leftover potato soup had splashed out of a pot down to the floor. A cat I had never seen before lapped up the spilled soup.

"No big deal," Manfred said. "Let the cat clean up and let's go to bed. I'll worry about the roof tomorrow."

Back in my crowded bed, it dawned on me that my enthusiasm for Chile had been tested severely. Would I ever learn to feel at home where the ground was unstable? I shuddered.

In spite of a strong wind, Gloria Toro came to see how we had survived last night's disaster. I already had a friend who was concerned and ready to help! She'd brought two of her children along, their age matching Little Bear's and Renate's: Pancholo, four, and Ana María, two. The four ran in the garden to play ball. Lilo was at school.

I told Gloria about the collapse of the kitchen roof and showed her how well Manfred had fixed it this morning. "You're lucky to have a handy man around," she said in her high-pitched voice. "Tremors like last night happen quite often. Real *terremotos* are rare."

"I hope I'll get used to it." I went to the kitchen for some apple juice. Then we sat down on the sofa.

"I would have called you earlier, but we don't have a telephone," I said.

"Neither do we."

"A doctor without a telephone?"

"Doctor or not — there are only a few lines in the suburbs. Only bakeries get them. Everybody goes out to make calls. That's Chile."

"Are you happy here?" I hoped for a song of praise.

Her brows knit and two vertical lines between them appeared. "The question is too general. I don't like to be a woman here, that's for sure. We have no rights."

I was all ears. "Can you give me an example?"

"Men can do what they want. They own everything and don't have to ask their wives for consent. In contrast, I can't even sell a chair without Ricardo's permission. And until recently, I couldn't even vote!"

Her emotion touched me. Was she just complaining about the Chilean culture or did she have a problem with Ricardo? If our friendship developed further she might tell me. "Why is Chile so different?" I asked.

"It goes way back in history. Over four hundred years ago the Spanish brought the concept of radical male domination to this continent, and," — her voice rose a step in pitch — "it has never changed."

"I have the impression that Chilean men are chivalrous, gallant and ready to flirt. They make me feel desired. I never had this feeling in Germany."

With a bitter smile Gloria said, "That's only as long as you aren't married to them."

I refilled our glasses. "How did you and Ricardo meet?"

A touch of smile smoothed out her face. "He attended the university in Berlin, got his M.D. there. My father was one of his professors. I met Ricardo at a university ball. We fell in love with each other, and when I turned 18 we got married. Then we moved to Chile and he got a job with the National Health Insurance."

"You have so many children. You must have enormous patience and strength."

"'Many children' here means ten or fifteen. We only have five so far. Ricardo and I are against any form of birth control because the Church forbids it. We are ready to have many more children."

"If ten to fifteen are the rule, you have quite a way to go."

Emphatically she put her glass down. "Be that as it may, there are many things that compensate for the absence of women's rights. For example, the Chileans' great love for children. The kids are carried, hugged and kissed a lot, and that's why they are so amiable as adults. What mother would object to that?"

I smiled with relief. It felt good to hear Chilean life praised. But it was time to discuss another issue. "Manfred is reading job ads."

"Ricardo could help him with his *cuñas*. Connections."

"But Manfred is an engineer, not a physician."

"That makes no difference. It's all a matter of *cuñas.*"

Skeptically, I shook my head. "There are lots of strange things here." I pointed out the window across the street. "Do you see the vacant lot? Some people live there in that window-less shack with lots of children. The pregnant mother washes clothes by hand under an outdoor faucet and the little children run around naked from the navel down although it's 50 degrees outside."

After a glance at them Gloria turned back to me. "These people are extremely poor and we call them *rotos,* the tattered, because of their ragged clothes. The mother lets the smaller children run around half naked because she can't afford diapers."

I listened to her account of yet another social problem. "The man of the *roto* family usually is an unskilled worker and terribly underpaid. Much of the little money he makes he spends for alcohol. To feed her kids the mother washes other people's clothes."

"My first impression of Chilean women was of elegant, flirting idlers. Now I see another extreme."

"And people like you and me live between the extremes."

"How many are *rotos?*"

"Too many. The tragedy is that the *roto* will always be a *roto*. They'll stay in their class, no matter how hard they try to get out of their misery. They can't get an education. The children have to go out and make money somehow. They're broken from birth."

"As refugees after the war, we all lived in poverty," I said. "But we had a good education and the government made every effort to get us out of the misery."

"Here, the government is made up by the upper class. They keep the poor from going to school to have more power over them."

"So, education is the clue." I felt a deep sympathy for the *rotos*. A pickup truck with the label *"Companía de Electricidad"* stopped in front of the vacant lot across the street.

"What's the electric company doing over there?" I asked.

Gloria glanced across the street. With a bitter smile she said, "Cutting the poor family's access to electricity."

"Why that?"

"The squatters' shacks have no plumbing and no electricity. Can you see the cable from the shack to the power lines on the street? To light their miserable interior they run clandestine cables from the power lines. Once in a while inspectors drive through the streets and destroy the cables. They can't collect fines because the *rotos* have no money."

"And then the poor sit in the dark?"

"Not for long. As soon as the inspector is out of sight, the *rotos* hook up another cable." She glanced at her wrist watch and got up. "I have to go. Tell Manfredo to ask Ricardo to help him get a job."

We collected the children from the backyard. I thanked her for her visit, hugged her, kissed Pancholo and Ana María and accompanied them through the tiny front yard.

The electric company's truck was gone. In the evening I saw the washer woman's husband and one of his sons hooking again a cable to the power lines. I smiled. I would do that too if I had to live in poverty. I'd always be on their side, I told myself.

My support had to be halved, I decided, when on a late Friday afternoon I saw the washer woman's husband coming home, staggering to her as she was rubbing clothes on her washboard. Shouting, he pulled her arm, she resisted, pointing to her wash. He beat her and chased her to their shack. Holding my breath, it dawned on me that he was going to crown his delirium with a sex act that would give satisfaction to him and pain and nausea to her. My heart went out to her. Yet I felt anger and disgust for the man. I remembered Gloria saying that the *rotos* had to stay this way all their lives. What in the world was wrong with Chile?

4. ROAD TO MUSIC

The day Manfred went to meet Ricardo for the job hunt stretched endlessly. Would he find work as an engineer? Because of the lack of shipyards naval architecture was out of the question, but plain engineering might offer a chance. In the afternoon Manfred rushed into the house like a fresh breeze. "I got a job!" He straddled a chair. "As some kind of an engineer." He grinned, recounting the interview. "They talked in rapid Spanish. I hardly understood them. The old Arab's name was Sa'íd. He seemed to be amazed at Ricardo's description of my qualities."

"No wonder!"

"Ricardo told him we were on our way to Sa'íd's competitor to sign my contract. Promptly, Sa'íd offered me a job in one of his factories. He called his son by phone. Young Sa'íd looked as if just escaped from *1001 Nights*. Pitch-black mustache and burning eyes. That young Arab took me in his Mercedes to a factory where they make copper cables, and told me to start work as soon as possible."

I jumped up and kissed him. "Congratulations!"

His smile disappeared. "There's a catch. I'll probably have to do things I know very little of. Insulation of plastic cables and natural rubber. I must order books about that. From Germany and the U.S. By airmail."

I sat down again. "So you'll study quickly what they think you already know."

"Everybody here thinks the Germans can do everything."

"It's good to be in a country that holds us in such high esteem." I got up to go to the kitchen. "By the way, what are the Arabs doing in Chile?"

23

"They dominate the textile industry and the banks."

"Well, good luck with *1001 Nights* I hope there won't be a Scheherazade around!"

Manfred winked at me. "Not at the cable factory."

As luck comes in pairs, the wooden crate with all our furniture and household goods finally arrived from Europe, including my piano, my accordion and the new sound recorder. Before the customs officer released the crate, we had to pay him "import taxes" of the value of two months' rent. Yet our own things helped us feel at home.

Every day Manfred rode the bus to the copper cable factory, one hour each way. "I'm learning about class differences by means of transportation. The upper class, including the Arabs, drive Mercedes-Benz's. The middle class commutes by bus. And the lower class, the workers, arrive by foot. They live in shacks near the factory."

"We take buses, so we're middle class now. Only one step down from being shipyard owner."

He grinned. "And before that we were refugees, therefore lowest class. Kind of dancing from one class to the other. See how ridiculous the classification is?"

Before he sat down to study, I asked, "What exactly do you do at the factory?"

He pulled a cigarette from a packet on his desk and lit it. "I supervise the fabrication of electrical cables and their insulation. I have sixty-five workers under me."

"Are they good?"

"They are skillful and cooperative, but hard work is shunned. There's no work plan, everybody just muddles along." He sat down. "The factory is like a museum — outmoded machinery and machine tools. Sometimes I think I'm transported back to the last century."

"Does anybody appreciate your knowledge and ideas?"

"I'm certainly expected to improve the working process. But it will take time."

"Do you mind the slow pace?"

"Not at all. It gives me time to practice my Spanish. Everyone likes to talk."

"Should be easy to make friends."

"I'm already good friends with the manager, Enrique Palma. He's a good engineer. Sophisticated and friendly. He was talking about inviting us for dinner."

He soon did, asking us to have dinner with him and his wife at 9:30 at the elegant Hotel Carrera. I could hardly wait to meet new people. "Why so late?"

"Nobody eats dinner before ten here."

At the hotel lobby a tall, robust and dark-complexioned gentleman greeted us: Enrique Palma. With his elegant mustache he looked like the typical handsome Latin. He smelled of English cologne. Best of all, his huge, brown eyes radiated warmth. He kissed my right cheek and introduced us to his wife Marlena, a diminutive brunette who took her long cigarette holder out of her mouth to place a kiss on my cheek. The first woman in Chile I saw smoking!

Transported back to former times, we walked over the thick red-plush carpet into the dining hall. The elaborate crystal chandelier spread its light over the white-clothed tables and the elegant china settings. Soundlessly the waiters scurried along, carrying aromatic dishes to the guests. My stomach rumbled.

When we approached our reserved table, an immaculately dressed, plain-looking, middle-aged man with a receding hairline rose from his seat to greet us: Enrique's brother, Roberto. They did not resemble each other at all.

Over *pisco sour*, the Chilean vodka with a slice of lemon, and hors d'oeuvres we chatted animatedly and I realized how slowly Enrique spoke to us and how well he enunciated his words, giving us a chance to follow him. I felt my heart go out to him in quick, warm sentiment.

As we were beginning our meal with a creamy asparagus soup, Enrique asked me the standard question, *"¿Le gusta Chile, Señora Eva?* How do you like Chile?"

"¡Bastante! Es maravilloso!"

"Your Spanish is perfect," he said with charming Latin exaggeration. "Did you get used to our greeting customs?" As I nodded he smiled. "I asked because sometimes it's hard to understand another culture. Last year I was in New York on business, and an American invited me to his home. When I met the hostess I hugged and kissed her as we do it in Chile. Her husband got angry as if I had raped her."

We laughed.

The waiter brought a delicious smelling beef roast with rice and "Chilean salad", tomato slices with an equal amount of onion rings. We had local wine, white and dry.

Even at this late hour many guests had brought their young children along. Some were dozing with their heads on the table, others, crying of tiredness, were consoled with pacifiers or cradled by the proud fathers, who were showing off their products.

I turned to Marlena. "Do you have any children?"

She put a fresh cigarette into her holder and lit it on the table's candle. "When I married Enrique after my divorce I insisted on being free for my work as a lawyer. No kids."

"I thought divorces didn't exist in Chile."

Marlena sneered. "To mate for life like owls?" After a long puff on her cigarette she added, "I was involved in getting women's voting rights. We still have to fight for them. Some people cling to the old idea that education would overheat women's brains." She was cool, detached and unsmiling and I didn't like her.

The waiter served the dessert — *chirimoya,* a fruit unknown to me, soft, mildly sweet and with heavenly aroma.

Suddenly I felt the floor move. The crystal chandelier began to sway and so did the wine in our glasses. Terrified I looked at Enrique. Yet he didn't even interrupt his talk. The other guests too continued to eat without a sign of surprise. The temblor subsided.

"Does this happen often?" Manfred asked.

Roberto nodded his head. "Every month or so. But it's

seldom dangerous." He finished his *chirimoya*. "If anything is dangerous, it's the growing political unrest."

"You mean among the workers?"

"Yes. They are stirred up. Soon they may go on strike."

"In Brazil they just had a small revolution," Manfred said. Marlena even produced a smile. "That kind of thing doesn't happen in Chile."

"That's right," Enrique said. "Let me tell you about the difference between us and others. A French, a German and a Chilean general boasted about the courage and the obedience of their soldiers. To demonstrate, the French general called one of his soldiers, gave him a pistol and said, 'Kill yourself!' The soldier shot himself to death. The German general called one of his soldiers and demanded the same. The soldier also shot himself to death. Then the Chilean general called one of his men, handed him the pistol and said, 'Kill yourself!' For a moment the soldier looked at his general, then patted him on his shoulder and said, '¿*Otra vez borracho, Capitán?* Drunk again, general?' He put the pistol back on the table and walked away."

We smiled, and I felt a strong love for the Chileans for scoffing at military rigidity. That was all we wanted from this country: tranquility and security from violence.

Shortly before midnight Roberto said, "Let's have our after-dinner drinks at the bar."

"It's almost midnight," I said.

"The night has just begun," Roberto replied. "There's a piano at the bar. I'd like to hear you play." I thought he was joking. We moved over to the dimly-lit bar where all the guests sat on small tables, drinking and listening to a jazz-piano player.

A delicious drink, *Cuba libre,* Free Cuba — coke with rum, got me in such a good mood that I felt little resistance to play on the grand piano when the hired pianist went out on a break.

Roberto led me to the instrument, I sat down and began to play a potpourri of classical and pop music. People began to call out songs they wanted to hear. I played them and each time they applauded wildly. I had arrived where I wanted to be in Chile, giving music to the people.

When a bald-headed gentleman asked for "Silent Night, Holy Night," I played it for him, although it was almost Easter.

After two more songs I looked up into Roberto's rapturous face. *"¡Bravo! ¡Fantástico!"* he said. "You are truly a successor to Claudio Arrau!"

"Thank you," I said and smiled at his exaggeration, comparing me to the world-famous Chilean pianist. "You should play on the radio!"

"What radio?"

"My station."

"Where is it?"

"Downtown."

"Could I have your address?"

He seemed a bit surprised, but then took out a pen and wrote on a paper napkin. "Bandera 156."

I couldn't believe my luck. "When?"

"Mañana."

"What time?"

"In the afternoon."

"Exactly what time?"

"Well, four o'clock."

Elated, I got up to join the general departure. We all said goodbye to each other with the usual excess of hugs and kisses which made me feel even more exalted. I knew I was a Latin at heart.

At home in bed, I could hardly sleep. I wondered if Roberto meant it to be a one-time stand or regular piano playing at his station. That early in the game my music was in demand! Well, tomorrow I'd be ready.

Next day, fresh and cheerful and in my best dress, I reached the modern highrise building on Bandera Street, downtown, and took the elevator up to Roberto's office. I checked my wristwatch: it showed exactly four o'clock. A chic young receptionist asked me what I wanted.

"See Don Roberto."

"Sorry," she said kindly. "He isn't in yet."

"Can I wait?"

"Certainly, *señora*. Please take a seat." At 4:15 I asked the receptionist when she thought he would arrive. "Maybe late. May I ask what he wants to see you about?"

"To play on his radio station."

Astonishment flowed over her pretty face. "He doesn't have a radio station. He is an import dealer." I tried to explain to her his proposal of last night. She shook her head. "He probably was joking."

Joking! I felt the blood rush to my face. How could she put me down like that? I was ready to shout at her, strangle her, until I grasped that the culprit was not the polite receptionist but her damned boss.

Fuming with rage I ran back to the street with its bustling crowd that, untouched by my frustration, went its way -- the women swaying their hips, the men devouring them with their eyes. Were they all liars like Roberto? Who could explain this all to me? Ricardo's olive-skinned face rose before me. He and only he could explain to me this outrageous betrayal. I went to see him immediately.

Ricardo was home, peacefully smoking his pipe and flipping through a magazine.

I sat down and told him about Roberto's hoax. "That scoundrel! I could wring his neck!"

Ricardo had listened to me attentively. Now he smiled. "He didn't mean any harm. It was just his little vanity."

"You call that 'a little vanity?' Telling me lies?"

He put the magazine away. "That is an example of Latin exaggeration. And you are a naive *gringa*, who can't tell a party gag from serious business."

"You mean I can never believe what anyone tells me?"

"There's a fine line you have to learn to detect. Our first desire is to make the moment pleasant. We create a warm atmosphere for the person so he or she will feel good."

"What about the consequences?"

"The consequences lie in the future. But who cares about the future? We live for the moment. Roberto provided for you a hilarious evening, and you were naive enough to take his fantasies seriously."

"I've had it for the day!"

But Ricardo hadn't finished yet. "One more thing. Don't make the *gringo* mistake of translating *'mañana'* into 'tomorrow.' It really means 'sometime' or even 'never.'"

"Jesus Christ! I have a lot to learn!" Later, riding home on the bus, Ricardo's words were still whirling around in my head. What kind of ethics was this, making promises without sincerity? To speak the truth at all times was the first thing I had learned as a child. Was this not taught in this country? How could I raise my children here?

A week later Roberto's hoax had somewhat paled into insignificance, as I sat down to count our money and realized there wasn't much left. The shock hit me as if I'd been taken by the throat. The shipyard director's income was gone. When I recovered I understood I needed to make money on my own. After all I was a pianist and an opera coach — someone would need me, I just had to find that person!

As if I were sleep walking, I went to the plaza where all kinds of buses stopped. I took the first oncoming bus, no matter which way it went, and gave the vehicle a mysterious power to decide my fate.

It took me downtown to the street where Vera Hermann's travel bureau was. So that's where fate wanted me to go! Not exactly a glamorous concert hall, but you never knew. Keep the flame of hope burning!

I found Vera before her typewriter, gray-haired, a bit old-fashioned, but radiating with warmth and compassion. "How are you, my dear?"

I hesitated. How could I suddenly fall upon her with my money trouble? Yet I finally sat down next to her. "We ran out of money. Do you have any idea how to make it quickly?"

She seemed to contemplate something. "A friend of mine is

the manager of a new sport club. She's looking for a man and a woman as cloak-room attendants."

Dammit! Instead of a shabby bus I should have given a limousine that magical power! Even if I could bring myself to do such work it would never be acceptable to Manfred.

Vera gave me an encouraging glance. "A good chance to meet people. Many newcomers start out that way."

I recalled the after-war time, when I learned to loot and haggle. We had no food then; now we had no money. "Sounds good," I heard myself say. "When would it be?"

"Every Saturday and Sunday. Nine to six. 500 pesos a day and you'll get sandwiches."

"Yes!" I said quickly, not to let the opportunity go. To persuade Manfred was my next job. At night I told him about our new job offer.

He flared up. "Are you out of your mind? Do you think we have to humble ourselves that much?"

"We hardly know anybody here. The Toros will understand. And I don't care what people think anyway."

"But I do! What if anybody knows I once owned a shipyard and now I'm a cloak-room attendant?" His face was red and pinched with anger.

"Then tell me where else we should get the money to pay our utility bills? They are due on Monday and you get your paycheck only in three weeks."

He frowned. "Where has all our money gone?"

"To the customs for our furniture, clothes for the children, who knows what?" Silence.

Then, without looking at me, he said in a joyless, but decisive voice, "All right, let's do it then. It won't be forever. And in the future we'll have a budget."

And so on Saturday morning Manfred, Little Bear and I marched from the bus's terminal station the two miles through rolling hills to our new work place in the basement of the club-house. Lilo, now eight, alert and very fond of her youngest sister, had to stay at home to take care of 18-month-old Renate.

She played with her, fed her, changed diapers and put her to bed. She often wrote us letters during our absence about her joys and frustrations of the day.

"Will we ever be able to repay her for what she's doing for us?" I asked Manfred.

"No. All we can do is thank her and love her." And we did just that.

Meanwhile, Little Bear had a good time, running around with the club members' children who all were watched by a life guard at the pool.

Soon I was genuinely excited about the new job. The simple task of hanging up bathers' clothes below the deck was quickly accomplished. What we didn't expect was the club members' interest in us. Every single one chatted with us for a while before ascending to the pool level. This way I learned about their needs and soon sold them safety pins, pain killers and candies and rented out my own swimsuit and bathing cap to forgetful bathers. When a club member suggested to put a box with a sign "tips" on the counter, I even provided that. Business was blooming. This was fun!

I even discovered a beauty secret. From our first day on in Chile I had envied the women for their slim waists. When one Sunday afternoon a pretty middle-aged bather peeped out from her cubicle, asking me for help, I rushed to her.

"Please hook up my corset," she said. "I can't do it myself. I must have gained weight."

Open-mouthed I stared at this remnant of a straightjacket, pulled the ends together until I feared her ribs would crack and tugged the hooks to the eyes.

"Thanks, dear," she whispered, quickly looking at my waist. "German women don't wear corsets, do they?"

"We prefer to breathe."

All told, I had a good time at the swim club. How Manfred adjusted to the menial job I didn't get to hear. He seldom shared his deepest thoughts and emotions. He refused to talk about it and just shrugged it off.

In March, summer and swimming season came to an end. On our last weekend I walked out with the lady whom I had straight-jacketed and who had always left good tips. A bald-headed gentleman approached us. "My husband," the lady said.

The gentleman seemed startled to see me. "I think I've seen you. You are a pianist." I nodded. "I heard you play in the bar of the Hotel Carrera once. You played 'Silent Night' for me." I smiled politely. "I've never forgotten your playing. A friend of mine is in dire need of a good pianist. Would you care to give me your address?"

I calmly ripped off a corner of my sandwich wrap, scribbled my address down and passed it to him. Consciously I enjoyed the "pleasant moment" and later discarded the memory, for I had learned my lesson about promises.

I was all the more surprised when I received a note from the bald-headed gentleman, asking me to see a certain concert agent, Ernesto Hall, downtown, who might need me. I showed the note to Manfred.

"Go see him," he said. "You never know."

Reluctantly I decided to meet Hall the next day. At nine in the morning, the city slept. Even the palace of the Moneda, Chile's White House, appeared lifeless. I knew the president of Chile lived and worked there, but at this early hour only two lonely soldiers stood in front of the palace, both half-asleep in the cool air. The echo of my footsteps bounced off the palace wall as I passed them. The drowsy soldiers opened their eyes and gaped.

Hall's office, two blocks away, was already open. A receptionist ushered me in. Upon my entry a pencil-thin man of about forty with a head way too big for his body rose from his desk. His large brown eyes gave him a steadily surprised look. He shook my hand gently. "Take a seat, please." His voice was light, almost feminine. After questions about my musical background as an opera coach he asked, "Do you know the operetta 'The Gypsy Baron'?"

"Yes, of course."

"I'm going to finance a production of the 'Gypsy Baron,' in German," he said, his huge eyes fixing on me. "I'm now in the process of hiring singers. One will come from Europe. I urgently need an opera coach. Are you available?"

"Yes."

"You'd be responsible for the musical part of all the soloists. Your honorarium would be 15,000 pesos." Ten times as much as Manfred's monthly salary!

"Besides coaching, what else would I have to do?"

"Play at the rehearsals. We'll start them in May. Opening night is September 20."

So, for 15,000 pesos I'd have to work four months. What luck! Without hesitation, I signed the contract. On my way home I almost danced. I had found my niche, I would pour music over Santiago until the end of my days!

Back home again, reality returned and our new budget came to mind. Hall would pay me after opening night — six months from now, but I needed money much sooner.

Pulling on my streak of luck, I walked into our small neighborhood church and met the pastor, Father Luís, a huge man whose girth made his cassock bulge like a wine barrel. I told him I'd played the organ in Germany for years and now needed work. It didn't take long to secure from him a job as an organist for all the weddings. My music was needed!

Through Ricardo's *cuñas* I also landed a job as a rehearsal accompanist at the Ballet National de Chile, part-time for one morning and one night a week. The pay was good and I would make music day and night!

Yet I still had a problem. "What do I do with Little Bear and Renate when I play at the Ballet in the morning?"

"Why don't you ask our friendly neighbor Elsa to take care of the children?" Manfred replied. "All Chileans love children."

I asked Elsa, a petite mother of twins across the street, and she agreed.

At night I thanked Manfred for his idea. "You're a genius!"

"No, just an engineer."

"'Engineer' comes from 'genius.' I always knew you were one."

He was already in bed. "Always trying to please Euterpe, the Muse of music," he said, pulling me to him. I was in his arms and in a fiery fusion he made me forget we were on earth.

5. LITTLE BEAR

Still happy with my success, I accepted Little Bear's request for an ice cream this morning. It would be just the two of us. Renate was playing at Elsa's house. I took five pesos for two cones, and Little Bear and I walked down to the ice cream parlor. It was one of those miraculous Chilean fall days, clear, warm, balmy, with just enough breeze to carry the fragrance of eucalyptus and roses that bloomed for the second time this season. I felt grateful for walking in so much beauty.

Since I was too slow for impatient Little Bear, she ran ahead, around the corner and out of my view. When I arrived at the parlor, she was nowhere to be found. Next door the barber in his white coat sat in front of his shop, waiting for customers. Once he recognized me he jumped from his chair. "Are you looking for your daughter?"

"Sí."

"Está atropellada," he said.

I had no idea what *atropellada* meant. I thought it had something to do with the ice cream parlor and looked again into the empty store. Little Bear wasn't there. Fear gripped me. What happened? What in the world did *atropellada* mean?

More people gathered and spoke to me with agitation. An older woman seemed to realize that I, the *gringa* didn't understand the situation. Using words sparingly, she showed me with gestures how Little Bear had crossed the street and was run over by a truck.

As soon as I understood, an icy hand seized my heart. I choked. Oh my God, was she dead? Please help me, God, let her be alive! I struggled to quell my panic.

"Señora," the woman said, "go to the police! The truck has

36

stopped at the police station." Gasping with fright, I ran down
the block to the police station. Two men followed me. Inside,
they both explained the situation to the officer on duty.

"The truck driver stopped here," the officer told me and in
my desperate alertness I understood him. "Your little girl was
unconscious and bleeding and we sent them to the Hospital El
Salvador. Take a cab and you'll be there in 15 minutes."

"A cab? I have only five pesos with me."

The officer raised his hand. "Don't worry about that, *señora.*
I'll get you a cab." He pulled me out into the street and blew a
loud whistle. Within seconds a cab stopped in front of us. I got
in and heard the officer give instructions to the burly driver.

In the torture of that 15-minute ride to the hospital I was torn
between fear and remorse. In what condition would I find her?
Why had I let her run ahead? What kind of a mother was I?

In front of the Hospital El Salvador I told the driver I had
only five pesos. *"Señora,* your child was run over. I won't
charge you any money. I'll help you find her." Tears came to
my eyes.

We asked our way through the ether-smelling hospital until
we finally found the emergency room and entered. I held my
breath — there was Little Bear, lying on a surgery table, her
clothes stripped down to her waist. Her forehead and shoulder
still bled although I could see both had been sutured. She was
sobbing. "Mami!!" she cried.

I rushed to the operation table and took her hand in mine.
"Little Bear, Mami's here. Everything will be all right now."
Amid tears, she smiled for a moment.

A nurse lightly touched her wounds and said to me, "You can
take her home. Give her an aspirin."

"In spite of the anesthesia?" I asked.

"The doctor sutured her without any," she said matter-of-
factly. "We don't give children narcotics."

They had tortured her! I wanted to strangle the nurse, the
doctor and everyone around here. I searched for the harshest
words but found none in Spanish. Unable to express myself, I

lifted my crying child in my arms. The nurse gave me gauze to handle the bleeding on the way home.

Ready to carry Little Bear out of the emergency room, I turned around and saw the cab driver stand at the door. "Let me carry her, *señora,*" he said and took her from me. "I'll drive you home." Exhausted, but grateful, I followed him. Seated in the back, I held Little Bear on my lap and soaked up her still oozing wounds with gauze. When we stopped in front of the house I asked the driver to wait a moment, I would be back with money.

He wiggled his index finger in the typical Chilean manner, indicating a denial. "No, *señora,*" he said. "I drove you to help your child. I have eight children myself. And I want you to keep yours." Carefully he took Little Bear from my arms, and carried her into the house. He put her on the bed. "God bless your child," he said and left before I could even thank him.

When Manfred came home that night and heard about the accident, he was out of his mind and hurried to Little Bear's bed. "My poor Little Bear, you missed your ice cream! Don't worry. I'll get you one tomorrow."

"Chocolate ice cream!" she said with emphasis.

"You'll get it!" He turned to me. "What bad timing! I must go out of town for a week and leave you alone with a sick child. I have to fly with my boss to Valdivia tomorrow. He wants my technical advice. And I can't say no."

I pushed away my disappointment. "I can handle it alone, Manfred. When you come back she'll be all right." I saw how torn he was between his responsibilities, but I insisted he go. "We have friends here. The Toros, Vera Hermann, the Palmas, the neighbors...."

"Be sure to get her ice cream whenever she wants it." Manfred left the next day — but not before he brought her a double chocolate-ice-cream cone.

I contacted the nearest physician, Dr. Larraín, an angular, plain-spoken man, who agreed to make daily house calls.

Meanwhile the news about Little Bear's accident spread

throughout the neighborhood. People whom I had never met knocked on the door, offering their help. Coming to see her, they always brought her something: cookies, a pudding, or a cat or dog to pet.

"I heard your husband is away from home," my silver-haired neighbor, Elsa's husband, said to me. "If you need any money, please let me or *Señora* Elsa know. You can come over any time, even at night if you have to."

I had tears in my eyes. This was a lower-middle class neighborhood, and many of these people had little money left after their own daily needs were met. But they showed me, a *gringa,* a camaraderie which was based on their inherent compassion and goodwill. Could I ever have come to a kinder nation?

The Toros, whom I had sent a note, came to visit Little Bear. Gloria was pregnant again and radiant. "You'll be well-served by Dr. Larraín," Ricardo said. "He's a good pediatrician."

"Imagine," I said. "For the surgery they didn't give her any anesthetic! Why not, for heaven's sake?"

"Many physicians think narcotics would hurt the child. Some even think children don't feel pain as much as adults."

"But that's bloody nonsense! I saw how much Little Bear was hurting."

"I agree. But even in the United States doctors usually hesitate to use anesthetics on children. They're afraid it would increase their heart rates and suppress their blood pressure."

"They are all a bunch of torturers!" I cried.

At least Little Bear's pain had finally lessened. Yet quite unexpectedly she became unable to urinate for two days. So I alerted Dr. Larraín. He prescribed medicine, but it didn't help. The same day Father Luís, the well-rounded priest from the church where I played for weddings, came to see Little Bear. "I understand she has trouble going to the bathroom."

"How did you know, Father?"

"When the kids on the street saw me walk toward your house they all told me, 'She can't pee, Father.'" He had brought her lots of assorted *santitos,* small colorful pictures of saints.

When neither medicine nor *santitos* helped, my motherly neighbor Elsa suggested an Indian remedy: strong tea made from parsley roots. I mixed the bitter brew with honey so Little Bear could swallow it. Ten minutes later the result was there, which not only relieved all of us, including the street kids, but also raised my respect for popular wisdom, brought down from the Indians.

From then on Little Bear was on her way to recovery. I was relieved. It came as the rehearsals for the "Gypsy Baron" began.

6. OPERA!

The singers for the "Gypsy Baron" were more than ready. We all received vocal scores and I worked out a rehearsal schedule with the soloists of the minor parts at my home.

Still confused with the reversal of the seasons here, I realized that now, in May, fall was in full swing. The vineyards thrived, wine was plentiful and the grape harvest turned out to be one of the richest. The delicious clusters came in subdued rainbow colors, green, pink, violet and almost black, and all had exotic names and their own delicious fragrance and flavor. We indulged in them every day.

Before the end of a rehearsal week three female singers canceled their coaching lessons for Friday. "We're going to join a rally for the presidential election," blond-tinted Carmen said. "It's the first year in Chilean history that women can vote."

"You've won! Now, who are you going to vote for?"

"Carlos Ibáñez," Carmen said. "He's the only one who can clean up the government."

The eagerness of these women surprised me. So far I'd been under the impression that most Chileans were only indifferent observers of public affairs. Alerted, I tried to broaden my political knowledge, and next morning I asked the milkman for whom he would vote.

"Salvador Allende," he said. "He's the only one who can help us. He's on our side."

"Your side?"

"Of the poor people," he said with pride in his voice. I realized I'd never really seen how the poor lived.

Still musing over this, I climbed into a bus to attend a meeting at Hall's concert agency. Many of the bus's leather-covered seats were empty and others were slit open with a knife and the wooly stuffing torn out — a hate message of the poor to the rich, although rich people never got to see this mute outcry because they rode in their own cars.

I arrived at Santiago's center and hurried to the meeting at Hall's, where he was going to introduce me to the tenor and the soprano, the two leads of the "Gypsy Baron."

When I entered the conference room, skinny Hall and our pale-faced conductor Bello were seated at the table, together with a handsome newcomer, the tenor from Buenos Aires, and — I gasped — Dolores Mannerheim next to him, my dear friend from Hamburg! A moment later we were in each other's arms.

"I hoped to find you somewhere in Chile," she said. "But I heard only this morning that you'll be my coach."

"Oh, I can't believe it's you!" I said, swallowing a few tears.

The three men grinned at our joyful reunion. "Surprise, surprise!" A trace of smile even appeared on Hall's thin lips.

Dolores would sing the role of the young gypsy, we'd rehearse every day, and we could continue our friendship! As we had done so often in Germany two years ago, we went to a coffee shop across the street for a talk. We ordered coffee and then looked at each other. She was as pretty as ever with her long, flowing blond hair that veiled her slim body like a coat. "I still think I'm hallucinating," I said. "Tell me about you, so I can believe it's you."

With both hands she pushed back her long hair and scrutinized me. "You're using much more makeup than in Germany and you wear earrings now."

"I've adjusted to Chile."

"It's very becoming." I felt as if Dolores and I had never been separated, as if we were just picking up where we had left the day before. "Shortly after your departure I filed for divorce from Vadim," she said.

"From your eternally absent husband."

"An opera singer should never marry a film director," she said, pushing back her hair again. "We finally became strangers, and I wanted to be free." She sighed and for a moment closed her eyes as if looking back at that painful time. "That's when I decided to go far away. When I read Hall's ad in an opera magazine that he wanted to contract a soprano for Santiago, I jumped at the occasion. I also remembered that you'd gone to Chile and I had this faint hope of finding you here as well. And I did." Her broad smile told me she had found a refuge, no matter how temporary.

Stage rehearsals began a week later at the two-story Teatro Municipal with its Greek columns resting on Romanesque archways like the Paris Opera. As a coach, I entered the august building with feelings of awe and expectancy. Under the cold work lights we gathered for the daily rehearsals, recreating the world of Hungarian 18th-century aristocrats and gypsies.

"You've got to be my interpreter," Dolores said. "My Spanish is close to zero."

Not only did we rehearse together during the next weeks, but deeply enjoyed our friendship, which helped both of us to bridge the differences between our European and the Chilean culture.

For opening night some of us had received complimentary tickets for our families. I was glad I had two for Manfred and Lilo, since the house was sold out. While the ticket holders flooded in, a commotion began at the entrance, which we all heard even from the stage, and I could see through the spy hole in the curtain.

"What's going on out there?" the tenor asked me.

"I can't figure it out," I said.

A minute later the stage director stormed onto the stage. "What a mess! Someone has sold duplicate tickets! For many seats there are two ticket holders." Through my peephole I saw that chairs were carried into the audience hall. Young visitors sat down on the floor, a few older people left the theater, loudly complaining. Meanwhile the singers were at their places, complete with gypsy rags and appropriate makeup. Everyone was excited.

Everyone except the fat, resolute prompter. She refused to

climb down into her prompter's box, constantly tapping on her vocal score and shouting, *"¡Plata! ¡Plata!"*

"Money! Money!" I translated for Dolores. Everyone was startled. We knew we'd all be paid two days after tonight's performance. "Why does she want to be paid now?" I asked.

"She doesn't trust Hall," the tenor said.

"There he comes."

Hall, his eyes bigger than ever, rushed in, right to the fat prompter. He gave her a pile of peso bills, she counted them and immediately descended into the prompter's box. The "Gypsy Baron" could now begin.

I watched the performance from the wings, always ready to send the soloists with their first lines onto the stage. Everything went well beyond my highest hopes. Hall wouldn't have to think he wasted his money on me. I was happy.

On our way home in the bus, Manfred told me how he had handled the double-ticket situation. "I put Lilo on my lap just like this," he said and pointed to the sleeping child on his lap. "She was wide awake for all three acts."

"You kept peace by giving up your comfort."

He smiled. "I've learned from the Chileans." I told him about the scene with the prompter. "When are you getting paid?" he asked.

"The day after tomorrow."

"I hope the prompter won't be the only one who gets her money."

"Pessimist," I said.

But the next day I felt hypnotically drawn to Hall's office. Very early in the morning, before shops and offices opened, I entered the concert agency. Without knowing what I would do I walked straight into the producer's office.

He stood cleaning his desk, throwing a bunch of papers in the waste basket, others into an open suitcase. When he saw me he looked surprised, even a bit shocked.

"Buenos días," I said. I felt a low-level electrical current surging through my gut as I always felt in emergency situations.

Immediately I slipped into the role of a desperate mother and knew what to say. "I came to ask you for my 15,000 pesos."

He made a helpless gesture. "I'm sorry, I don't have the money here today. Payday is tomorrow."

"But I need it today," I said with tears in my eyes. "It's my last day to pay my electricity bill. If I don't, they'll cut the power."

He raised his shoulders. "I'd like to give you your money, but it will not be here until tomorrow morning."

I frowned and stepped closer to his desk. "My children are crying of hunger and cold. I can't stand that anymore." I looked around the office for a valuable object. On a shelf stood a beautiful antique desk clock, richly adorned with pearls and inlays of ivory and gold. I stepped over and grabbed it. "If you don't give me my money now, I'll take this clock and keep it until you've paid me."

He went pale. "I'll give you a check. The bank will pay you."

"I want cash," I hissed, my hand still on the clock. "Cash or I'll get the police."

The double threat broke his resistance. He went to the open suitcase, rummaged in it and turned around with a package of peso bills in his hand. Without a word he counted out 15,000 pesos in front of me.

I grabbed them, murmured, *"Gracias,"* and fled from his office.

Late the next afternoon, Dolores stormed into my house. "Where were you this morning? He's gone! This damned Hall has fooled us all. He's run away! Escaped to Paraguay with five million pesos!" She threw herself on the sofa. "None of us got our money," she added with anger. "Not only that. Hall was the one who sold the false tickets!"

Spellbound I listened. That scoundrel! My hunch had been right. I told Dolores how I'd outfoxed him.

She stared at me in disbelief. "You got your money? You and the prompter!"

I showed her my shopping bag full of the money I forced from Hall. "That's the booty. Let's split it!"

Without a look she pushed the bag away. "Thanks, but no thanks. Keep your well-earned pesos. I brought enough of my own money to Chile."

"By the way, the less money people make here the more generous they are." I told her about the neighbors' compassionate actions after Little Bear's accident.

At first, Dolores listened carefully. Then she shook her head. "Maybe the poor people are this way. I'd thought Chile was South America's most advanced country. But here I'm experiencing a grand theft on myself. And worse, judging from people's reaction, it's even taken for a sport!"

Somehow I felt I had to defend Chile. "I know there's something wrong with law enforcement in Chile. Probably it can be explained by the Chileans' love of freedom. It's their special charm. They just act as whimsy dictates."

She chuckled. "Like flirting. The men here are the biggest flirts I've ever seen. I can hardly sit in a bus without being 'accidentally' touched. Or walk on the street without being whistled at."

I laughed. "It's springtime! And you are blond and pretty. No wonder, men get crazy." At last she smiled again. "Please take half the money I got from Hall."

"No, really not!" She pushed her long hair back over her shoulders. "I'm not angry with Chile. I'm going to stay here. I'm also looking for an apartment."

Her determination aroused my admiration. With all scheduled performances of the "Gypsy Baron" canceled, Dolores might feel unneeded. I played at church and ballet, but she didn't have any other musical outlet. An idea flashed into my mind. "Dolores, how would you like to sing in a chamber group?"

Astonished she stared at me. "What chamber group?"

"Together with another musician and me."

"Explain!"

"The idea just popped into mind. A small group like this is

missing here in Santiago. We could perform in churches, at the University and so on." The idea quickly took shape in my head. "The third musician should be a flutist. The instrument would blend beautifully with your great voice."

Her face began to glow with radiance. "What a brilliant idea! Do you think you could set this on foot?"

"Why not? Chileans are hungry for good music. And two-thirds of the group are already established. You sing and I play piano or organ. I'll find the third musician within the next days."

Dolores put her arm around my shoulder. "Thank you for giving me hope for the future. I'll help you whenever you need me."

A rosy color crept through the window. I got up, took my friend's hand and pulled her from the sofa to the window. The giant crests of the Andes were visible. The sun sank in the west, flashing its last crimson rays upon majestic peaks, where snow gleamed and sparkled.

"Incredible," Dolores whispered.

"We get this spectacle every night. It repays us a thousandfold for all our troubles."

7. PROMOTIONS

I found the desired flutist sooner than I had assumed. Riding in a bus to downtown, a man sat down next to me. To prevent any possible advances I stared out the window, ignoring him. "Excuse me, *señorita,*" the man said to me. "Aren't you the opera coach from the 'Gypsy Baron'?"

I turned to him. "Yes. How do you know?"

"I saw you at the rehearsals. Have you recovered after the disaster with Hall?"

"I survived. Has it effected you?"

"Not really. I'm part of the National Symphony Orchestra. We replaced the canceled performances of the 'Gypsy Baron' with symphony concerts."

Then I recognized the instrument case on his lap. "Are you a flutist?"

He nodded. "My name is Arturo Castañeda."

As a member of the National Symphony he undoubtedly was good. I asked him right away if he would be interested to play with a newly created chamber group. "Any time. I always wanted to do that, but nobody is willing to organize such a group."

I told him about Dolores, whom he of course knew from the "Gypsy Baron." We discussed the possibilities, exchanged addresses and made an appointment for the next day at my house. I couldn't believe my luck.

Dolores suggested I had used some magic to conjure up the flutist. In any case the three of us were of the same stamp — professionals, hungry for music making. We knew we'd have to start without being paid. We discussed, played and laughed together until we had a program ready for performance. "What

48

do we call our chamber group?" Dolores asked.

"MÚSICA," I suggested. The two agreed it was a good name. "I'll start making contacts now," I announced.

"Wait 'til after the presidential election," Castañeda advised. "It's always a big event in Chile." I made a list of potential clients and waited until the election results were broadcast.

On the day of the election our middle-income neighborhood was euphoric. Small Chilean flags hung between the iron window gratings; neighbors on the street chatted animatedly with each other and there were more drunkards on the sidewalks than ever. The year was 1952 and Carlos Ibáñez had been elected president of Chile, above all because during his campaign he had shown compassion for the underprivileged majority.

"Everything will be better soon," a lame, old neighbor assured me after Ibáñez' victory.

"God had His hand in this," his cross-eyed wife said. "He also took away that sleazy woman in Buenos Aires." I knew she meant Evita Perón, the glamorous wife of Argentine's dictator. Evita had just died of cancer.

The most enthusiastic were the politically active women. "We made him win!" they shouted in parades and in the media. "He'll thank us for it and give us more rights!"

No flags waved from the rich people's homes. The poor people didn't even own flags. And their candidate, Salvador Allende, had lost again. But from the leftist newspapers headlines screamed his prophesy:

"WE'LL MAKE IT NEXT TIME !"

My pious neighbor Elsa across the street also thought he'd win one day. "Then we'll be rich. All of us."

I wished her wealth with my whole heart, because she had developed into my most appreciated neighbor, who was always at hand to help and came over to take care of my girls, whenever the need arose. The Chileans' proverbial love for children showed its best example here. Her loyalty gave me the freedom to approach the potential concert hosts on my list.

To my surprise almost all responded positively and set up

performance dates. "We always wanted something like this," the director of the National Education Institute said. "It took a German to launch such a group. What would Chile be without the Germans?" he joked.

Beyond setting a date for the concert at his institution he volunteered to take charge of advertisement. Within days our names and pictures were in the newspapers and on the radio. Manfred was proud of me.

Coincidentally, on the day of Ibáñez's victory, Manfred's manager, Enrique Palma, left the cable factory for a better job and Manfred took over the technical management. "Good news," Manfred said. "Better work, more money."

"Congratulations!" I produced a bottle of wine, and we celebrated the welcome changes, Manfred's promotion and the new president.

Evaluating Ibáñez, Manfred said, "It's time someone assumes the reins of government. Now we have hopes of getting imported spare parts for machines."

"How's that?"

"Ibáñez' first action will be to borrow new money from the United States. Soon we'll get spare parts from there. Faucets, electrical switches, everything."

"Can't you use those made in Chile?"

"Sure. But they are poorly made because there's no quality control here."

"You should introduce quality control to Chile! You had a strong hand in that in Germany."

"The government supported me then."

"You should look for help here too!" He grinned at my naivety. Yet I was as full of hope for the future as the people around me.

More good news came from the Toros, when Ilona, their oldest daughter, brought us the announcement of Gloria's sixth child, a boy. I decided to see mother and baby immediately.

In the bus I stared amused at the huge, colored picture of the Virgin Mary, who was used to advertise Mejoral, the Chilean equivalent for aspirin — she and Mejoral made all *mejor*, better. Mary, the symbol of hope and consolation, was an indispensable lifeline for all those who suffered. Patiently she also bore her lot as a pill advertiser.

As I arrived at Gloria's house and entered her small, fresh-smelling bedroom, she lay pale and small between the bedsheets, nursing her tiny, black-haired baby. On either side she held her arms around one toddler; both were sucking on pacifiers. Noises of fighting children came from the next room.

I congratulated her and praised her wildly sucking boy. "How can I help you, Gloria? Anything I can do for you?"

"Not really. Filomena is doing everything necessary. But thank you anyway. You are getting busy and famous, aren't you?"

I smiled with a denying gesture as Ricardo rushed into the bedroom. He beamed with pride at having created another boy, which showed his, Ricardo's, fertility to the world. For the first time I resented his presence. "Congratulations," I forced myself to say.

"Thanks," he said in a hurry. "And goodbye. I must leave for my evening duty." He glanced one more time at the baby.

"I'm leaving too." I kissed Gloria. "Take care."

Ricardo didn't kiss Gloria goodbye, but I'd already learned — marital affection was never displayed, whereas men freely courted other women. Once in the cage, wives weren't worth a smile.

Ricardo and I walked together toward the bus station. In the east a half-moon stood vertically on the crest of the mountains, casting its pale shine on our surroundings. The fragrance of jasmine and honeysuckle waved through the air.

Assailed by fierce dogs barking and snarling, I had to raise my voice over the canine noise. "You are a rare doctor. No car, no telephone and no attack dog."

"I don't need any of them." He pulled me away from the barking hellhounds and we walked in the street in order to hear each other. "By the way I would rather live with the poor than with the braggarts of this neighborhood."

"Then why do you live in this place at all?"

"Because Gloria dragged me into it."

"She's right. A doctor's family doesn't belong in a shantytown!"

"But the poor need doctors badly. During my evening duty I can attend only to the most severe cases."

"Is this part of your job at the National Health Service?"

"No. It's voluntary."

"I didn't know you did social work."

"That's all I live for."

The barking died away while we passed by the high walls which still bore the graffiti NERUDA and ALLENDE. "The message of the poor to the rich," I said.

"That's all they can do. They are caged in eternal poverty. We have a sharp class division here. There are a few dozen landholding families who keep the lower class down so that they are little threat to the rich."

"How do they do that?"

"By underpaying them. The children are undernourished and therefore have learning difficulties. In rural areas there aren't even school buildings! No blackboards, no books, no chairs, no toilets. In other words, the rich exploit the poor and there's little hope this will change unless — "

" — unless you folks do something about it?" I asked.

His voice rose. "As long as we make excuses for our social injustices, we just perpetuate the misery."

I strongly felt his determination and was going to ask him what he could do about it. Yet as we were approaching the main street an unusual crowd had gathered, some calling for help. We arrived at the same time as a policeman.

A young man in shabby clothes lay on the street. Black hair strands clung to his pale, haggard face. His lips had a purple color. Blood oozed from his chest through his torn shirt.

Ricardo knelt down and checked the man's pulse. He talked to the man, who tried to answer, but only gurgling sounds came from his mouth. Shortly after, even those stopped. After a long time Ricardo checked the man's pulse again and then declared, *"Muerto.* Dead." He arose and briefly discussed something with the policeman.

Ricardo said to me in a matter-of-fact voice, "The man was stabbed in the chest. His lung collapsed. He died from inner bleeding."

"My God, who murdered him?"

He shrugged. "We'll never know." The policeman opened a path through the crowd and searched left and right for something on the street. In no time, he whistled to a horse-drawn cart, which stopped immediately.

"Why did he stop the cart?" I asked.

"He wants the coachmen to take the dead man away." Indeed, with a minimum of fuss the body was carried onto the cart and driven off.

"Where are they going?" I asked Ricardo.

"To a common grave at the edge of town. Now you can see how the poor are treated. They are on a par with animals. Some snobs even call them 'animals with names.'" Seeing the horror in my eyes, he added, "Look, Eva, you've just seen the worst of Chile. And now you'll understand why I stand up for the poor." I sighed and nodded. "There's your bus coming," he said. "I'll take one in the opposite direction. *Ciao,* Eva." He helped me into the bus, and I waved back to him.

The lack of a reliable mail service or a telephone did not keep the communicative Chileans from contacting each other. When in a hurry, one just flagged down a taxi. Therefore I assumed something important was brewing when, one day later, I saw a cab stopping in front of our house. Ricardo Toro rushed out toward our door. I opened it before he reached it. There he stood, with shining eyes. "Hola, Eva."

"Come in. Sit down."

He wiggled his index finger in denial. "How would you like to be in a radio program?"

With both hands I warded him off. "Not again radio!"

"This time it will be different. Trust me. Come along." My mind sped as fast as it could. Lilo was at school and Little Bear and Renate at a birthday party; none of them would be back before evening.

"I'm ready," I said. We climbed in the cab and the taxi sped away.

"I talked with a friend of mine, Miguel Fuentes," Ricardo said. "He's technical manager of Radio Agricultura. His wife does advertisement for the SAS on the radio."

"SAS?"

"Scandinavian Airlines. Miguel's wife is Austrian and produces a children's program in German. She's going to Europe on a concert tour for three months and is looking for a substitute. I suggested you." He knocked out his pipe and began to fill it.

"Radio shows! You have a finger in every pie," I said.

"This way one survives."

Since I was used to buses stopping on every other corner, I was surprised how fast the cab arrived downtown at Radio Agricultura, just half a block away from the Teatro Municipal of "Gypsy Baron" fame. Upstairs we entered the technical manager's small, smoke-filled office. Ricardo introduced me to his friend Miguel Fuentes and his wife Lonny. Miguel instantly extinguished his cigarette and stroked his wavy brown hair. He was about 40, impeccably dressed and solemn; his deep-set blue eyes gave him a melancholy appearance.

"Ah, the leading lady of MÚSICA?" He spoke German fluently with a Chilean accent. "I heard you and your group last week at the University. You played very well."

His Viennese wife, Lonny, a charming, blond, with dimples in her cheeks as she smiled, was about my own age. She too recognized me from newspaper pictures. "You may be the right person for this job," Lonny said. "I need someone who speaks German without an accent," she said. "Who understands music and isn't microphone-shy."

"I qualify for the first two," I said. "I'm not sure about the microphone. But I could try it out on my sound recorder at home."

"You own a sound recorder?" Miguel asked with surprise. "What kind?"

"A magnetic one with wire reels."

"Wow! You could record it all at your home and bring the reel to us so we can air the program?" Miguel asked.

"Perfect!" Lonny said. "Why don't we record the whole next session on your wire recorder?"

"Fine. May I ask how much SAS pays?"

Lonny smiled and the dimples formed again. "You'd make about 12,000 pesos in three months. How'd you like that?"

I smiled back at her. "Not bad." Hurrah! A new experience and a well-paid one! And I'd use a lot of music.

Impatiently I awaited the day when she appeared at my house with five children between eight and twelve years to tape her next session. Clever as she was, she'd already put me into the script. She let me speak the lines of a fairy, corrected me a few times and coached my transformation into a supernatural being. Although I was nervous, my voice didn't project it on the replay. "You did well," Lonny said. "The job is yours."

I couldn't believe it, couldn't imagine I'd made it to the radio world. "It's unreal! Thank you!"

She gathered her papers. "Here's a list of names, ages and addresses of the eligible kids." She motioned the children to the door. "I like to write stories for the program myself. But you can use any plot you like."

So I'd use "The Little Mermaid" and cast Lilo as the mermaid, Manfred as the prince and myself as the witch.

Next morning Lonny took me to the SAS office downtown. Elated, I signed the contract for the three months she'd be in Europe. From then on Scandinavian Airlines put my picture with their advertisements in all newspapers. Never before had I received so much publicity. Lilo and Little Bear cut out as many pictures as they could get hold of.

I wasn't the only one getting a good job offer. A few days

later Manfred came home with news. "Enrique Palma called me
at work today. We met for an espresso downtown. He's now the
liaison between a sulphur mine in the Atacama Desert and the
office in Santiago."

"We haven't seen him for a while."

"Because he's busy flying to the desert and back. He needs
an administrator for the mine, who can handle technical affairs.
He offered me the job."

Had he told me he'd go to the moon, my shock couldn't have
been bigger. "Where in the world is the Atacama Desert?"

"About 800 miles north. Near the border of Bolivia."

I had little conception of deserts besides the Sahara sand
dunes. "They're digging for sulphur in the sand?"

"In the rocks," he corrected me. "The Atacama is the driest
desert in the world. There are all kinds of mines up there, gold,
silver and copper mines. This one is a sulphur mine. Named the
Vilama Plant."

I was speechless.

"I'd make four times as much money as I'm getting now," he
said. "And I wouldn't even need money in the desert. Everything
is free for the employees. Imagine how much we could save!"

He was already considering the offer! I stared out the window
at the palm trees, which stood unperturbed in the December
heat. "Would we all have to live in the desert?" I asked.

"No. You and the children would stay in Santiago." I'd be
alone! Alone in a culture that hadn't become my own yet. "The
owner of the mine has a private plane and a pilot and its use
would be free for us," Manfred said, trying to make the
would-be separation appear easier.

"How come you decided this so fast? You said Enrique talked
to you about it today."

"He's mentioned it to me before. And today he made me the
offer. If I worked there for two years, we could save one million
pesos."

Was I still in my radio-fairyland where I conjured up dream
castles, elves and mermaids? A million pesos in just two years?

And unlimited flights to the desert? Who would refuse that? Not Manfred, chasing his rainbow. As I surmised, he accepted. And he had to leave for the Vilama Plant even before Christmas.

After a desperate try to adjust to Manfred's departure I finally decided to give a farewell-garden party for him. Everyone I invited showed up: the Toros, the Palmas, Vera Hermann, Dolores and Miguel Fuentes.

"We'll miss you, Manfredo," Ricardo said in a farewell speech. "But I know that your lust for adventure and your pioneer spirit drives you on to new realms."

"I may become invisible," Manfred told our guests. "But if you want to hear my voice, just listen to my conversation with my boss in Santiago on this frequency — " he gave the number. "Every Friday at two in the afternoon."

So he flew to the desert and our separate lives began. All that was left of him was his radio voice on Fridays, speaking Spanish to a stranger as if he were in another world, where I didn't exist. Each time I wept. I didn't know if he could hear my German program on Saturdays. I couldn't even expect to receive a letter from him; domestic mail took weeks to be delivered — if at all.

In time I developed a sense of abandonment like a lost, unwanted animal in a cage. I fought this feeling as best as I could, hoping a magic door would suddenly open and I could walk into Manfred's new world with just one big step.

I well knew that magic didn't appear on a wish, no matter how strong. Yet I found out that misery and desire both could forge fate.

8. LOVE'S WAYS

High summer! The infamous January heat that stifled the city with its hellish glare made those who could afford it escape to the coast or go abroad. All my friends had gone on vacation; even the Toros with their six children had left.

The squatters across the street had torn down their miserable shack and disappeared. Construction was now beginning on the lot.

Schools, the National Ballet and many churches closed and concerts weren't in demand in the summer, which to me meant no music making. Only my SAS radio program continued.

"Mami, do you have time now to give me piano lessons?" Lilo asked.

"Of course, I do. You deserve it for playing so many roles for the radio show." She also took guitar lessons and ballet, and Little Bear got swimming lessons. Renate was too young to ask for anything more than climbing on my lap.

I regarded it as a consolation that Dolores Mannerheim decided to stay in Santiago. We were still very good friends. Divorced in Europe, she had come to start a new life in Chile. I was alone too — so we could share our misery. Instead of an expensive apartment near downtown, she rented a less costly bungalow on the lovely outskirts of Santiago, a few blocks away from me.

One morning, before the dry, suffocating heat began to subdue my energy, I walked to Dolores's house. In the front yard, blooming bougainvillea, hibiscus and strong-smelling roses spread out against the majestic backdrop of the Andes. A full chorus of birds was singing.

I found Dolores on a lounge chair on her terrace. "Like an

allegory of luxury and happiness," I said.

"I can't complain," she said with a roguish smile.

"What is it, Dolores?"

She fixed her eyes on me. "Miguel and I are in love."

"Miguel Fuentes from the radio station?" She nodded. "Oh, my God," I cried, "he's married! And his wife is coming back in three months!"

"Three months is a long time."

"But then what? A divorce? There are no legal divorces in Chile."

She shook her long, blond hair. "Neither of us thinks in those terms."

"Then just an affair for three months?"

"Just for three months," she said with wistfulness.

"The two of you met — "

" — at your farewell party for Manfred in December."

I sighed. "You just escaped from your marriage. And now this affair. Why, Dolores, why?"

"Loneliness, I guess."

Loneliness — I knew about that! "And he is lonely because his wife left him alone for three months?" Dolores didn't respond. "I am happy for you," I said. She was my dear friend, and I would always be on her side.

"Miguel moved in with me soon after Lonny had left for her concert tour in Europe," Dolores said.

They weren't even trying to keep their romance secret! "I wouldn't want to be here when Lonny comes home. She's a spitfire."

"I don't even think about it. Live for the moment, as the Chileans say."

We talked until the violet glow slid down the mountains and the sinking sun took the day's heat away. Just as we were back in the house, someone unlocked the door and Miguel Fuentes entered.

When he saw me, he quickly glanced at Dolores. With a slight nod of her head, she made him realize I understood the situation and would not interfere.

"Hola, Eva," he greeted me, kissed my cheeks, and then went to Dolores, hugged and kissed her with a lot of familiarity. He belonged in this house as much as Dolores. And no longer was there melancholy in his eyes. He went to the wetbar and poured wine for us.

Staring at the two lovers, I felt envious. They were together; Manfred and I were separated. This never-before-experienced envy threw me into confusion. How could I develop such a bad feeling by seeing my dear friend's happiness? Yet the feeling intensified and finally turned into anger. Hot, red anger with our separation. Right then I decided to take steps to join Manfred.

When I finished my drink I got up to say goodbye. They accompanied me to the garden door. I kissed them both, said, "Enjoy the summer!" and left their lovenest.

At the bakery I called the office and asked for Enrique. He was in the Atacama Desert, and so I had to ask the secretary when I could fly to the desert.

"We're flying only once a week to the Vilama Plant," she said. "And then, the boss has preference. But I could put you on the list for February."

Bang! A nice blow to my ego. My frustration grew into an overwhelming desire for Manfred. Could I really be sure they would fly me there in February? I had to force myself to be calm.

Impatiently I waited for February.

9. THE MYSTERIOUS DESERT

Finally, on a February morning of 1953, Felipe Svensen, the mine owner's pilot, came to pick me up in his Mercedes. His tall, erect Scandinavian appearance was a surprise in this country of short, quick, dark-haired people, but I liked his friendly, elongated face -- like that of a noble horse. He was already dressed for the desert: white polo shirt and gray trousers.

I kissed the children. "Mami is coming back in a week. Elsa will take good care of you."

"A thousand kisses for Dad," Lilo said.

Little Bear tapped on my arm. "Tell Daddy I caught a flea this morning. All by myself!" Renate just reached up her arms to be kissed again.

Svensen grabbed my small suitcase and the accordion and put them in the trunk. True to his Nordic looks, Svensen was extremely taciturn during our drive to a small private airport on the outskirts of Santiago. We were so close to the giant Andes, they seemed to collapse on us.

Svensen stopped the car and walked into a hangar. He piloted a one-engined Cessna onto the tarmac and waved me aboard. I climbed in and fastened my seatbelt. "You'll be my only passenger today," he shouted over the engine's roar. "You and the mail and medicine for the employees." He taxied to the runway, stopped, switched the radio on for permission from the control tower and waited.

"When are you flying back again?" I hollered.

"The day after tomorrow. With three others."

"When are you coming to pick me up?"

"Don't count on me. We don't have a fixed schedule. And most of the time the plane is full."

Confused, I asked, "How will I fly back then?"

"There are commercial flights from Calama. Sixty miles from the Vilama Plant. Just a stone's throw." He got the permission to fly, readied for take-off, gave full throttle and ascended into the deep-blue sky.

Flying, my secret desire! To be free as a bird, defy gravity, soar into the sky — I'd always been fascinated by the myth of Icarus, who soared so high that the sun melted the wax, detaching his wings so that he fell into the sea and drowned. If I could only conjure him up to show him that we had achieved what he had dreamed of!

To my surprise even the taciturn Scandinavian had changed, transformed into a man who wanted to share his knowledge of this wondrous country. His voice rose over the now subdued engine noise. "Do you know what 'Chile' means? It's an ancient Indian word, meaning 'the end of the world.'"

"Did the ancient Indians know how endless the coast was?"

"Surely not." He chuckled. "Chile is like an elevator, running for 3,800 miles through different floors. It passes through all climates and landscapes. Chile has everything; deserts and geysers in the north. Lakes and forests in the middle. Volcanoes and glaciers in the south."

I listened with fascination. "Have you seen all these parts of Chile?"

"I've flown over all parts of South America."

"Which country do you like the most?"

"Chile is my big love." An acknowledgement, a confession, a final statement.

A warm feeling overcame me, for the pilot and for the country over which we winged. We flew parallel to the snow-capped Andes, the spine of South America, above the fertile central valley, which baked under the midday sun.

For refueling we descended outside the town of Vallenar, a lonely place, filled with succulents and cacti.

"Look around," the pilot said. "You won't see green stuff for quite a while." He was right. In flight again, the landscape under us changed from green grass to brown lifeless rocks. When the rock formations grew more rugged and steeper, Svensen had to ascend more and more. "We're now over the Atacama Desert. The driest place on earth. Only a few Indians live here."

"Do they speak Spanish?"

"Most do. But they all speak Aymará or Quechua with each other. They stick to their old religion and mix it with Christianity."

"What's their old religion like?"

"They have gods and goddesses and spirits for every event and emotion. They are intimately united with their gods and pray to them before each event or action."

"Were they ever baptized?"

"Some were, and the majority of the Indians practice Catholicism on the outside. But they don't trust it. For instance, they still sacrifice the living heart of a llama or a lamb to the sun god every year. Blood must flow. That's what the gods like. Then the animal is roasted."

"Have you seen that?" I asked.

"No. They won't let any non-believer see it."

"How do you know all this?"

"Señora Eva, I have lived here in the Great North for fifteen years. Researchers and missionaries know about these rites and sometimes, when an Indian is converted, he tells."

I was deeply touched by Svensen's account. Was this really going on in the 20th century? Below us I saw a large, white area. "Is that snow?"

"No. Salt. A salar, a dried-out salt lake. We've just flown over the Tropic of Capricorn. We are now in the tropical zone."

Dry west winds swept in from the Pacific. Once in a while the winds tossed our airplane like a leaf. I felt cold sweat breaking out. "Dammit," Svensen said. "These afternoon turbulences over the pampas...."

I asked myself if I was intoxicated by the altitude or by Svensen's stories, fearing the gods that dominated this desert were trying to keep us away.

While Svensen concentrated on navigation, he became as taciturn as he'd been before the flight. He began to descend, slowed down, and at last approached a barely recognizable rocky runway. Carefully he touched down on the bare gravel, taxied and finally stopped the plane.

Impatiently, I climbed out into the sharp-scented air and stood rooted to a desolate barren wilderness. West, toward the ocean, the high plateau was strewn with gray rocks and boulders as far as the eye could see. Yet east, toward inland, a chain of strange pyramids protruded from the horizon, like a barricade before a forbidden world — menacing volcanoes, one of them steaming from several outlets. The wind hummed around my head, its voice sliding up and down. There was no sign of any living being.

Yet from afar I heard the noise of truck engines and saw two pickups approaching us. The driver of the first waved his arm from the cabin. Manfred!

Both trucks stopped. Manfred, dressed in dark-blue mechanic's overalls, jumped out and a minute later I was in his arms. The hug was endless. How much had I missed this!

"I saw the plane come in," Manfred said. He took a moment to greet Svensen, but then turned back to me and left the pilot to supervise the transfer of the cargo to the other pickup. "I'm sooo glad you're here," Manfred said, driving with one hand and squeezing me against him with the other arm.

"It was terrible without you in Santiago."

From a stone building a Chilean flag fluttered high in the desert wind. "What's the occasion?" I asked.

"Your visit!"

In front of the building, made of huge, flat stones, were two gas pumps, where trucks lined up for gas. They had no hoods and their engines were exposed. "Why's that?" I asked.

"This way the dust can't accumulate, and the engine won't overheat in this altitude," Manfred replied.

We parked and walked through the opening of the stone building, which was built around a sandy patio. Manfred led me into his large living-room/bedroom, primitive as a soldier's lodging with two iron beds along the walls. In the corner of the room, a wash basin was fastened against the wall and in the middle stood a clean-scrubbed wooden table and two chairs — all lit by only a bare bulb that hung from the ceiling. I sat down and laughed. "A real millionaire's home!"

He locked the door, pulled me from the chair, hugged me with one arm so hard I couldn't breathe, kissed me and began to undress me with his other hand. Finally we could be ourselves and unleash our long-restricted desire — too stormy, too swift, leaving a thirst for more.

"Christ, I've been waiting for this!" he said.

I buried my head on his chest. "Hold me." I heard his heart beat and inhaled deeply his unique scent. For a long time we remained in each other's arms.

Later we dressed and sat down at the table. I looked at his radiant blue eyes, his perfect nose, his straight high forehead, his perfect body — so near, so dear. "You are worth more than a million."

He smiled. "We really could be rich in two years."

"Do you still think you'll make that much?"

"I think so. You see, the sulphur we're refining here goes to the United States. Good business! And we are well-paid by Don Francisco."

"I haven't had the honor of meeting him yet."

"You will, sooner than you want. He's a strange guy. Rich and taciturn." He got up, stretched his hand out to me. "Let's get dressed. I'll show you around." Arms locked, we went through the stone building complex to the outside.

"Walk slowly," Manfred warned. "You have to get used to the altitude. We are at 8,000 feet here."

A rotten smell of sulphur lingered everywhere. "Where does this hissing come from?" I asked.

"The refinery."

"How many people work here?"

"350."

"As many as you had at the shipyard in Germany! Now you've become a mining engineer, haven't you?"

He chuckled. "Every few years I change my field of expertise." We came to Manfred's pickup. "Ready for a ride?" I nodded and we climbed into the driver's cabin.

He stopped before a young Indian woman. "She's packed a lunch for us." He motioned to her to put the basket on the truck bed. "Now I'll show you the desert." We took off.

As though produced by magic, a world of bizarre mountains and empty canyons opened before me, rocks in sizes from pebble to boulder were strewn everywhere. "Look at those tiny, pale-green plants!" I said. "How they force their way out! Is it sage?"

"Could be. I'm not a biologist."

After we rounded a rock-littered hill, a chain of pyramid-shaped volcanoes appeared in the distance, blue and purple, capped by snow. Huge white clouds hung above the peaks, severed by the winds like torn-up sheets.

"Like an artist's vision of a strange planet," I said. I sniffed at the air. "It's so dry here, I can hardly open my mouth."

Manfred pulled a water bottle from a car pocket and handed it to me. "Never be without water in the desert."

Without warning we suddenly came to a river. With his typical daredeviltry Manfred drove right into it. I clung to dashboard and side window. The water rushed around the truck, but a minute later we drove up the other bank. "I thought you'd drown us!" I said.

"Just crossing over the Vilama River."

"Rivers in the desert?" I asked, still breathless.

"When snow melts on the mountains, it feeds the rivers."

"Do you have more surprises for me?"

Manfred stopped the car. "First a kiss. Then I show you more." He took me in his arms and I strongly felt what I had suppressed for so long, the urge to unwind, to be held tight, to be protected. Silently we withdrew from each other, but remained holding hands. I felt as though still in his arms. He spoke first. "It's hell to be without you."

"It's a waste of time to live alone."

He squeezed my hand. "I'm grateful that you are here." He took his hand away. "Shall we go on now?"

I nodded and he restarted the motor. The higher the pickup climbed the more barren the landscape became until all vegetation vanished. Driving up a slope, he stopped the truck almost at its peak. We climbed out and stood in the thin, windless air. I felt my tongue cleave to the roof of my mouth, pulled the water bottle out and drank.

"Let's walk up to the rim," Manfred said. Even walking slowly in this altitude was a chore. My heart pounded, I gasped for breath, but finally we made it to the rim.

I stared down at a gigantic valley, filled with gray craters and myriads of small cones, pointing upward. Not a blade of life. "The moon!" I exclaimed.

"Valle de la Luna, moon valley. I knew you would guess the name right away." With fascination I took in the moonscape, whose images I had seen on many space paintings. "Do you think humans will ever walk on the moon?"

"I'm sure. Wernher von Braun is doing his best to get astronauts there. He's now director of NASA's Space Flight Center in the U.S. — "

" — and my personal hero," I said.

Manfred smiled. "Approved."

"If an astronaut would walk on the moon," I said, "what do you think he'd feel?"

"I can't imagine."

"I can. He'd feel as lonesome as I felt in Santiago without you." His hand searched for mine, found it and held it. Still gazing at the desolate moonscape, we were engulfed in a great solitude.

He disrupted the silence. "During the day I was killing my loneliness with a lot of work. But at night I was all by myself."

I felt the warmth from his hand flood into mine. "I was alone night and day. Like the only human in that gray crater down there. And no hope to get out of it," I added.

"You are here now," he said softly. He lifted my hand to his lips and kissed it. I had come home.

We turned away from the rigid moonscape and descended on slipping rocks to the pickup.

"Whew!!" I said. "Are there any humans in your desert?"

"Indians. Let's drive to their settlement. We can have a picnic there." He drove uphill again, sand, rocks and boulders on both sides, until tufts of green sage and river-smell signaled the nearness of water. "Wherever there's water, there's plant life and there are humans."

Four windowless stone shacks, covered with cactus wood and dried mud came in sight. Two dogs fought ferociously before them. "Indians live here," Manfred said.

"So far from civilization!"

"They live in their own world of nature gods and magic." He stopped at a small, isolated adobe structure, shoulder-high and in the shape of half an egg. Its opening was just right for a child.

"Is this an outdoor oven?" I asked.

"No. This is an Indian chapel. You'll see how they mix religions." We stooped over to enter, and once inside, had to stay bent over. Opposite me, as if on an altar, the notorious poster of the advertisement for headaches: the Virgin Mary with a compassionate look and the name of the pills, MEJORAL.

"The Christian disguise of their worship," Manfred said in a low voice as if someone was listening, a god or a spirit. "The Virgin is a manifestation of the Earth Mother." He pointed. "Look at the craft work."

Four colorful, hand-woven baskets contained different offerings: one filled with yellow corn, another with brown beans, a third with rice. The largest basket held magic pipes in different sizes and a wooden, hand-hewn drum. I stood spellbound in the middle of living shamanism and pagan worship accessories. There was a world here which most of humankind didn't know about, and I was privileged to set foot into it!

Outside, between two of the stone shacks, an Indian woman in shapeless, drab clothes stared at me. Two long black braids hung down from under her gray felt hat. A child held on to her long skirt. As soon as the woman saw us, she ran toward her stone shack, followed by the child. "They are scared," Manfred said. "Afraid of the spirits and of humans other than themselves."

As we turned away from the settlement, a little girl of about ten years old walked toward us. Her black hair fell unkempt over part of her tiny, cheekboned face. Barefoot and dressed in faded rags, she was distracted by a small bird in her hands.

I stopped before her. *"Hola, mi'jita,* hi, little girl." She looked up at me, her almond-shaped black eyes and small mouth large with amazement. I pulled a chocolate bar from my jacket pocket and offered it to her.

She stared at the candy, apparently unknown to her. Then, as if driven by fear, she ran toward the shacks as fast as she could. Dumbfounded, with candy in hand, I gazed after her.

"She probably understands only Aymará and no Spanish," Manfred said. "And she was afraid of you."

"Oh, I wish she'd stayed." I felt sad.

Back in the pickup, we drove on until we were out of any Indian's sight and then stopped for our picnic. Manfred unfolded a canvas cover and laid it on the ground. We sat down and pounced upon the water bottles, bread and cheese and oranges. "That Indian girl," I asked, "is she ever going to have an education?"

He shook his head. "No schools in the desert. That's why our girls are with you in Santiago." He stared at the ground. "I miss them terribly. Tell me about them."

"All send you kisses. Lilo already plays songs on the guitar. And she plays Mozart minuets on the piano. Little Bear swims and dives, and Renate already says Spanish words."

He sighed. "I'm losing all this. What would I give to have only one here with me!"

"You won't be here forever," I said, stroking his hand.

"Every day without the family is a lost day."

"Do you want me to move up here?"

"Listen, if you think you could live in the desert, then move up here. Little Bear and Renate would come with you. Only Lilo would have to be in a boarding school in Antofagasta, just four hours from here."

"I do like the desert. Let me think about it." A cool breeze of air began to drift around us.

"Sunset," Manfred said, getting up. "Within minutes it will get very cold. Let's go back."

When I looked at the distant volcanoes, lowering clouds had veiled them as though a curtain was drawn to hide the change of a stage set. Dreamily I snuggled up to Manfred. He put his arm around my shoulder and kissed me.

Later we entered the large dining room with its many tables for six. Several employees stood around, smoking and talking. Two men stood out from the crowd, Svensen with his Scandinavian height, and an equally tall but very thin, stiff figure of a middle-aged man.

"The man who is talking to Svensen is a VIP here," Manfred said. "Emilio Delgado. Our warehouseman. A hybrid of a male nurse and a medicine man. A frustrated physician. He treats everybody here. We call him *el doctor.*"

We stepped over and Manfred introduced him to me. Stiff and without a smile, "the doctor" shook my hand without a word. Through his thick lenses he only fleetingly looked into my eyes as if I was a piece of furniture. I wondered if he were a woman hater or just ill-mannered.

I also met a jolly, bald-headed engineer from Germany. "This is Herr Wolters, who supervises the installation of the new chemical plant," Manfred said. "He's here only temporarily."

With Svensen and Delgado, we sat together with Wolters, who often stroked his bald head as if remembering hair that had once been there. "Don't you miss Germany?" he asked me.

"Not really," I said. "Chile is such a beautiful place and the people are very nice. I just love it. But how do you like it here?"

"It's damned dry," Wolters said. "During the day we work. But the evenings are boring. There's not even music from the radio."

"I brought my accordion," I said. "We could have music after dinner."

Everyone nodded and smiled. A few clapped their hands. Meantime the kitchen maids brought red wine and served cazuela soup, tough beef with rice and carrots, and chocolate pudding, all of which tortured my stomach at this late, nine o'clock dinner.

After the dessert Manfred brought my accordion. The men lit cigarettes and turned around to watch me. I played everything that came to mind, classical and pop music. Soon my audience called out names of songs they wanted to hear, I played them and they sang along and clapped. I could spread music even in the desert!

Pilot Svensen stared at my left hand that manipulated the eighty bass-buttons. "I'm trying to find out how you know which button to press. They all look alike."

"You are saying that?" I asked. "How do you know what all the buttons in your cockpit mean?"

The pilot shook his head. "I don't have that many." More wine was brought, the air got bluer and thicker, and soon everyone sang to my tunes.

When the party came to an end, Manfred and I slipped out of our roles as hosts and went to our room. In his narrow iron bed we made love again. We finally had time for exploring each other, responding to every word and touch, delaying the ultimate climax for as long as possible until no wishes were left, and I was aware of having arrived at the summit of a mountain-chain. When I opened my eyes, I couldn't see anything in the darkness, but Manfred's arms still held me tight and beyond that I had no wishes.

Next morning, the curtain was drawn away from the volcanoes, showing the mountains covered with brilliant snow down to the valleys. The glare was blinding; I quickly turned away and followed Manfred to the dining room for breakfast.

Svensen and Delgado joined us at the table. I enjoyed seeing the pilot's friendly horse face again. Delgado, however, sat, tall and aloof like a statue, before he condescended to tackle his breakfast. I attempted to pull the indifferent man out of his shell. "We saw some Indians yesterday. I wonder how they can survive in this desert."

Delgado calmly finished chewing his roll and wiped off his mouth with a napkin. For a second he glanced at me through his thick glasses. "They hunt and grow corn. They live closely with one of the few animals that resist high altitude." The statue had spoken!

"The llamas?" I asked.

"Yes. Llamas are their best friends, unselfish and obedient. They transport loads, give milk, meat, wool and leather. Indians and llamas are inseparable." He took a sip of water. "The Indians' panacea is coca. They chew themselves into a narcotic euphoria."

"Are they drug addicts?"

"Not at all. The coca leaf contains less than one percent cocaine. It alleviates hunger and fatigue for the chewer and also repels insects. The coca leaf also supplies vitamins and minerals."

"They probably know quite well what's good for them," I said. Everyone else listened to the question-and-answer session.

"They've lived here for thousands of years," Delgado said. "Long before the white man invaded this continent and deprived them of their land."

"In the 16th century. I thought they were converted. Why are they still pagans?"

"Maybe once in a year a priest gets up here. He says mass, baptizes whoever they bring to him and then leaves something religious like the advertisement of Mejoral with the Virgin Mary."

"We've seen that in a tiny chapel. It was right in front of the volcanoes."

"One of them is sacred to the Indians," he said. "The Licancabur."

"I haven't seen it yet. But I've seen how afraid the Indians are of other people. And maybe of natural phenomena. Are they afraid of death as we are?"

Delgado stared at me. I became very uncomfortable, but held out against his gaze. "I think not." He got up, said, *"Hasta luego,* Goodbye," and left the table.

"I have to congratulate you," Manfred said. "Delgado never talks that much. You must have impressed him."

"At least I should get credit for pulling info out of him."

"You'll get your award," Manfred said, getting up. I followed him. "Today I'll introduce you to the Licancabur."

"It seems, that monster has a personality."

"It does." We went out to his pickup. The vehicle jolted with us over gravel and rocks until we reached a small creek, which worked its way through the pebbles.

"Do you recognize this?" Manfred asked. I shook my head. "It's the Vilama River from yesterday!"

"Impossible!"

"It's true. No melting snow on the mountains, no river. Just a creek. Sometimes it even ceases to exist and after days it appears again."

"Mysterious Atacama," I murmured. Before us the desert expanded in its virgin state, an immense void, nature reduced to the elements of light and heat, sand and rock. The scanty vegetation consisted only of grayish succulents, and low shrubs with green, thick leaves.

"That's *boldo,"* Manfred said. "They make a tea of the leaves for stomach aches. It works like a miracle."

"It would be good for your sensitive stomach."

"I drink it as often as I can."

I put my hand on his knees. "Are you happy living here?"

"Except for the loneliness, I'm fascinated by the Atacama Desert."

"And Chile in general?"

"I'm very glad we left Europe. The Russians will never come this far. And then this great climate! Warm days and cool nights. And the sun! Remember North Germany's eternal rain?"

"I just look up at the Andes to feel grateful."

Manfred shifted to a lower gear. "And then — can you imagine? I no longer have stomach pains!"

"The unhurried life in Chile, no distractions in the desert, all that was good for your health." I smiled at him. "Including the *boldo* tea."

"You know? I realized that in the thirty-six years of my life I've achieved what I wanted. I'd been on submarines, built a shipyard from scratch and have switched continents at will."

"You are a devil of a fellow!"

"Thanks, my treasure!"

Passing a giant boulder, which had blocked our view, we saw the long chain of volcanoes before us, bigger, closer to us. One loomed above the lesser ones like a monster, breathing heavily and waiting. "The Licancabur," Manfred said.

"Wow! It's fuming from..." I counted, "...seven vents!" My eyes caressed the extraordinary mount. "Delgado said it's sacred to the Indians. It's a monster, breathing heavily. Strange, no sound comes from it."

Manfred broke the silence. "Do you think you can brace yourself for a 12,000-foot level? It's that high up to paradise."

"With you, paradise is everywhere."

He put his arm around and squeezed me. "Well, even paradise is graded. Let's step up."

We drove uphill through a dry landscape dotted with sage scrub. Llamas, those wooly-haired relatives of camels, watched calmly as we traveled up. Some had ivory-colored coats, others dark brown. Their banana-shaped ears erect, they stared at us, while others majestically strutted along, giving life and beauty to the desolate wilderness.

"Can I go touch them?" I asked.

"You and your need for stroking fur! The llamas would run away before you reached them." He stopped the truck. "Here we are." He pulled me over a rim and I looked down into the loveliest valley I'd ever seen. Its depth was wildly overgrown with giant pampas grass, whose flower plumes stood motionless in the thin air. The source of the green luxury was a brook that babbled over the rocks, disappearing and reappearing between the shrubbery and ending up as a small waterfall.

In the middle of all this wonder lay a green fountain that sparkled in the sun, softly bubbling like a spa. "The Thermal Waters of Puritama," Manfred said. "Most people don't even know they exist."

In the thin air we cautiously descended into the ravine that looked like an Inca prince's private resort. On one side of the spring stood a roofless stone cabin, which could have been abandoned a thousand years ago. We were almost at the bottom when we realized we weren't alone. A huge black bird right out of a fairy tale stood motionless at the spring's edge, watching us with one wide-open eye.

Fixed by its stare, we stopped. "A condor," Manfred said softly. "The soaring spirit of the Andes." In mutual respect we and the bird of prey stared at each other, my heart pounding from lack of oxygen. At last the condor decided to abandon his realm, spreading his huge wings, ten feet across, and regally soaring into the sky.

"This is as far away from the Russians as we could ever get," Manfred said. "And now we are alone." Leaving our clothes in the abandoned Inca "bath house," we stepped into the emerald pool. The well-known aroma of much of the Atacama Desert ascended from the sulphuric water, which had a temperature of about 90 degrees and reached up to my shoulders.

My body felt wonderfully caressed by the fountain's silky fizz. But then it was Manfred who caressed me, and for a while I didn't know if it was my beloved man who excited me or the bubbling water. As his tenderness heightened into vehemence and breathlessness, we merged into one creature — until the ground began to move, jets of water sprang up, the pampas grass swayed violently, and rocks and streams of sand dashed down from the canyon rim.

"You made the earth tremble!" I said, laughing. "You are just too stormy."

"No wonder. With you around all nature gets wild."

When the earth stopped shaking, the pampas grass calmed down and the pool bubbled softly as before. We dressed and set out on the bouncy ride home — just in time to see the snow-covered mountains bathed in an unreal, deepening orange-pink glow. But the magic shine was short-lived. A blue twilight sank over mountains and valleys. Tomorrow the hot tropical sun would melt the snow and swell the Vilama Creek into a respectable river again.

On request I played the accordion for the diners every night. Their thirst for music seemed unquenchable. "I've never seen so much harmony between these rough men," pilot Svensen said to me. "You make them even sing together. Can't you stay up here?"

"Sorry, I'm here only on vacation. I must return." Yet I told Manfred about it. "You've got a radio. All you need is one loudspeaker in the dining room and one in the workers' dorm."

"There isn't a single one in the entire desert."

"Why don't you ask the boss in Santiago for one?"

Manfred scratched his head. "He'll think I'm crazy. But I'll try." He told the boss it was absolutely necessary to keep employees and workers happy to counteract lurking political instigations. Two days later, when Svensen arrived from the capital, he brought two loudspeakers along. From now on music flooded over the Atacama Desert!

Freed from playing after dinner, Manfred and I prepared for a walk. He put his parka on and I slung a blanket around me. "Take at least two," he said. "It's chilly."

I grabbed a second blanket and we stepped out into the cold air. The moonless night had spread its dark, wide-stretched wings over the desert under a dome studded with a myriad of stars. A broad band of densely-packed galaxies crossed the sky from the horizon to the volcanoes like a fresco. He put his arm around my shoulders. "I ordered those millions of stars for you."

"You made me a millionairess."

We walked in silence, the cool, sharp-scented air around us. "It's so good to know that all the heavenly bodies are everywhere. No matter where we are." I stood before him, flung my arms around him. "And you are here. The man I love."

Next morning I was putting on my desert sandals as Manfred, who had worked at the office since dawn, opened the door to our room. "Ready for the *salar* and Toconao?" We climbed on the big truck next to the driver. The twelve staff members were already seated in the back. We followed the bumpy dirt road, sand and rocks on both sides, the volcanoes to our left, the glaring desert sun above.

We entered a fairyland of snow-white hills and roads, blinding so much we had to put sunglasses on. "Snow in the tropical sun?" I asked, unbelieving.

"Salt," Manfred said. "The beginning of the *salar.* A dried-out salt lake, hard as crystal. Sixty-five miles long." Car tracks led right into the *salar.*

"I can't believe it," I said. "Real salt?"

"Want to lick it?" He said to the driver, *"Pare aquí,* stop here." The truck halted and I jumped out. I brushed my wet finger over the lake's hard, glassy surface and then over my tongue. Salt! No doubt about it.

As we continued over the white, solidified lake, huge pink birds circled above us, inspecting the truck monster. "What are they?" I asked. "I've never seen such large birds."

"Flamingos. They stand five feet high." As fast as they had appeared, they flew away. "The only living things here," Manfred said. "No animals or humans. The desert has no mercy."

We drove on. When the first signs of low scrubs appeared, the driver turned east, following the vegetation until we entered the lush oasis of Toconao. With its paved street and 350-year old wooden church it looked like many of the tiny villages throughout Latin America. The peasants' homes were built of light-brown adobe, the sun-dried mud, molded to bricks. Roofs were thatched with straw. An Indian woman in a white shirt and wide, dark skirt shuffled by, balancing a basket on her head.

The driver parked the car before one of the adobe houses, and we strolled along the lone street that quickly became a dirt road. Mongrel dogs, cats, ducks and a baby pig crossed our path. Two chatting Indian women with long, black braids and beige boiler hats, colorful shawls and long skirts approached us from the other end of the street. Each carried a child on her back, tied up in a shawl. When the women saw us they fell silent and lowered their eyes in passing.

I turned around to watch them. They continued their walk, then stopped. Lifting their full skirts, they squatted. After relieving themselves, they got up and walked on. I could see two wet spots on the roadway. In the dry air they would disappear within seconds.

I hurried to catch up with the others. Carlos Gómez, Manfred's technical manager, marched in front of the group. Bald-headed, robust, in his forties, he was not much taller than I. I wondered what kind of a man he was with his thick lips and fast-shifting gray eyes. If the eyes really were the window of the soul, Gómez would be a rogue. Nevertheless, I appreciated his quality as a guide.

"You should see the bar they've got here," he said. "I need cigarettes. Want to come along?" He turned to the others. "We'll meet you at the barbecue place."

Manfred, Gómez and I entered the "public" adobe house. Once my eyes adjusted to the dark, I realized that the dirt ground I stood on served as a floor. There were three straw chairs and a simple iron-framed bed under dangling onions and a saint's picture. Above a charcoal fire on the ground stood a long-legged iron pot in which a woman in a brown blouse and a half-long gray skirt stirred some soup.

"Is she Indian?" I whispered to Gómez.

"Not a hundred percent. But the admixture of Indian blood is still very strong here in the north." He asked for a pack of *Particular*. The woman left and reappeared with a carton of the popular cigarettes. Manfred ordered grape juice for us and both men indulged in smoking.

Through the open back door we saw the woman talk to a young man, who soon jumped on a bicycle and began to pedal. "Strange," I said. "It's a stationary bike."

"What's he doing?" Manfred asked Gómez, who obviously had been here before and was now proud to be the only one in the know.

"He has a small generator on his back wheel that provides electricity."

"What does he use it for?" Manfred asked.

"To entertain us with music," Gómez said. Through a mysterious device the bike activated an old gramophone so that the turning record produced squawking noises. By straining my ears I could identify it as an old American song, "The Battle Hymn of the Republic." Eventually the music slowed and the pitch sank: the bicyclist was tiring. When the music went down, he pedaled harder and the sound rose again.

Trying not to laugh, we clapped. When we finished our drinks and left this hospitable place, we heard the Battle Hymn of the Republic sink and finally die.

From there we crossed the street and entered a small forest, a wilderness of strong-scented eucalyptus, peppertrees and dense underbrush. Fruit trees, flowers, and blooming vines created a jungle of green richness, dotted with fire-red blossoms and juicy berries. The fragrance in the warm, humid air intoxicated us, and we brazenly picked whatever we could reach.

"What do you want?" I asked Manfred. "Figs? Oranges?"

"Not exotic enough," he said.

"How about a prickly pear?"

When I picked one of the pear-shaped, green fruits from the huge cactus, Manfred's warning, "Don't touch them!" came too late. The prickly pear was in my hand, and I felt its fine hair penetrate deep into the skin. I dropped the fruit, but the almost invisible stings stuck to my skin. I tried to pull them out, but I only spread the spikes. It was so painful it brought tears to my eyes. Manfred grabbed my arm. "We must see *el doctor.*"

We found Delgado in a clearing, where Gómez and Co. were preparing the barbecue. "Señora Eva has touched a prickly pear," Manfred said to Delgado.

Without a word, Delgado walked over to a fig tree, plucked one of its large, three-lobed leaves and passed it on to me. "Rub the affected areas against the leaf," he said. "It will remove the stings." After a lot of rubbing the pain was gone. "Where there's a natural injury there's a natural remedy," he said. He's learned this from the Indians, I thought.

We sat down on grassy mounds. The aroma of smoked meat filled the air. I looked at the lamb on the spit. Its fleece removed, the animal was stuck horizontally on the skewer, turned by Gómez with relish. Once in a while, the dressing dripped into the fire, where it created tiny, sizzling explosions. As I watched, the smoke assumed strange forms, encouraging mystical interpretations.

When Gómez opened red wine bottles, I watched with amazement as he poured some wine on the ground. Only then did he fill the wine glasses. "Why did he do that?" I asked Delgado, who sat beside me.

"It's an old custom in the desert. An offering to the thirsty demons."

"But Gomez is not Indian!"

"We've lived up here for so long. The cultures overlap, and one learns from the other. Why do you think we're roasting a lamb?"

"Because we're hungry."

"The emphasis is on lamb. Only a llama or a lamb should be sacrificed to please the gods. Since llamas are highly valuable, we use the much cheaper lambs." I was strangely impressed by the religious rites, no matter how watered down. Besides, the pieces of lamb roast, which Gómez cut and offered to each of us on the tip of his knife, were delicious and the wine heightened the spirits — ours and perhaps also the supernatural ones, whose power the Indians feared so much.

For dessert we chose from the many fruits within our reach

— figs, grapes, oranges, raspberries galore. A feast!

"So much is growing here, there must be water somewhere. Why can't we see it?" I asked Delgado.

"All these rivers are nothing but intermittent washes. Most come from the mountains. Except for one they never make it to the ocean."

Inscrutable desert! I thought.

We packed up and drove out of Toconao. The vegetation diminished in size, until we entered the *salar,* which was glazed with a bluish shine. In the middle of the salt-lake we happened upon a small pile, something darker than the salt. When the driver stopped we realized the pile was a human being in the middle of the dry salt lake. My God, was he dead or alive?

We jumped out and placed ourselves around the crumpled body: a slim man in a white shirt and blue shorts. An empty water bottle next to him indicated he had run out in the middle of the merciless desert. Most of our companions made the sign of the cross.

Delgado was the first to kneel down. Carefully he turned the long body over onto its back. The man was young and his blond hair and fair skin suggested his European origin. Salt was stuck on his cracked lips. *El doctor* took the man's pulse and nodded. "Heat stroke. But he's alive. Let's get him in the shade."

Delgado and three others lifted the body and carried it over to the truck's shadow. Delgado sprinkled water from his own bottle on the unconscious man to wet his face, clothes and legs, and fanned the patient to cool his skin. The man moaned and seconds later he opened his eyes — blue as the sky.

"*¡Haló!*" Delgado said. "*¿Quién es?*" There was no reaction from the young man.

I tried it in German. "*Wer sind Sie?*" No answer.

Manfred bent down to him. "Who are you?" he asked in English.

"Ralph Marston," the victim said with great difficulty.

"Where are you from?"

"Los Angeles, California."

"Norte Americano," the employees said to each other. The poor North American — had we come in time to rescue him?

Delgado encouraged him to sit up, supported his back and put the water bottle to his lips. He looked at the men around him. "Let's lift him up and put him on the truck. Put a canvas cover over so he can lie in the shade."

Everyone followed Delgado's orders. How could this young man have undertaken such a dangerous walk through the world's driest desert? I only hoped he would recover fully under Delgado's care.

With the Yankee temporarily taken care of, we took off again. Without another incident we arrived at the Vilama Plant by sunset, and Marston was carried into Delgado's sick-bay — a tiny room with two iron beds and shelves full of medical paraphernalia. I trusted he was in good hands with Delgado. Before I fell asleep that night, I said a prayer for the young American.

On my last day in the desert Manfred and I came back from the shrunken Vilama creek where I had picked up several colorful rocks to take back to the children. On arrival at the plant we saw Emilio Delgado pumping gas and packing bags into a pickup with its hood off.

When Manfred stopped next to him, Delgado said, "An Indian woman in labor has complications. Her shack is at 12,000. I left a message at the office."

"Do you need any help?" I asked boldly.

He looked directly into my eyes through his thick lenses. "I sure could use a hand. But it's at 12,000 feet."

"I've been that high up before."

"Take water along, Ev," Manfred said.

"I've got enough," Delgado said. He jumped into the driver's cabin and started the engine. I slid in next to him. As the pickup rolled down the path, I waved goodbye to Manfred.

Surprised by my own boldness toward this distant, taciturn man, I was immediately distracted by an unforeseen struggle for survival in his truck. In comparison to Manfred's careful driving on the gravel, Delgado took off like the devil, whirling up huge clouds of dust. The car jerked and jolted over so many rocks and potholes that I thought my inner organs would be torn from their appointed resting places. To absorb the shocks I propped up my outstretched arms against dashboard and side window.

When the terrain leveled out a bit and the jolting diminished, I regained my composure and felt exaltation take over. I was needed in the Atacama Desert to help an Indian woman deliver her baby! So far I'd been a sightseer in a fascinating spot of the planet. Now I was called, if only by chance, to be part of it. Not used to traveling in silence, I made an attempt to communicate with Delgado. "You're used to this altitude, aren't you?"

To my delight he condescended to answer me. "This is small fry. I'm often at 18,000 feet. Treating the miners."

"Are they all Indians?"

"Oh no! They are all ordinary Chileans. The Indians consider it an insult to Mother Earth when we dig up the ground for minerals."

"What a different world! I heard they sacrifice animals to the gods. But I don't know if it's true."

"It's true. Either a llama or a lamb. The gods want to see blood flow."

"They do their sacrifices at night, don't they?"

"Not necessarily. The one I saw was outdoors and in the daylight. It was a llama. They let the animal bleed to death, saved the blood and then cut out its heart. The heart has to be exposed to the sun, because it's the sun god that asks for it."

"Fascinating! How come they let you see it?"

"The Indians consider me their *curandero,* medicine man. I've learned Aymará and have healed many Indians."

When I shivered and began to pant for breath Delgado glanced at me. "The air is thin. We're at 12,000 feet. Almost there. I wonder what's going on this time. Usually the woman delivers her baby alone. She cuts the umbilical cord, picks up her baby and walks out of her hut to show the new human to the sun." I listened with wide-eyed awe.

Soon three shacks, built of the rocks that lay on the ground everywhere, came into view. An old Indian woman, wrapped in her woolen dress and a poncho, her head covered with a gray man's felt hat, stood before one of the huts. Delgado stopped, jumped out and exchanged a few words in Aymará with her. She stared fixedly and without moving her eyes.

Delgado turned to me. "The woman in labor hasn't delivered yet. It's unheard of to bring a visitor to a patient, but you'll be my assistant." He handed me a bag while he carried another.

The old woman followed us into the Indian dwelling. Six-foot tall Delgado and even I, at five-three, had to bend down for the low entrance. Once inside, my eyes were still blinded for a while. The entrance was the only opening in the shack, not enough to light up the room, yet the darkness was relieved by an open fire. Beside it a young Indian woman in her abundant woolen skirts and a jacket sat on a blanket on the earthen floor, bending back and forth in pain. Tears ran down her cheeks. I wanted to dry her face but wasn't sure if that was appropriate. The old woman crouched next to her. I heard Delgado ask her something in Aymará. When she answered, I saw his usually stony face distort in horror. He turned to me and said in Spanish, "The old hag forced her to drink wine with ground glass. To help her push out the baby. I doubt she'll survive that." The poor woman writhed with pain, moaning. Finally she screamed.

Delgado knelt beside her. "Give me the small bottle from the bag," he said to me.

Trembling, I handed it over to him. He tried to make her drink from the bottle, but she refused, still crying. In the flicker of the fire, the sweat glistened on her face. My heart went out to her. If I could only help her! "Probably the glass splinters have already entered her digestive system," Delgado said.

Not allowed by Indian standards to remove her skirts he held his ear to her stomach, feeling all over her abdomen. Then he spoke to the other woman in Aymará.

He turned to me. "Hold her hands down so she won't tear her

blouse to pieces. I just told the old one I'm going to break the taboo and check her friend out."

I knelt down behind her head, bent over the panting woman and held her wrists down. Delgado reached his hand under the woman's many skirts.

She began to scream again, and only with effort I understood Delgado. "A part of the umbilical chord is hanging out. It's not pulsing. I feel the baby's head — it's stuck. Christ, she's bleeding like a slaughtered sheep!" He removed his hand. It dripped with blood.

The grip of the woman's hands were now loosening, so I removed mine from hers, took two pieces of cloth from the bag, handed one to Delgado and with the other one gently rubbed the sweat from her face.

Delgado wiped off his hands to get ready for a final checkup. Blood oozed from under her skirts. Her groans weakened. "She's bleeding to death," Delgado said.

"And the baby?" I asked.

"A stillbirth. It's been too long in the birth canal." All this torture in vain! I gently stroked strands from her forehead. Her moaning had turned into a whimper.

"Take a candle out and hold it close to her face," Delgado said. I did. The color of her high-cheekboned face turned gray and her lips bluish-white. In the flickering candle light Delgado pulled her eyelids back. She had stopped whimpering and was breathing her last. But she would not be alone; together with her baby she would now make the journey into a better world.

Delgado made the sign of the cross over her body and turned to discuss last matters with the old woman. She kept her eyes cast down and I couldn't read any thoughts or feelings in her stony face. We gathered our bags, left the shack and climbed in the pickup.

"Oh God," I said. "All her pain for nothing."

For a while there was silence. "Life is a struggle, and then we die," Delgado said.

Sadly, I looked at a new desert before me. Rocks, sage tufts and the eternal sun hadn't changed. It was I who was undergoing a transformation. What was my place in the Southern Hemisphere anyway? Not rich, not poor, a *gringa,* now and then making music, worshipping Chile's nature, yet not belonging to the Chilean nation yet, but struggling to be needed. And now it was Delgado who had elevated me from a sightseer to one who in the future might have the privilege of serving the Indians. "I want to thank you for letting me help," I said.

I became aware of the pickup's occasional jolts. No longer in a hurry, Delgado drove more slowly and carefully on the gravel. "If you like, you could help me now and then," he said. "There's no end of misery among the people here."

I swallowed. "I'm flying home tomorrow."

"Then forget the whole thing," he said gruffly.

"But I'll come back," I heard myself say as though to seize the opportunity. I would come back!

"Maybe then," he grumbled and fell taciturn again. I shall come back! it rang in my head all the way home.

When we reached the plant I was so absorbed in my thoughts about the future that at first I didn't see Manfred. He opened the truck door for me. "How did it go?" I was still too overwhelmed to tell him of my experience, so I only nodded.

"The woman had been given ground glass to swallow. She bled to death," Delgado reported. "Her baby was stillborn."

"For heaven's sake," Manfred said. "Can these people ever be taught?"

"To change their way of life? Who should do that?"

Manfred fell silent. After a while he said, "Now we have to report the death to the San Pedro police."

"I'll do that," Delgado said.

Only when we retired to our room I was able to give Manfred the details of what happened in the Indian's shack. Manfred shook his head in exasperation. "It's a rough life up here. How do you feel now about moving?"

"I'll come back. I want to be with you. And I want to help out here. As soon as I have wrapped up things in Santiago, I'll be back."

He took me in his arms, holding me tight. "I can hardly wait to have you all here."

After a delicious night of love-making he drove me early in the morning to Calama for a commercial flight to Santiago. Outside the Calama oasis the "airport" was nothing but a rough road, where the biggest rocks had been removed. No buildings, no flight personnel, nothing but the naked desert in the sun. Manfred parked the pickup in the middle of nowhere. Holding hands, we approached the "road," which had been rutted by taxying airplanes.

More or less on time a propeller-driven commuter plane with the letters LAN CHILE appeared above us, descended onto the rocky road and came to a halt. A door opened, a four-step ladder unfolded and two passengers climbed down to the desert floor. A taxi cab picked them up and sped away.

The pilot called from inside. *"Suba, no más, Señora,* please come in."

One last time I hugged and kissed Manfred, thanked him for the wonderful vacation and climbed in the commuter plane. It took off with me as the only passenger. From above I saw Manfred waving at me. He wouldn't be alone for too long. I'd leave Santiago and its fascinating life behind me and move with the children to the wondrous desert.

10. SETTING OUT FOR THE NORTH

In March the summer drew to a close, vacationers returned from the beach and students prepared to go back to school. I wrapped up most of my obligations. Without much difficulty I found a pianist to replace me at the MÚSICA chamber group. She also took over my jobs with the Ballet and the neighborhood church. Only a little did I regret giving up all my musical alliances. Manfred was waiting in the solitude of the desert, and the Indians were on my mind.

One evening a loud whistle came from the street, aimed at our house. The mailman had a letter for me. "Ten cents, please," he said. I paid my fee and went to read the letter. It was from Manfred.

"Planta Vilama, March 1953.

"My beloved Ev! Yesterday my boss, Don Francisco, arrived at the Vilama Plant with news. He wants to enlarge the export of sulphur and needs me in the near future to do this in Antofagasta, a city of 100,000. Hurrah! We can all be together in the beautiful harbor town, the children can go to school there, and we'll be living in civilization! It's a very nice promotion for me. We can save much more money in Antofagasta than living separately. The Palmas are moving to Antofagasta too and so we'd find old friends there.

"Break camp in Santiago, sell as much as you can. I'm waiting for you. We'll buy new furniture in Antofagasta, where everything arrives by ship from all different countries.

"Contact Svensen about flights for you and the children. Even if we had to stay in Vilama for a short time, remember, I miss you and I can offer you the most splendid desert in the world with geysers, grand volcanoes and fabulous sunsets.

"My bed is so cold without you —

"I take you in my arms. Love, Manfred."

My hands let the letter drop in my lap. This was Manfred, my dynamic husband of eleven years, storming through the world and sweeping me along. Hardly had I settled in this great, sizzling metropolis, then he pulled me into the desert and on to Antofagasta.

But what about my planned work for the Indians? Manfred didn't say how long we would stay at the Vilama Plant. Well, time brought wisdom. Once there, I'd see where I was needed most. Already I felt my old lust for adventure surface. Don't waste any time, I told myself. Put a sales note in the bakery, sell what you can, store the piano, call the office for a flight, pack and leave! I accomplished much of that in two weeks.

The day before our departure I visited the Toros to say goodbye. I took Little Bear along, who begged to play with her favorite Pancholo.

After three long summer months apart, we had a jubilant reunion. "Hello!" I said. "How was it in Viña del Mar, the Pearl of the Pacific?"

"Hot beaches and a cold ocean," Gloria replied. At the luncheon table we were twelve. While Filomena served cazuela soup and open-face sandwiches I told them about my pending departure.

"You'll leave Santiago after you have established yourself here?" Ricardo asked indignantly.

I nodded. "Can't you understand that I want to be with my husband?"

"I do. But you are a rising star in the music world! Do you realize that?"

"That's exaggerated," I said. "But no matter what, Manfred is more important to me."

"We just don't want to lose you," Gloria said.

Ricardo leaned back. "Sooner or later you'll be back. Nobody can stand the desert for long."

I dismissed his prophesy on the spot.

Later, over coffee and cake, Gloria exploded. "What about your friend Dolores Mannerheim? She soon will be in the gossip columns of the magazines."

I glanced from her annoyed face to her husband, who had already lit his pipe and hid behind the blue smoke. "Just back from vacation and you have already heard about her?" I asked.

"They're talking about her and Miguel Fuentes everywhere," she said. "His actress-wife is in Europe, and Dolores immediately sidled up to him."

I had always felt so close to the lovers that I was unable to come up with a judgment. I decided to evade the issue. "In the theater world this is very common."

The tension in Gloria's face rose. "Does anybody think of the betrayed wife?"

For a second I wondered why she was so upset about people who actually were far removed from her. Maybe the affair between Dolores and Miguel reflected her own problem? I decided to toss the ball to her smoking husband. "How do you feel about it, Ricardo?"

With relish he sucked on his sacred pipe and produced a beautiful blue smoke ring like an Indian wise man. "The usual situation. If a wife doesn't care enough for her man and goes away for three months, he looks elsewhere."

"Women have no rights in this country," Gloria said reproachfully.

Ricardo knocked out his pipe. "That's grossly exaggerated. Yet a married man can certainly have a mistress. It even enhances his status as a virile man. If a married woman has a lover she's condemned. That is extremely important in our culture. Miguel Fuentes' star has actually risen because of his affair with Dolores Mannerheim. Beyond that, she's pretty, European and a well-known figure in Santiago's opera world. By the way, what's she going to do when Miguel's wife comes back?"

"Withdraw and let time heal, I guess," I said.

Ricardo shook his head. "It won't be easy. Miguel's wife is a spitfire. She may blow up."

I remembered his words when Dolores stormed into my house the next day. "She's back!" she cried, tears running down her cheeks. She threw herself into my arms and sobbed without restraint.

I held her for a long time. When she quieted down, I led her to the sofa and sat next to her.

Dolores wiped her tears. "Miguel moved back to his apartment two days ago as we had planned. His wife came back the next day." She blew into her handkerchief. "I always knew it would come to this. But it's different when it really happens." She shivered. "It's terrible to be alone."

Seeing the tears come again, I put my arm around her shoulder. And now when she needed a friend the most I was leaving Santiago! "You once said you had your music to carry you over the pain. What about the operas this winter?"

At least her tears had stopped. She nodded. "'Aida' first. Later 'Tosca.' But I won't be able to do 'Tosca.'"

"Why not?"

She looked me full in the face. "I'm pregnant."

Her words hit me like a bomb. The lighthearted summer affair had turned into a nightmare. "Oh, my God," I said.

Dolores sat there, composed, her attractive features calm, her still slim body erect. "I have accepted the fact," she said in a controlled voice. "I'll do 'Aida' and then go back to Europe."

We'd be even farther apart! "Have you thought of abortion? It's illegal in Chile, but I heard it's easy to get it anyway."

She shook her head. "No, I won't do that. It's against my belief. I'll have this child in Europe. People over there don't care if a child is legal or illegal."

"True. But won't you miss Chile? You said you love it."

"I'll never cease to love it," she said, her voice shaky, her eyes filling with tears. "But I have to think of the baby. It would be best for him or her — " a slight smile came to her face — "to be far away from any gossip."

"When do you expect it?"

"In December."

I gave her a long hug. "I'll miss you."

She held me tight. "I'll miss you too."

Next day Svensen flew us to the Atacama Desert. As Santiago disappeared in the distance my thoughts rushed back to my friend in trouble. My farewell from Dolores had taken its emotional toll. But her last words built a bridge to the future.

"How do you feel leaving Chile?" I'd asked her.

"I leave it only physically," she'd said. "My child is half Chilean, so I'm taking this wonderful country with me."

Now at the end of my separateness from Manfred I allowed my own wishes to flood in. On my way to be reunited with him for a long future, I was ready to fulfill my wish for another child. Born either in the desert or in Antofagasta, he or she would be Chilean — way ahead of us!

Hours later the Cessna descended over the Atacama and landed on Vilama's rocky road.

11. FRONTIER LIFE

There he was as I had dreamed of him, tall and slim in his dusty overall, his sun-tanned skin darker than his blond hair, his blue eyes radiating warmth and love. He took me in his arms, held me tight, murmured, "My treasure," and hugged and kissed the children.

The Vilama River was swollen. As our truck sank into the flood, Lilo's eyes widened in horror, and I took her hand in mine. "We'll be through in a minute." Now I was an old-timer in the desert!

When we were out of the river, I turned to Manfred. "I brought you lettuce, black bread and liverwurst."

"I can hardly wait. I'm slowly getting fed up with stews, tough meat and gluey rolls."

The flag was not out for me this time. At the two gas pumps they were busy filling up trucks as usual.

Manfred's large room now held five beds, lining the walls, and a dresser and two more chairs had also been added.

"Remember this is only a temporary solution," Manfred said. "A transition period before Antofagasta."

"Never mind! We are in this wonderful desert."

"It's totally safe here. No streets, no street crimes."

"And no pediatricians!" I said.

"Emilio Delgado cures young and old, whites and reds."

"And we are finally together."

After dinner I put the children to bed, and Manfred and I talked until they were sound asleep. We didn't have to be concerned about sleeping with them in the same room, knowing that they had inherited Manfred's deep-sleep pattern.

Manfred and I lay in each other's arms all night long. He

held me tight. Wordlessly, we let nature take its course. Intuitively I knew I had conceived a new child, a Chilean child, and it would be born in Antofagasta.

In the morning I discovered a human skull on the wash basin shelf in the corner. From its open top protruded a tooth brush and a tooth-paste tube. "My God, what is that?"

"When they dig at construction sites, they find all kinds of fossils," Manfred said while he put on his socks. "I have more of these bones in my office. All this may become valuable as soon as archaeologists take over. So far, nobody cares."

I stared at him. "What else is new in the desert?"

Ready to go to his office, he grabbed his papers from the table. "There's a new restlessness among the miners."

With a bitter smile I asked, "So the music hasn't helped?"

He shook his head. "They won't take their terrible living conditions anymore."

"Are they going to revolt?"

"I don't think so. At least not now. But don't worry about it." He kissed me. "See you at lunch." Despite his unconcern I hid the skull in the dresser.

At midday, as we entered the dining room, "my" speaker obtruded itself on me with blaring marching music. The employees began to file in. Some smiled at me. One said, "Our music lady."

"What kind of music are you going to make this time?" Manfred asked.

"None. I hope to be of use to Delgado." My eyes searched for him. He was one of the last ones who entered. I thought I even saw a trace of a smile on his face as we greeted each other. Again I met Wolters, the German engineer, and Gómez, the technical manager.

We sat together with Gómez and Svensen. The pilot animatedly told hair-raising flight stories, while Gómez sat taciturn; his thick lips opened only for the food.

"I heard the workers have found more fossils in the mine," Svensen said. "There are rumors the government will finally step in and organize the digging."

"Good idea," Manfred said. "Apparently we're sitting here on a historical site."

A kitchen helper served the popular cazuela. Gómez wiped his thick lips with a napkin. "I have more news. The miners may go on strike. They want more money."

Manfred looked up. "They just got a raise."

Gómez turned down his lips in contempt. "Bribery in a wasteland! They want more."

"President Ibáñez recently forced a bill through Congress that the miners get tax deductions for each of their children," Manfred said.

Gómez's face remained stern. "They are still angry."

"Who's stirring them up?" Manfred asked. "Do you have any names?"

"Salvador Allende," Gómez said calmly. "His men hold meetings with the miners after work."

Svensen's face reddened. "Allende lost in the presidential election. Now he's making trouble. Even here."

"He said very clearly he'd be back," Manfred said. "And as we can see, he means it."

Back in our room, I said, "What a job for you! To take a strong line with both sides!"

"The restlessness is definitely political," he said. "Chileans generally are very peaceful and conservative, but I have a hunch they won't stay this way for long."

"Why are they more rebellious than before?"

"Miners have a difficult time. Their life is hazardous with the constant danger of avalanches. They got more benefits, but they still want more." After a moment he added, "I don't blame them."

"I guess it's no fun having to juggle with the poor and the rich."

"That's the administrator's job."

"It's good you are such a diplomat. You'll manage this too."

"Thanks, my darling."

The family was reunited at last! I began to teach the children to read and write in both languages. They always spoke Spanish to each other and German to us without hesitation. The switch from one language to the other happened automatically, and I understood what I had heard before: the second language, if imposed early in life, is just another acquisition.

I took the children to the Vilama River, which overnight had shrunk to a shallow creek, barely squeezing itself between the pebbles. "Bah!" Lilo cried.

"What's the matter?"

"I drank the water and it's salty as hell!"

"Don't drink it! The whole desert is soaked with salt."

"How come?"

"Thousands of years ago everything here was under water, under a great ocean. Fish were swimming where the tree branches are now."

"Mermaids also?"

I smiled. "No mermaids. Just fish 'n stuff."

Lilo was sitting on the pebbles, warmed by the sun, her eyes open in awe. "What happened to all the fish when the water went away?"

"They died." She began to cry. "What's the matter, Lilito?" I used the affectionate Chilean form.

"Because all the fish had to die.," she sobbed.

I stepped over the creek to her side, putting my arm around her shoulder. "We all have to die, Lilo. There's nothing bad about it." She sobbed one more time, then playfully splashed the creek water onto her sisters, who screamed and splashed back.

The lack of toys was of great concern to me, but the children's creativity overcame the defect. One cold morning Lilo put a night desk against the wall, camouflaging it with a bath towel on three sides.

"What's that going to be?" I asked.

"A manger." She put her doll in, whose head she covered

with a handkerchief. "This is the Virgin Mary." She looked around. "How about baby Christ?" There was no other doll.

Little Bear came to her help. "Take this." She offered her tiny teddy bear. Carefully Lilo placed it on an empty cigarette package next to Mary.

I suppressed a smile. "And angels, kings and sheep?"

Lilo, seldom at a loss for ideas, had the answer. "We'll clip them out of carton." With firm lines she drew the whole bunch of followers on a discarded folder, cut them out and placed them around baby bear Christ.

"She'll become an artist," Manfred said.

As soon as the sun rose the three ran out to the patio, romping around. I stayed in the room to read. A few minutes later the door opened and Lilo stormed in. "Mami, I need newspapers. I want to make costumes."

"What for?"

"We're playing carnival."

Together we went to the storage room and took out several old newspapers. Beginning with a hole for slipping the paper over the head Lilo made several incisions at the hem to create the equivalent of fringes. She fitted out her sisters and herself for the imaginary carnival.

"I'm sure Lilo will become a fashion designer," Manfred joked as the kids paraded before him.

Meanwhile, my desire to help the Indians in some way still simmered on the back burner. Delgado was elusive. One morning I decided to go look for him. On my way to the warehouse, which Delgado managed, Manfred called me back. "I have to go to San Pedro to see the mayor. Want to come along?" Torn between being with Manfred and my hope for involvement, I decided not to turn him down; he always tried to make my life in the desert as pleasant as possible. So I left the children in the care of Matilda, a friendly kitchen maid. I knew if I could count on anything in this country, it would be the people's love for children.

Manfred threw a cardboard box in the pickup's bed and we climbed into the driver's cabin.

"What do you have to see the mayor for?" I asked.

"I want to urge him to prop up the bridge over the Vilama River. It's part of the only road to Calama, where we get our supplies, our water, our spare parts. If a rainstorm comes, the bridge might collapse and we'd be without water."

He had just started the engine when a worker came running up to us. He panted. "Don Manfredo, one of my children was very sick this morning when I left for work. Could *el doctor* look at her? He says he needs your permission."

"Certainly, the doctor can get a ride with us. Where's he now?"

"At the warehouse."

"Go get him."

The man ran to the adjacent building. A moment later he returned with Delgado, who carried his bag with the medical paraphernalia. He climbed up to us.

"Un millón de gracias, Don Manfredo," the worker said.

"De nada, it's nothing," Manfred said and started the car. "What's wrong with the child?" he asked Delgado.

"Probably a bad sore throat. He said the girl had a high fever, can't eat or drink, can't speak." He turned to me. "Still my assistant?"

"Anytime."

The route down to San Pedro de Atacama, the capital of the desert, was another washboard road. We left the majestic chain of volcanoes behind us and bounced through the desert, sand and rocks far and wide, unrelieved by vegetation.

"You are now more needed as a doctor than a warehouse-man," Manfred said to Delgado.

"Because there are more injuries than ever."

"Why?" I asked.

"More political unrest, more fist fights, more drunks, more knifings," Delgado said.

"Why have the Indians become so rebellious?" I asked.

"Not the Indians, Señora Eva, the miners! Their wages have shrunk because of inflation. All their attempts to earn more money are in vain. In their resistance against the rich landowners, they are the losers. They starve all their lives and die young."

I'd seldom heard Delgado speak that much and certainly not that passionately. His description of the social unrest sounded like warning shots.

With the first view of the greenbelt at the horizon I relaxed. The color of life was back, intensifying as we drove into the outskirts of the oasis San Pedro de Atacama. Stunted pepper trees grew everywhere, shading several shacks, which were composed of cardboard and corrugated iron, weighted down by rocks. A dirty, barrel-like sow with eight piglets rummaged on the ground, and chickens picked their way through the dusty dirt.

Delgado pointed to one of the huts. "Halt over there please. That's where the sick child is."

Manfred stopped, Delgado jumped down and turned back to grab his bag. He looked at me. "Come on, nurse," he said. In no time I was next to him.

Manfred grinned, understanding. "Let's meet at the main plaza!" he said as he shifted gears.

When Delgado and I approached the shack, two barking mongrels leaped out from nowhere. Then a woman of about 25 in shabby clothes appeared at the open door. Her black, tousled hair framed her round face, and her skin was the color of a hazelnut. *"Buenos días, señora,"* Delgado greeted her.

She led us into her dark one-room hut. Light came in only through the door, which also served as a window. The sick child was lying on a blanket on the earthen floor.

"A candle," Delgado said to me. I took one out of his bag and lit it. The child was covered by a sackcloth. She seemed not more than five years old. Strands of unkempt hair stuck to her thin face and her dark eyes looked sad and imploring. I yearned to cradle her, promise her a bright, warm house and a clean, soft bed. Instead I saw next to her a box filled with newspaper, in which a small baby and a puppy lay in shared sleep. How could human life exist in this environment? Where was its dignity?

"Open your mouth," Delgado said to his patient. The girl choked and coughed.

Lured by our arrival, three other children, staggered in size, came in, barefoot, in rag clothes and with runny noses, obviously the offspring of this same woman. Every year a child; she might have fifteen more. Trapped this way, she wouldn't live very long. Wasn't this hell on earth?

Meanwhile, Delgado had taken the girl's temperature and examined her small body through her cover and clothes. "Get the *manzanilla* out," he said to me. I sniffed at the many bundled herbs, pulled out a twig of strongly-scented chamomile and passed it to him.

"Make a tea from it, cool it and give lots of it to the girl," he said to the mother. "It's not serious. She'll be better in two or three days." He made the sign of the cross on the girl's hot forehead and turned to leave.

"Un millón de gracias," the woman said. "May the Virgin bless you!" That's all she had to give him in return.

I followed Delgado out the shack. We began to walk toward San Pedro's main square. "How can people live this way?" I asked.

"They have no choice. They've been kept in illiteracy and poverty for umpteen generations."

"By the rich landowners and factory owners?"

"To make sure cheap laborers are available."

I burst out. "But the church must see the misery! Why doesn't it intervene?"

"Because the church is supported by the upper class, the landowners. Financially and politically."

"I thought the church is essentially there for the poor and the wretched?"

"Señora Eva, that's the view of a child." Few people had ever spoken to me this way, but I accepted it from Delgado, whom I

saw as a guide into a world I had never known. His abruptness
didn't bother me, and to be considered by him an "assistant" on
his visits to the sick meant an honor to me.

Before us lay a treeless street with box-like cube-shaped,
adobe houses, attached to one another, all white-washed,
windowless and with open entrances. Beside the sidewalk ran a
ditch filled with fast-running water. I saw a man with a bucket
gather water from the ditch.

"San Pedro's irrigation system," Delgado said. "Also its
waste disposal. No wonder the children die by the dozens."

"How can the government allow this?"

"The government is a bunch of crooks."

I gave up my fight against the invisible authorities. Women
carried loads on their heads, while little children held onto their
mothers' wide skirts. After a quick, furtive look they always
turned their eyes from us. "Indians?" I asked.

"No. They are mestizos, as we all are. Spanish blood mixed
with Indian. Some more, some less."

"Some people in Santiago told me they were of 'pure'
Spanish blood. Not a bit of Indian."

"They were racists and liars."

Our street led us into the main square. Shaded by
fully-grown, lush pepper trees, the small area was covered by
dried-out grass. The white church gleamed in the midday sun,
dominating the plaza as well as the inhabitants' souls. The
typical square tower carried the belfry and a simple cross.

"The churches in this area originate from the time the
Spaniards conquered the land 300 years ago," Delgado said.

"Not very old in European terms."

"In the New World 300 years mean antiquity."

"Hello!" Manfred's voice called behind us. He didn't look too
excited.

"How did your meeting go?" I asked.

His eyebrows knit. "I got a *mañana* answer. I told the mayor
the bridge could collapse any minute, and he promised to get it
fixed *mañana.*"

"Meaning some time in the future," I said.

"Or never," Delgado grumbled. We climbed in the truck.

"I'd like to do it myself," Manfred said. "But I don't want to step on his toes and make him my enemy. So I must wait." He made a turn into a narrow street. "I have to go to the village priest."

"Do you need a special blessing?" I asked.

"The opposite. I'm going to pay him for coming up to Vilama the other day to give the last rites to a worker. And we'll need him soon to bless the new chemical plant." He stopped in front of a flat adobe house, jumped down, pulled the box from the truck bed and walked through the open entrance into the house.

"He's paying the priest with soap," Delgado said. "He can't pay him with the company's money. It's easier to use merchandise from the warehouse."

"But what's the priest doing with all the soap?"

"He sells it piece by piece in the village. Soap is hard to get here in the north. He needs money because he's only on God's payroll."

A minute later Manfred came out of the house. We drove up the dirt road back to Vilama, toward the snow-covered volcanoes. "You said the priests deal only with the rich," I said to Delgado. "But this village priest seems to be different."

"He sure is," Delgado said. "He serves the poor and sticks up for their rights. But the official church despises him and his kind."

"So the church is divided?"

"There's a lot of fighting going on."

After turning a corner the steaming volcano Licancabur came in sight. "It looks like an engine ready to go," I said lightly.

"No," Delgado replied. "Like Chile waiting to explode." I was still brooding about the meaning of his allegory when he asked, "Don Manfredo, would you mind if Señora Eva helped me in the sickbay or when I'm called out to see patients?"

"I think she'd be happy to be needed," Manfred said. I looked at Manfred with gratitude. He always supported my ideas and wishes. I couldn't have a better husband. What a contrast to the machos who surrounded us!

A day later, during the children's naptime, I went to the sickbay to see if Delgado needed me. Each bed in the tiny room was occupied by two men. *El doctor* was giving one of them an injection. Delgado looked up. "You're coming at the right time. Do you know how to give an injection?"

Blood rushed into my face. "Sorry. No."

He went to the other patient. "Look how I do it."

"Penicillin?" I asked.

"Yes. At the next chance you do it. Under my supervision."

"Where do you get the drugs from?"

"Svensen brings them from Santiago. I also use a lot of Indian medicines. Often they work better than the drugs."

The two men lay on their backs again. "Can I do something for you?" I asked them.

"It's payday," one said. "Could you get us our money from the office?"

"No problem," I said. "Give me your names." I jotted them down and walked over to the main building.

At the office bespectacled Alfredo Cerda, bookkeeper and treasurer, sat at his desk, flanked by two men, one spindly, one portly, like Laurel and Hardy. Workers patiently stood in line, waiting for their money. Cerda counted out the peso bills to a miner. "Count them and sign here."

With considerable fuss the man counted the bills and nodded. Instead of taking up the pen for his signature he pressed his thumb on an ink-pad and then on the line on Cerda's wage list. Four out of five "signed" this way.

"They are illiterate," Manfred said to me in German.

"What are Laurel and Hardy doing here?"

"They are witnesses and guards at the same time. In case there's a fight."

"Where do you get the cash from?"

"The bank in Calama. I send a trustworthy man there."

"That far? Sixty miles?"

"That's no matter of importance in the desert. Besides, we pay only once a month. On the last Friday."

I stepped over to Cerda. "Could I have the money for these men? They're in sickbay." I showed him the two names. He looked up at me with surprise, but didn't say anything. I got the money, put it in an envelope and signed.

Just as I was about to leave the office, two bald-headed men rushed in, Wolters and the technical manager, Gómez. Wolters' face was red and tense. He panted. "Herr Krutein," he said in German. "All our welding rods are stolen! I have to stop all work!"

Manfred jumped up from his chair. "Whaaat?"

No one understood German, and the disbursement went on. Manfred, Wolters and Gómez left in the direction of the sickbay and I followed them. Reaching Manfred, I asked, "What are welding rods?"

"Custom-made rods for welding the new pipes. They can only be used for the construction going on here."

"Then why would anybody steal them?"

"To try to sell them at the flea market or elsewhere."

Not far from the office building Wolters showed Manfred the shack where the rods had been locked up. It was empty. "It will take three months to get replacements from Germany. Everything stands still now," Wolters moaned.

"I'll call the police immediately." Manfred stormed back to the office.

I continued to the sickbay and handed the money over to the two patients. Drowsily, they thanked me and went back to sleep. On my return a police pickup truck with three officers stopped in front of our building complex. At the office the disbursement of pay to the 350 workers continued, when the three policemen in their khaki-brown uniforms entered. Their faces showed more Indian features than their counterparts in Santiago. I wondered if they were as slow and dispassionate as their colleagues in the capital.

"The rods must be found," Manfred said.

The sheriff nodded. "I want to talk to six of these men." He pointed to the line of about twenty, who were waiting for their money. The men's faces become tense and hateful.

At random the sheriff poked at the shoulders of six men, counting: *"Uno, dos, tres, cuatro, cinco, seis..."*

"Please tell the sheriff I can take him to where the welding rods were kept," Wolters said in German. Manfred translated it.

The sheriff made a contemptuous gesture. "I just need six large sacks," he said to Manfred. The six selected workers now looked scared, like cattle ready to be slaughtered.

"Is there an empty shack?" the sheriff asked. Manfred pointed to a wooden storage hut thirty yards away.

The sheriff chased the six men toward the hut, wielding his rubber truncheon. His subordinates carried the sacks. They entered the shack and closed the door.

All activities in the office halted. Everyone now listened for sounds to come from the shack. And they came. Blows and cries. The policemen's shouts: *"¿Quién era?* Whodunit?" Blows, cries. *"¿Quién era?"* More blows and cries.

"Oh my God!" I asked Gómez under my breath, "What are they doing?"

"Trying to get the names of the thieves."

"What are the sacks for?"

"They cover the men's heads so they won't know when the blows are coming."

At that moment the door to the shack opened, and the six hapless miners stumbled out, their faces black and blue from the punches, one man's nose bleeding.

The sheriff, proud of his victory, strode behind them. "We got the names," he said to Manfred.

I glanced at Manfred. His face looked pale and tense. The sheriff said the names, Manfred jotted them down and handed the slip to Gómez. "Get those guys up here."

Gómez left and returned with three defendants.

"Ah," the sheriff called out scornfully, "here are the culprits!" He kicked all three men in their behinds. "Move!"

The defendants stumbled but preceded the policemen and disappeared into the shack. The ordeal began again. Blows, cries. *"¿Dónde están las barras?"* Where are the rods?" More blows and cries. *"¿Dónde están?"*

Minutes later the door opened and the workers stumbled out. The victorious sheriff and the two torturers, carrying the sacks, approached the office in triumph. "The welding rods are hidden in a ravine over there," the sheriff said to Manfred, pointing into a northern direction. "Let's go get them."

The three thieves tottered out with bleeding noses, puffy mouths and bruised cheeks. Feeling sick to my stomach, I staggered to our room.

The children had awakened, but I was unable to play with them. I told them I was sick and went to bed and turned to the wall so they wouldn't see that I was wide awake. I heard Lilo take over my role as she made her sisters get up from their nap. I heard their cheerful talk, but it didn't pull me out of my feelings of wretchedness, shame and guilt.

The sounds and images of the torture kept replaying in my mind like a horror movie. I had been a witness to a crime and a medieval distortion of punishment. In an obviously well-known manner innocent people were tortured to get a denouncement. Manfred and I as bystanders, hadn't intervened and had so become accomplices. How could I live with that? How do I like Chile now after this? I buried my head in my arms and cried. If I only could get out of the desert!

At dinner time I joined the staff in the dining room.
"We found the rods in the ravine," Manfred said.

"What happened to the thieves?" I asked.

"The police took them to jail in Antofagasta," Gómez said, obviously pleased with the outcome.

"What a way to find and convict people!" I said. "Aren't there any lawyers, trials or judges in this country?"

Gómez chuckled. "Sure! But that's just for the rich people. Lawyers and judges cost time and money. The poor have no money and the police have no time. Force is cheap, quick and effective."

"I never thought this was the way of the desert."

Gómez grinned. "In Santiago they not only beat them with rubber truncheons, they apply electrical shocks to their tongues and genitals."

I covered my ears with my hands. Enough of these exaggerations!

When we were already in bed I said to Manfred, "What I don't understand is why the six men didn't fight back when the police beat them."

"They are poor and powerless and the police have the guns. If they get their back up, they're called communists."

"Isn't there a solution between the rich and the poor?"

"I hope so," he replied. "One day justice and fairness might come to the underprivileged. But that would mean a big revolution. Which is unlikely because of the people's political apathy."

"Couldn't it be done without a big revolution?"

"Erasing illiteracy, providing medical care and enough food for everybody? Not an easy task."

I thought about it, but didn't find an answer. "How did you feel when you heard the beating?"

"Horrible. As administrator I was supposed to retrieve the rods, but as a human being I should have intervened and stopped the police from the beating. But then the police would have dropped the interrogation and the company would have lost months of work." He sighed. "We can't change this world."

"I think we can," I said. "As you said, start with erasing illiteracy. All of us can do it. I can do it."

He took me in his arms. "Try not to worry about it anymore. We won't be in the desert for very long. Look forward to the 29th, St. Peter and Paul's Day."

"What's so special about it?"

"Peter is San Pedro's local patron saint. There'll be a big fiesta. You'll see the Indians in their fanciful costumes dance in honor of their saint."

"I thought they were pagans?"

"Whatever that means. They manage to combine the two religions. Remember the little Indian chapel?" He kept talking to me about the Indians until I calmed down and fell asleep in his arms.

On June 29, the day of St. Peter and Paul, I woke up early and went to the window to see how high the sun — my substitute for a clock — had risen. My view was blocked out by a big, long funnel of cloud in the distance, dark gray, spinning like mad and coming right at our house.

I woke up Manfred and the children. When they rushed to the window, the twister had already turned into violent gale-force winds which howled through the desert as if to prevent the Indians from performing their ancient pagan rites.

"Damn! That's all we need today!" Manfred shouted.

Strong sand drifts swept over the plains and coarse sand and pebbles whipped against the windows. Even before Manfred had finished putting his clothes on, the fine sand was already penetrating through the cracks into the room and soon covered everything that was near the window. Because the wind originated from the volcanoes, which towered into heights where only snow and ice ruled, it also brought a chill into the room.

"Wrap yourselves up in blankets," Manfred said before he went to the office.

We took them from the beds, wrapped them around us and stared out into the madness as the winds kept twisting, turning and raging through the canyons with ferocious power, whisking a trash can up onto the flag pole and hurling wooden benches and unprotected tools through the air. The howling of the winds reminded me of the air-raid sirens of the war.

Manfred ordered all windows boarded up. We had to turn on the lights in our room.

Soon he stormed in himself. "The winds come in at 100 miles per hour. Too dangerous to drive to San Pedro now."

My voice sounded unstable as I asked, "How long will this last?"

"Maybe an hour or so."

Indeed, as if by command, after an hour the winds calmed down a bit. I prayed for their total cessation.

The employees and workers scrambled for the ride. It was the Saints' Day and everyone was in a festive mood. All available trucks, one after the other, filled with people wrapped in ponchos, left, heading for San Pedro.

I finally decided to take a chance and go. I packed water bottles and vaseline for our lips. For the biting cold of the winds, the children and I wrapped ourselves in blankets even for the few steps from the building to the pickup. The wind's whistle was so piercing and intense that it hurt my ears. With Manfred as driver we squeezed into the protective driver's cabin, while all the others sat in the open back, hidden under canvas covers and blankets.

During the four-mile drive through the open desert, dust and pebbles swirled around us. Our view was greatly diminished. All we saw was dust. Dust and dryness. We all prayed for better weather.

Once we arrived in San Pedro, the storm had lost its power considerably and our view improved. The town itself had come out of its slumber, and the streets were filled with its 700 townspeople and their visitors.

"Most will be drunk after a few hours," Manfred said. "I'd like to be out by then."

The crowds came from all directions, heading for the snow-white Spanish church. The nave was already filled to capacity, whiffs of lighted incense flowing out to us.

The children had discovered Matilda and insisted she stay with us. With luck we found a place under a fully grown pepper tree, which cast its wide shadow over us.

"Listen to the strange music inside," Manfred said. I heard a harmonium play, an organ-like instrument, where the player had to operate the bellows with his feet.

"The player is using the five-tone scale," I said. "He's playing Indian music."

A movement and rhythmic noise behind me made me turn. A parade of Indians in fantastic costumes approached the church, marching to their own drum beat. "How will they get into the crowded church?" I asked.

"I don't think they are allowed to enter at all, with all their pagan costumes and instruments," he said.

He was right. They stopped their march in front of us to begin their own dance-worship. And so we turned our backs on the indoor Catholic mass to watch a group of spirits and demons, who danced before us to the sound of drums, flutes and panpipes.

All the dancers were males, young to middle-aged, with strong Inca faces. They were dressed in imaginative costumes — all different — including regal head pieces, decorated with eagle feathers. Some were barefoot, others wore moccasins. Dried seeds, bundled at their ankles, made rattling, percussive sounds with every move. Stamping one foot after the other to the drum beat and stirring up the desert dust, some dancers swung their wide coats like wings, imitating the first flight of young birds; others portrayed hunted deer.

"Watch," I said to Manfred, "they all have different dance styles."

He nodded. "A dance is a prayer and everybody prays differently."

Half the dancers played strange melodies on high-pitched flutes or on low, throaty panpipes, while others jingled hand-bells. The rest sang "Hei-ah, hei-ah!" All seemed mesmerized by the rhythmical music, including me. I felt a strong desire to dance with the troupe and I closed my eyes, imagining I was one of them.

Manfred pulled me out of my trance. "I wish we had color film. These dancers look fantastic!"

The strangest person in the group was at the same time its most important musician. A fat woman in her thirties, who had placed herself on a low stony fence, held her baby in one arm and hit a drum with such strength and regularity that the ground vibrated. Her child was shaken by each of her beats, and I was afraid it would go crazy — or become a drummer itself.

"I've been told that drums have very little value in the Indian culture," Manfred said. "Therefore women get to beat them. They aren't allowed to play the flute or pipe."

Even the woman's outfit showed her low standing. A green, machine-knit sweater stretched itself to the limit. This and a red-checkered woolen skirt were both obviously from a cheap store — as if she wasn't worth an ancient costume. Long, black braids hung from under her felt hat. Her face remained like a mask.

"Imagine," I said, "As if I would play the piano with Renate on my lap."

"Why not? You may become a celebrity."

When the mass ended, the Indians broke up their dance. Breathing heavily, they wiped the sweat from their faces. Gómez was behind us. "Want to see what they are doing now?" His voice sounded as if he were announcing a new act. Without waiting for an answer he said, "Follow me."

I asked Matilda to play with the children on the shady plaza and we followed bald-headed Gómez, pushing behind the Indians, who set off at a slow trot.

Four of the dancers squeezed through a narrow entrance to one of the adobe houses. Gómez followed them, and Manfred and I walked in his foot steps. For a moment I was torn between intruding into a stranger's house and my curiosity. As usual, the latter won.

We stepped into a tiny patio and faced a niche, which served as a shrine. A candle flickered next to tiny figurines with horrible heads and long, white garments. They stood erect and threatening, as vapor rose from a pot on the floor containing burning sage and resin — sweet-smelling, purifying, elevating. The four Indians we'd followed, still in their fanciful costumes, were in a trance and didn't notice us. One spread something yellow before the figurines.

"Sacred cornmeal," Gómez whispered in my ear.

All at once the Indians began chanting. Their words were unintelligible to me, but not their chant — monotone lines, interrupted, as if for emphasis, by a higher note. Solemnity overcame me as in all religious ceremonies, Christian or otherwise. The hypnotic singing evoked in me a feeling of community with them and the wish that the singing would never end.

But before the chant was over, Manfred signaled us and we sneaked out, picked up the children from the village square and climbed in our pickup.

Manfred tried to drive through the throngs of people. As he detoured in hopes of finding a less crowded street, he found he had miscalculated. The mob pressed toward San Pedro's only bar. "Juanita will be busy today," Manfred said.

"That's the bar owner?"

"Yes. A real character. With half the population drunk today it will be good business for her. Like payday."

"The Atacama Desert is a perfect stage for frontier life," I said. "With pagan ceremonies and Hollywood scenes. I almost regret we have to leave it."

Next morning I said to the children, "Let's go to the Vilama creek before it dries out again." Some lovely white-and-pink ball-of-cotton clouds had sneaked over the famous Andean barrier — a rare sight in the Atacama.

At the gas pump an old man with a cane was talking to Manfred, pointing up to the sky. "A rain storm is building," I heard the man say. "A big one!"

Manfred reacted fast. "Stop all work and bring in all things lying around!" he told the bystanders. Seeing us, he said, "Go back to our room. And stay there."

As we returned to the building the harmless-looking pink clouds had already metamorphosed into massive violet thunderheads. Manfred's shouting, "Keep all windows and doors shut!" could be heard even in the courtyard.

Once in our room, I heard the first rain drops fall. Quickly, they became stronger, hammering on the roof like sticks on a kettledrum. The percussion turned into rolling thunder when the rain came down in sheets as though our house sat under a waterfall. The sky had flung open all its floodgates as if trying to drown the Atacama Desert.

Manfred burst in, canvas cloth over his head.

The drumming of the rain was so loud I had to shout. "How long will this last?"

"At least several hours," he shouted back, shaking out the canvas over the wash basin. "Dammit! The rain is coming in here!" A rivulet ran from the window into the room. The kids shrieked and jumped on the beds.

"It comes through the roof too!" I yelled.

Manfred dashed to the washbasin, grabbed a bucket and water glasses and put them under the dripping holes in the roof. With the dirty clothes and towels he soaked up the water from the windowsill.

"It's raining on my bed!" Lilo cried.

Manfred and I rushed to her bed. "Get down!" Manfred hollered. We both pushed the bed away from the ceiling leak.

"It rains on my bed too!" Little Bear cried. We kept pushing beds until they stood in dry spots.

Yet Manfred's face was still tense. "I'm worried about the bridge. I know the mayor never fixed it."

"The only way to Calama?"

"Yes. In two days it's payday. If the bridge collapses, I can't send a driver to the Calama bank for cash."

Outside, rivers of rain water rushed down to lower areas, carrying mud, rocks and debris through the plant, sounding as if a train was passing by.

Manfred grabbed his canvas cloth. "Sorry, I have to leave you alone here. Must get a flood-control crew together. Sooner or later this downpour will end." He left to brave the rains.

The children and I huddled on the scattered beds. I told them the story of the Great Deluge and we counted the animals Noah might have put in his ark.

Suddenly there was a silence in the air. We stared out the

window. The rain had stopped! Abruptly, as if someone had shut off the valve.

I opened the door to the outside. The smell of rich earth penetrated my nose. Small rivers were still running through the courtyard, but the clouds were disbanding and exposing a brightly shining sun. The kitchen helpers carried out clothes, blankets, socks and sandals and hung them on lines to dry. "It was God's will," they told each other.

"Can we go out now?" Lilo asked.

"I think so. Put on your desert sandals. We may have to wade through water." Outside the building complex we were confronted by newly created rivers, which were rushing from higher elevations through the plant, carrying mud, rocks, tools, half of a door and a drowned cat.

"Mami, look at that building," Lilo said. "It has no roof anymore." The roof of the refinery had been blown onto our building.

"It looks like after an air-raid," I said.

Nearby, Manfred was supervising the operation of the bulldozers. The clean-up crew was trying to unite the several storm-induced rivers into one confluence.

Manfred saw me and called over, "All canyons are full of mud and the roads are washed out. The Vilama creek has swollen to a torrent, six-foot deep. Don't go there!"

"Our toys!" Lilo cried.

"We'll get new ones," I said, hugging the children.

"The power line is knocked out," Manfred said. "I've sent out a truck to Calama for the money."

"I'll keep my fingers crossed," I said. Despite my attempted magic, the driver came back after an hour and reported that the bridge had been swept away.

I've seldom seen Manfred so red and so furious. "That damned mayor! That lazybones! I wish I could shake him! Let him swim through the river and get him to Calama on foot to bring me the money!"

"Can't the workers wait until the bridge is fixed?"

"They are already whipped up politically. Not getting their money on time may lead to an open revolt." Manfred worked long into the night, supervising the clean-up and assessing the damage. I went to bed, feeling totally useless.

When I woke up next morning Manfred was already dressed. His anger had turned into resoluteness. "I'll get the money."

"What are you going to do?" I asked. I believed him capable of anything if he set his mind to.

"I'll show you. Ask Matilda to watch the children for two hours." More than curious, I climbed into the pickup with him. Five young employees sat in the back. I found nothing special about this, for many businesses were included whenever a truck went to San Pedro.

The desert had lost its ever-present dust layer, and the sparse shrubs shimmered in the brilliant sun. "It looks like after a giant clean-up," I said.

"Not only that, but the rain has penetrated the soil and reached all the dormant seeds. Within two months the desert will be a blooming paradise."

"Too bad, we'll be in Antofagasta by then," I said.

At the outskirts of San Pedro the stunted trees looked as refreshed from the rare rain as the stones and rocks we passed. But the shacks of the poor were in total disarray. Roofs hung aslant and the dirt around them had turned to mud. Blankets on a wire, wet from the rain, swayed in the wind. Where were the church and the city officials, the charities to help the children of the poor?

Yet as we entered San Pedro, which now was rainwashed and sleepy again, my anger subsided before my curiosity. "I can't wait to see your mysterious bank," I said to Manfred.

After a few turns he stopped at one of the windowless adobe houses. *CASA JUANA* it said below the roof in big faded letters, Juana's House.

Manfred stopped in front of the bar. "Here we are."

"Are you planning a hold-up?" I followed him inside. My eyes gradually adjusted to the darkness, only dimly relieved by a naked bulb which dangled from the ceiling. There were several small tables and chairs and a bar with six stools. Completely empty, the place looked like a Hollywood frontier set, waiting for its director and actors. I wondered where the owner was.

She appeared from a back room to check on her customers — corpulent and in a wide black skirt and blouse. "Don Manfredo! Our famous administrator!" she exclaimed.

"Hola, Señora Juanita," Manfred said, addressing her with the affectionate form. "This is my wife."

She opened wide her arms. *"¡Hola, mi hijita! ¿Cómo está?* Hi, my dear, how are you?" As we exchanged hugs and friendly words, her huge eyes studied me closely. She used her wide skirt to clean off a table. "Sit down!" We did and she grabbed a third chair for herself.

While Manfred explained that he needed to borrow money because of the inaccessibility of the Calama bank, I looked at her chubby face. She couldn't be older than forty-five. Her disheveled black hair was already graying, but her shrewd eyes were alive. She was very much the independent woman who stood up to the machos of the frontier.

"How much?" she asked Manfred.

"I don't know if you have that much," Manfred said. He told her the huge sum.

She grinned. "Want to try? Come on in!" She led us to a windowless room, where a naked light bulb on the ceiling shone coldly on her unmade bed.

While I looked in vain for a safe-box, she reached for a broom and began to sweep enormous amounts of crumpled peso bills from under her bed. "These are the wages your husband's workers leave here when they get drunk on payday," she said to me. She swept out more. "Is that enough?"

Manfred didn't seem impressed. "I don't know."

"More?" she asked, and kept sweeping.

"I think that will do," Manfred said.

"Did you bring your guys along?" she asked.

"Claro, of course," Manfred said. He walked outside and

called his five helpers in, who grinned, crouched down, smoothed out the crumpled bills, sorted them and put them on separate heaps.

"Here's the list for the peso bills for the pay packets," Manfred said to one young man. "Make sure we get them exactly."

I felt sick and looked around for a restroom. Juanita noticed. "Around the corner, *mi'jita.*"

On my return, I sat down at the table, exhausted. Juanita saw that too. She moved her portly body to the doorstep, from which she could overlook both rooms. "Do you want something to eat, *mi'jita?*" Before I had time to answer, she called "Aurora!"

A thin girl of about thirteen with strong Indian features appeared from the other door. "Fry two eggs for the lady," Juanita said.

The girl disappeared. After a few minutes she returned with a soup bowl full of oil in which the two eggs had been cooked. A small mongrel appeared, lured by the same smell that made me sick. I let it all cool off and then furtively put the bowl under the table. The dog devoured eggs and oil with lightning speed.

The five money counters had now bundled the peso bills in three packages of 150. Manfred insisted that everyone sign the receipt, including Juana. He also paid for the eggs.

"Thank you, Señora Juanita," I said and gave her a hug. "You saved us all." Everyone was happy, and we left the bar.

On the ride back to Vilama, money and money-counters in the back, I asked Manfred, "Do the workers really spend all their money on alcohol? How much can one drink?"

"They tell me, when the men are so drunk they fall asleep on the floor or even on the toilet, she pulls the rest of their money from their pockets. You've seen where she keeps it."

"And when they wake up from their stupor and notice their money is missing, then what?"

"Then she yells at them and throws them out on the street."

"A woman who stands up for herself."

He nodded. "This is the law of the frontier. If you don't play the game, you'd better go back to Santiago."

"You really have adjusted to the Wild West mentality." We drove to the Vilama Plant in silence.

But he was probably right, I thought, as I entered our quarters. Little Bear stood in the middle of the room. "What are you doing?" I asked.

"We're playing hide-and-seek."

A ghost rose from behind the bed. "Hooooh!" it moaned. Wrapped in a white bed sheet and crowned with the skull I once had hidden, the ghost moved up to me. "Hooooh!"

Should I scold or laugh? I decided for the latter, loosened the skull and unwrapped the ghostly bed sheet until Lilo's fresh, laughing face appeared.

I carried the skull to the office and had Manfred lock it away. A few days later the Chilean government ordered all relics to be turned in. Chile began to awaken to the value of its ancient remains. The spook was over.

After the rainstorm destroyed our bridge to the civilized world, San Pedro's mayor finally replaced it. Manfred got the cash from the Calama bank and paid Juanita back what he owed her. I hope the new bridge will hold for the next few months," Manfred said. "After all, our drinking water is brought over in barrels from Calama, sixty miles away."

The bridge did hold, but the water trucks did not make the trip on the day they were supposed to. Manfred immediately ordered rationing of the drinking water. Soon the news spread: "The workers of the water company in Calama are on strike." Everyone knew it was the only water supply facility in the Atacama Desert.

"What does that mean for us?" I asked Manfred when we prepared for going to bed.

"That the workers' anger and frustration have turned into open protest and strike."

"Who's behind these strikes?"

"Unions and leftist parties. Allende and others."

For a fleeting moment Delgado's remark of Chile being ready to explode came to mind. I chased the image away. "And what's going to happen to us without water?"

This time I got no answer. He threw up his hands in despair. At lunch time it became clear how we'd have to cope with the absence of fresh water. Instead of water glasses, Coca-Cola bottles stood on the table, and the cazuela soup was horribly oversalted.

"The cooks had to use the salty water of the Vilama river," Manfred explained.

"We'll get pretty thirsty," Gómez said.

"Drink Coca-Cola," Manfred said. "We've got lots."

"Oh goodie!" Little Bear shouted.

Yet I felt strangely removed from the water problem. After the meal the children ran off to the Vilama river that had shrunk to a creek again.

Under a leaden sky I shuffled like a somnambulist to our room, and without really knowing what I was doing, took paper and ballpoint from a drawer and began to write. The words flew from my pen, as if it were the key to my pent-up despair. I wrote:

>"Again the sun rises over the desert and again I wonder about the meaning of desert and sun.

>"Sand and rocks lie sterile and useless, sand and rocks time and again, in random pattern as if a careless hand had cast them away. Gray, dark-brown and black, flat or mountainous, their color offers no solace, their shapes no beauty.

>"I am looking through the screen window, which was put in to prevent flies from coming into the room, and despite my inner resistance the picture of the bars of a prison window intrudes upon my mind.

>"Surely, the analogy is absurd, for I could go out! If I wished I could run for miles and miles. Yet to what end? I would see nothing but sand and rocks, sand and rocks time and again.

"How unfair I am to the desert! Truly, it is also blessed with beauty. I have to remember the rugged lava fields, formed millions of years ago, suddenly damned to solidify — now looking like threatening points of knives. Or the Valley of the Moon's craters, boggling by the sheer size of them. Or the red stillness of the Valley of Death. Or the snow-white salt mountains.

"When blinding snow enshrines the volcanoes down to the plains so that the eyes can't bear to gaze for long, this splendor lasts until the unsurpassed Chilean sunset adds its crimson brilliance onto the snow-covered peaks, setting them ablaze!

"But only fleeting is the magic shine; quickly extinguished, it leaves a bluish twilight that spreads over plains and mountains. The day after, the hot tropical sun begins to melt the snow, and soon the loveliness is forgotten.

"It's winter now, time for cold, sandstorm and aridity. Here, so close to the equator, the days' length is the same, summer or winter. Nothing blooms or wilts to set the seasons apart.

"Tonight billions of tropical stars will arch over the sky and the crescent moon, like a silver bowl, will make its steep ascent to the zenith, awakening within me a nostalgia which will soon burn like an uncontrollable fire. Within weeks, spring will make its entry in Santiago and I must go! I must immerse my senses in that splendor, inhale the jasmine's perfume and absorb the beauty of the peach blossoms! Pink and resplendent, they wallow through streets and gardens, and along with the countless, sun-bright mimosa push among the green, delicately fibrous leaves, transforming Santiago into a paradise of sights and scents.

"Until one day I inexorably must return to the desert, where the sun rises fast and senseless, and where nothing happens but the sweep of the sandstorms.

"My mouth, my nose and my uncovered skin are now
dried out. My hands are wrinkled like those of an old
woman. Horrified I rush to the mirror to see whether my
face too shows these signs. But it is only the face of
someone who has cried a great deal."

I noticed how much the writing had relieved me; I felt as if
I had shed a burden. A new sensation gripped me: deep
satisfaction with putting words on paper. I put the pages in an
envelope and addressed it to Dolores in Santiago.

As I walked to the office, the sun broke through the leaden
clouds in another triumph over the day's gloom. I became aware
of the rotten-egg smell from the sulphur refinery, but it didn't
bother me a bit; I had transformed my sadness into writing. I
knew I could do this again if I needed to.

Fortunately, the absence of fresh water came to an end after
a week. The demands of Calama's workers were met, and water
trucks linked us again to the civilized world and its life-giving
resources.

Even so, the dissatisfaction of the lonely men in the desert
showed its ugly face. Bickering, name-calling and fist fights
gained ground, and Manfred, peaceful by nature, had a hard
time standing up to the rowdiness of the mob.

"The only thing that really works in the desert is the stick. Or
at least a kick in the ass," Gómez said to Manfred at the dinner
table.

Later, in our room, Manfred told me: "Sorry, I just can't
treat people that way. I'd feel like a Gestapo hangman."

The general tension rose as one of the jealous office workers
brought to Manfred's attention that Cerda, the bookkeeper, had
embezzled company money.

I happened to pass by the office when Cerda and his accuser
began to shout and to beat each other. The young office helper
slapped Cerda's face so that his glasses fell to the floor, breaking
into pieces. Cerda, though half-blind now, slammed his fist in
the young man's face. Blood streamed from his nose, which he

tried to wipe away with his sleeve.

When he ducked for his next blow I pressed my handkerchief against my mouth and ran through the courtyard to our room. But even from that distance I heard the shouting and beating. I stopped my ears but couldn't keep back my tears.

A little later Manfred walked in, pale, his face distorted. "These damned scoundrels!"

"Did they finally give up their fight?"

"It took me some time to separate them. They almost beat each other to a pulp."

I yearned for deliverance. "When are we moving to Antofagasta?"

"Not before the boss flies up here."

Seldom had I waited for any man's arrival as I did for Don Francisco's. In my fantasies our family lived among rough, lawless men, and Don Francisco became our rescuer, who would deliver us from Vilama's misery and take us to Antofagasta with its comforts and amusements.

Finally, in August, in the middle of winter, as cold, strong gales howled through the desert, pilot Svensen, using a narrow window between two hurricanes, flew the Cessna into Vilama. Shortly after Manfred pulled up in front of the plant with a bald-headed gentleman in the passenger seat. Don Francisco! The day of deliverance had finally come.

I danced with the children in our room, and they couldn't get enough of it. I took them to the dining room where the employees gathered for a late supper. We were already seated when Manfred and Don Francisco approached our table. The tall middle-aged giant wore an ice-blue sweater and black pants. His glacier-blue eyes were expressionless, and he didn't smile as we shook hands and exchanged a few polite phrases.

Manfred didn't appear too happy, and I knew at once that Don Francisco had brought bad news. Still, I decided to try a positive approach. "I hope you brought good news, Don Francisco. We've been waiting for your arrival for quite a while."

He didn't look at me, neither did he smile. "It may be a surprise to you, señora, but the world has changed out there."

I crumpled the napkin on my lap. "In what regard?"

"The Korean War is finally over." He was so un-Chilean, so cold, so stern-faced.

"Does this affect us here?"

"Very much so."

Silence.

His ice-blue eyes, matching his sweater, focused on me. "Since the Americans have signed the armistice in June, they no longer need our sulphur. So I'm going to close the Vilama Plant."

The broken pieces of our dreams and plans were tossed around and trampled to dust by this man. Manfred kept his eyes on his plate, slowly chewing his tough beefsteak.

"The closure of the Vilama Plant will take a while," Don Francisco said. "Of course, all plans for Antofagasta are canceled."

My cup was filled to the brim, and I no longer cared where Francisco's mutterings went. As a matter of fact, I was unable to listen further, and after dessert the children and I left for our room. We went to bed right away.

When Manfred came in and sat on my bed, he first said nothing as if to gather strength for the decision he had to make. Then he summed the situation up in one word.

"Shit!"

12. NEW WAYS

After only five months I left the desert again. Caught by a thunderstorm, we braved the shaky flight until we finally arrived in Santiago. Late at night I took a taxi to Dolores' house. I had only Lilo and Renate with me. Manfred had to dissolve the Vilama Plant, which would take at least a month, and Little Bear had begged to stay with him in the desert.

Dolores, advanced in pregnancy, was the same wonderful friend she'd always been. Although she was in the process of packing and leaving for Germany, her house, already in chaos, became my haven and springboard for our new life.

"I received your essay on the desert. You're quite a writer." Dolores said at the breakfast table. "What are you planning to do? Back to your music? MÚSICA is still going strong. You'd just have to give some interviews and the offers would come."

I shook my head. "First I have to find a house."

Every morning I studied the for-rent ads in the newspaper and went to see those homes within our budget.

With concern I noticed the people's growing discontent, written in graffiti on many walls:

ALLENDE PARA EL PUEBLO

Allende for the people. The hope of the underdog.

I found a brand new bungalow on a street called Vista Hermosa, Beautiful View, correctly named. White-painted and with large windows and a pointed roof, it lay at the foothills of the Andes. Every single room had a French door to the outside. It was surrounded by a large patch of land, untended and overgrown with knee-high weeds, which needed to be eventually cultivated as a garden.

The one feature that made me decide to rent this house was

the huge, snow-capped mountain wall behind it, rugged, unconquerable, a fort, eternal, eternity itself! Turning my eyes upon its majestic peak, I felt my own problems shrink to thimble-size. I was under the protection of the Andes again. Deep gratitude filled me: to be back in Santiago, to live so near the mountains, and to be challenged to begin a new act in the drama of life.

Within one week I enrolled Lilo at the German school, got my piano out of storage, bought Dolores' furniture and moved it into my new house.

One day later I accompanied Dolores to the airport. I cried as she vanished from the country we both loved.

As soon as I had readjusted my life I went to see the Toros to let them know about the changes in our lives. Gloria told me she was expecting her seventh baby. "I'm happy about it," she said. "Besides, men's respect for their wives grows the more babies they give them."

Her assertion didn't convince me a bit. Obviously she was rationalizing her situation to herself to keep her marriage together. As for me, I felt angry with Ricardo who forced her to be so at his mercy. But I didn't say anything. I had my own problems to solve.

I tried to organize our household. The whole house still smelled of fresh paint, and compared to the single room in the desert, this bungalow was a castle.

I stepped through a French door into the warm sunshine. Small, immature maple trees had been planted on the edge of the sidewalks. Their sparse branches allowed a good view to the opposite side of the street.

The lot across from our house was vacant and taken over by squatters. From their shanty of packing crates the notorious clandestine cable ran from the shack to the power lines. On the vacant lot several small children played in the weeds. The toddlers were without pants for easier access to toilet needs in the bushes. Near the stone wall to the adjacent property stood a woman, washing clothes on a washboard. She had put her wooden trough under a faucet, the only water on this lot.

As if she had felt my stare, she turned around and looked at me. I raised my hand and slowly waved it in greeting. She answered the same way.

The next morning there was a knock at the door. A petite woman with a Madonna-like face, beautiful dark eyes and wavy black hair said, *"Buenos días, señora. "* Immediately I recognized her as the washerwoman from across the street.

"I wash other people's clothes," she said with a gentle voice. "May I wash yours too? I can pick them up."

I had a load of them! "Fine. Tomorrow morning I'll have everything together."

Her name was María and she was, like me, thirty-two years old. She already had eight children. Visibly her husband had demonstrated his virility, and there was no reason he wouldn't continue to do so in the future.

"Like all men," María said with a bitter smile, "he gets drunk on paydays and brings little money home. To keep my children from going hungry, I wash."

My desire to help was frustrated by my unfamiliarity with groups who organized aid for the poor. At the moment I could only say, "If you or your children ever need injections, let me know. I learned how to do that up north."

Yet she never complained, and I never heard her children cry. She was always with them, giving them all her love and the meager food she could afford. I decided to regularly bring over meals for her children.

Since a neighbor catty-corner across the street did the same we soon became friendly. Alicia Hurtado was ten years older than I. I admired her expressive features with beautifully arched black eyebrows over gentle gray eyes. She offered me help if I ever needed it. I was very grateful for this beginning friendship.

It was now September, and spring began bursting out in overwhelming splendor. Thousands of streets were lined with trees loaded with pink peach and plum blossoms, and white buds

on the cherry and apple trees. Since none of them would ever
bear fruit, they seemed to live for beauty alone.

I missed Manfred. At night as I lay in my bed and watched
the crescent moon rise over the Andes like a symbol of rebirth
and hope, I thought of the myriad of stars that now arched over
Manfred in the far-away desert, and I wished with all my heart
he would come home soon.

A shock seized me. He'd be without a job! How long? I tried
to fight the nagging thoughts and finally pushed them on the
backburner. After all, I could hardly be of help. And in two
months I'd have my new baby.

"Time to see a midwife," Gloria told me as she visited me.
She was visibly pregnant, but energetic as usual.

"Why not a doctor?"

"Because a midwife is cheaper and does the job as well as a
physician. I always go to Señora Ida. She delivered all my six
children and will do so with my next."

So I went to the hospital where she worked. Señora Ida was
the most petite and the most charming woman I had ever met.
Her intelligent black eyes sparkled with amiability. "I'd love to
deliver your first Chilean baby. When labor starts come back to
me. I'm always here."

"How much does it cost?"

"Medical care is free in Chile."

On my way out of the hospital I ran into Dr. Larraín, who
once had made house calls for Little Bear. He greeted me as if
we'd been old friends, asking in the Chilean way about Little
Bear and all my family members he had never seen.

"Your husband is an engineer and looking for a job?" he
asked. "He should try at F. L. That's short for *Fundición
Libertad*. My father-in-law is working there. He sure could help
him." A job possibility for Manfred! I'd never heard about the
foundry, but that didn't mean anything. Dr. Larraín told me
where it was.

"Your father-in-law's name?" I asked.

"Alberto Espinoza."

I thanked him and took the bus down the Alameda and walked the two blocks to the foundry Libertad. At the entrance yard a middle-aged worker crossed my way. *"Perdone, señor,"* I said. "Do you know where Señor Espinoza works?"

He stopped. "No. But let's ask the bookkeeper." He led me to an office where a corpulent gentleman with a big, red nose sat at a desk.

"Espinoza?" the bookkeeper asked. "I've worked here for twenty years, but I never had an Espinoza on the payroll."

"But I'm sure he works here."

"If you don't believe me, señora, you can ask the technical manager of our company himself."

"Yes, I'll talk to him."

The bookkeeper led me and then introduced me to Pedro Martínez, who rose from the chair behind a huge desk, receiving me with a surprised look. Pregnant women probably didn't come to his office too often. For a moment I thought I was seeing Wernher von Braun — tall, broad-shouldered, with dark hair and eyes. He offered me a chair opposite him. "What can I do for you, señora?"

"I'm looking for Alberto Espinoza. Apparently an engineer." In a flash I thought Martínez might think Espinoza was the father of my baby.

"I'm sorry, señora, we don't have a man of this name at our company."

"But I just talked to his son-in-law, Dr. Larraín."

Martinez slowly shook his head. "Sorry, señora." Had Larraín's "helpful" suggestion been another of those nice promises? Dammit! "May I ask, señora, what you wanted from that fictitious man?"

"I hoped he could help find a job for my husband," I said, on the verge of tears.

"What kind of a job?" he asked politely.

I told him about Manfred and our peculiar situation.

"A German engineer?" he asked, obviously interested. "I sure could use such a rarity. When is he coming to Santiago?"

"In October when the sulphur plant is dissolved."

"Be sure to tell him to see me as soon as he's back."

We shook hands. Again I thought he resembled Wernher von Braun who was expected to lift up humanity to the stars. Martínez certainly had uplifted me today. Besides, he would get a brilliant engineer. Manfred was a man with no limits to his potential.

Four weeks later Manfred came home, together with Little Bear, who had grown two inches and couldn't wait to go to school and laughed with joy while she climbed into her upper bunk bed.

How wonderful, he was home and was holding me! I bent away from his arms to touch his face. "Is it really you? Thank God, you are here! It's been so long! Our baby wants to greet you when it's born."

"From now on we'll stay together, no matter what." He kissed me.

"I may have a job for you!" I blurted out. I told him about my adventure with F.L.

He smiled and shook his head. "This Eva is really something!" He hesitated. "It may turn out to be a bluff. But I'll go see Martínez."

In the afternoon he came home beaming. "Guess what! I got a job as chief engineer! With a good salary. I'm starting tomorrow." He kissed me softly. "Thank you for leading the way to F.L."

"Actually it was just an accident."

He sat down opposite me. "F.L. needs an experienced engineer for the planned production of industrial boilers, water pumps for factories etc. I'll be in charge of it all."

"Do you know how to make boilers?"

"I made ships. Don't you think I can make boilers as well?" He hardly had time to adjust to civilization, to family life and Santiago's summer heat. But we would have a Christmas without worries or frustrations.

Yet Manfred had little time to enjoy the summer. He plunged himself into the new job with his usual enthusiasm and love for perfection. "It's my lucky day," he said on the day he started his new job.

My own lucky day came on January 5, 1954. While I was polishing the floor with the heavy floor conditioner, I felt the first labor pains. My time had come.

Because of summer vacation all three girls were at home. I told Lilo that I was going to the hospital, and she offered to take care of Renate as she had done so often. Little Bear ran over to María's hut to play with her favorite little friend, a black-haired, eight-year-old boy, called José-Stalin.

I carefully stepped over to my neighbor Alicia to alert her. She immediately went out to flag a taxi. The jalopy arrived and I climbed in.

María, who had seen this, left her wash, walked over to me and said: "I hope it'll be a boy!"

Her wish became true, as Señora Ida, the petite midwife, delivered my baby boy, skillfully removing the cord around his neck.

"*¡Felicidades al hombrecito!*" she called out. "Congrats on your little boy!" She held him up high so her assisting nurses could see him. "Look at the *gringuito's* blue eyes! And his blond hair!"

For me he was a Chilean, for her a *gringo,* one of foreign descent, affectionately called *gringuito.* He protested loudly while he was bathed and wrapped up.

Only then did Señora Ida put him in my arms. I looked at his tiny face with mouth wide open, crying out his anger. I kissed his face and his tiny fists that were clenched as if ready to fight the world. My fourth child! And at last a Chilean. Thank God!

"What shall we name him?" Manfred asked when he and the children visited later that evening.

"How about Wernher?"

Manfred smiled. "After Wernher von Braun?"

I nodded. "He'd be a great godfather."
Manfred promised to write to von Braun, NASA's director.

During my three days in the hospital I received so many
flowers that the nurse was at a loss where to put them.
MÚSICA, my brain child, the Scandinavian Airlines, churches
and institutions where I had played, sent flowers. Gossip traveled
fast in Santiago. Here and there little notes were stuck to the
bouquets: "When are you coming back?" They made me feel at
home, appreciated, desired.

Gloria, whom Manfred had notified, visited me. As ever, her
tight curls sat on her head like little soldiers. When she heard
that I had polished the floor with the heavy floor conditioner she
scolded me. "When are you going to get a maid? In this country
we don't do these chores!"

I struggled for words. "We've just started a new life, and I'm
trying to be frugal."

"Maids are cheap here and they all love children."

So the day after I came home from the hospital I asked María
if she knew of someone who'd do housework for me. The news
of my request spread and the next day an elderly woman, her
flat-brushed, gray hair pinned up in a bun, asked for the offered
job. In her gray dress, decorated by a snow-white apron, she
looked like an old-fashioned housekeeper of a farm mansion. Her
name was Rosa, and delight and kindness radiated from her face
as she saw my children. She said she wanted to live with her
husband on a vacant lot a few blocks away. She asked for so
little money I was ashamed to agree.

Life gradually became easier for me. Rosa and the children
were delighted with each other. I was still in a streak of good
luck.

All the more I felt I had to give, since I had received so
much. No Indians lived in Santiago, but there were enough poor
people. Yet how could I come in contact with groups that dealt
with social problems? To send over meals to María's children
across the street was not enough. If I could find some

organization....

I asked Padre Luís from the neighborhood church.

"The poor people are all communists," he said. "They would throw rocks at me if I approached their shacks."

Where in the world was the place or the person I could get information from?

The place manifested itself. I received an invitation from the German newspaper CONDOR to see the director, Klaus von Plate. "We'd like to know if you'd be interested in doing concert reviews for our paper," the note said.

Writing, my old desire! And what a challenge! Certainly I had the musical background for the task and in the Atacama Desert I had begun to write.

So I squeezed myself into a bus headed for downtown, then walked to the big building where the CONDOR had its headquarters. The old-fashioned elevator, with bars like a prison cell, stopped at the fifth floor. I got off and without hesitation entered the newspaper's office. It was almost like science fiction. With a few steps I walked back in time — back into the German culture.

The sweet, red-haired receptionist led me to the paper's director, Herr von Plate. A tall, slim, white-haired gentleman in his fifties, he rose from his desk chair, shook my hand firmly and offered me a seat. "I'm very glad to meet you in person. I've attended many of your concerts and listened to your radio shows. What we need is a concert reviewer. Would you be interested?"

"I'll try."

"Good. We pay 150 pesos per line," von Plate said. "First, of course, we have to see your work. Check the local papers for musical events. If you think one is important let us know and we'll purchase two tickets for each concert." Even a ticket for Manfred! I thanked von Plate and left his office. The elevator took me down. Back into music! This time as a critic! My euphoria persisted.

After the first concert I set my alarm for five in the morning, wrote the review in bed with pencil, typed it two hours later and presented it to von Plate before nine.

He read it, smiled and shook my hand. "Excellent German. I like your style. Now we have a new music critic! And a German one! Invaluable to our readers."

He took me to chief-editor Klaus Paschko, a short, thickset man with big, observant gray eyes. "Frau Krutein writes well," von Plate told him. "I suggest you let her review books also."

Paschko pulled a book from a heap of volumes. "A Chopin biography. I've been waiting for someone who understands music. You can get started right away. I hope it won't take you more than two weeks to read it."

"I can do it in less than a week," I said.

He looked me over from top to toe. "A fast lady."

Although I perceived the double meaning of his remark, it didn't bother me; I just filed it away as a compliment. The feeling of being needed in music and literature uplifted me. Besides, I'd be paid even for the joy of reading books!

There had been so much good news lately that I had to unload it somewhere, and the best place to do that was at the Toros' house. Ricardo's widowed mother had died and he had inherited her money. The Toros had moved into a newly-built home in Vitacura, a well-to-do neighborhood on the outskirts of Santiago.

All the houses were brand-new residences, surrounded by manicured gardens and high stone walls. Full garbage cans stood in front of every house, scavenged by hungry, stray dogs, snarling at me in fear of competition.

Chile's well-known hospitality allowed anyone to visit any time of the day. If one appeared at meal time, the maid just put another setting on the table and prepared more food. Hospitality was sacred in Chile and no visit was ever inconvenient.

I studied the white exterior of the Toro's spacious two-story house as I rang the doorbell at the iron garden gate. Good old Filomena appeared, unlocked the gate and let me in. The living room, also painted white, was furnished with many comfortable sofas and chairs. Two walls were completely covered by bookshelves — a paradise for bookworms like me.

In one of the armchairs sat Ricardo in his favorite position: legs up on a low table, reading a book and smoking a pipe.

"¡Hola, Eva!" he said, visibly glad to see me. He got up to hug and kiss me.

"Congrats on your ascent to the upper class," I said with a roguish smile.

"Appearances are deceptive. Gloria insisted on this environment."

"Are you still working at the slums at night?"

"Four nights a week." We sat down, and he picked up his pipe again. "We haven't heard from you for a while."

"If you had a telephone, I would have called long ago."

"As long as the phone company has that old-fashioned telephone system we'll never get a line out here," he said.

"Why don't you protest?"

"What for? Life is much quieter without a phone."

"Is it really quiet nowadays?" I asked. "I see Allende's name everywhere on the walls."

Ricardo's eyes flashed. "Rightly so. Allende fights for shifting powers from the rich landowners and factory owners to the working people."

"Fights are going on everywhere. In the Atacama Desert, the miners were rebelling too."

"No wonder."

A door opened and Gloria appeared, baby in arms and followed by three of her pre-school children. "¡Hola, Eva!" Lots of hugs and kisses. Nevertheless the two wrinkles above her nose were deeper carved than usual. "I hope you can stay for lunch." I accepted and thanked her.

In my honor, Gloria had the children fed before we sat down for lunch, so we could have a quiet meal. Filomena served fish and salad, red wine and coffee. "How does Manfredo like his job?" Ricardo asked, sipping his favorite red wine.

"He's very happy," I said. "He feels needed and appreciated. The cooperation between him, his boss and the workers is ideal."

I told them about my writing job for the CONDOR.

"Congratulation," Ricardo said. He refilled our glasses with wine.

Filomena brought coffee and *torta de mil hojas,* the over-sweetened "1,000-layer-cake."

"How was Wernher's baptism?" Gloria asked.

"We had to wait for Wernher von Braun's answer. He accepted and became Wernher's godfather in absentia."

While we attacked the cake, Gloria said, "You look well. Your new child gave you more radiance."

"I am feeling good. Señora Ida was a good midwife."

"Good for next time too," Gloria joked.

"There won't be a next time."

"Don't be too sure."

I was sure. After all, I didn't have a husband who felt he had to demonstrate his virility till death took us apart.

"Before you go home you must see the house," Gloria said. As I followed her out of the dining room, I had a hunch she really wanted to tell me something.

The two-story chalet was spacious with five bedrooms, two children in one room. "Your house is wonderful," I said. "You must be very proud of it."

"I?" she asked belligerently and blew air through her nose with contempt. "Ricardo is the sole owner. According to Chilean law, nothing of it belongs to me."

"What are your rights then?"

"I may live in his house and bear him one child after another to satisfy his masculinity. With other women he's more careful."

"What do you mean?"

"A few days ago I was going to send his suit to the cleaners and checked all the pockets. I found an open box of condoms."

Silence.

"Keep the condoms," I said. "And tell him, 'No more sex without one!'"

She shook her head. "The church prohibits birth control. And with *relaciones diarias,* you know the results."

"What relations? Daily? What do you mean?"

"Sex."

"It means sex every day?"

"Here it does. And no birth control allowed. Which means a dozen or more children."

It was the first time I not only became angry with the church, but I also seriously questioned its wisdom.

13. INDEPENDENCE DAY

The 18th of September, Día de la Patria, Chilean Independence Day! The day, when Chile threw off the Spanish yoke in 1818, was celebrated with great jubilation, flags on display, people dancing, eating and drinking, the latter in abundance — a holiday for everyone.

"I don't mind seeing people play and dance," Manfred said. "But leave me alone with the parade. I can't stand that military crap."

"Neither can I. Those puppets doing their goosesteps! Let's go see real people."

So the six of us took the overcrowded bus to the park grounds where hundreds of citizens had gathered. It wasn't easy to shove ourselves between the joyous people in the streets and on sidewalks. Out of open booths drifted the smell of *empanadas,* the popular turnovers. Others offered candies, shoestrings and ice cream and even tea for impotence. Photographers with ancient cameras on wobbling tripods covered themselves and their magic instruments with huge black cloth and produced family pictures for eternity. Excitement crackled in the air like summer lightning.

The sound of guitars and harps thrilled me. As we turned a corner we discovered a pair dancing the *cueca,* Chile's national dance. The man wore a striped poncho over his black trousers, silver spurs and a straight-rimmed straw hat. The woman in a short-sleeved white blouse and wide black skirt had pinned a red rose onto her black hair as the only decoration. Both danced opposite each other, but never touched. Instead, they twirled white handkerchiefs above their heads as a symbol of flirtation, teasing and eluding one another over and over again..

Suddenly a young, handsome boy of about eighteen, approached our Lilo, stretched out his hand at her, inviting her to dance. They began the lively *cueca* steps. He was a good dancer, who waved his handkerchief with charm. Lilo, who liked to dance to all music but had never seen the *cueca* before, danced with him as though they had done this together for years.

Seeing that she had no kerchief, Manfred rushed forward and handed her his. Soon she was using it like a seductive siren.
When the guitars fell silent the dancers stopped, their faces red, their eyes shining.

"That was wonderful!" Lilo laughed, and while we walked to the bus station, she danced along.

Somber thoughts crept into my head, how a wonderful encounter between girl and boy would end with the woman's abuse soon after the wedding.

At night, after the children had gone to sleep, I told Manfred about my fears.

"I had the same thoughts when Lilo was dancing," he said. "But we can't take the bad marriages we've seen and generalize from them."

I tried to shake off my worries, but they kept haunting me.

14. HIDDEN PATHS

Spring was turning into summer when I suddenly got sick to my stomach and could no longer eat. I dragged myself to concerts and wrote music and book reviews, until I collapsed. Manfred demanded I should see Ricardo next day.

In the morning I woke up long before sunrise. Above the dark wall of the Andes in front of our window dawn approached, heralding the rise of the sun. One bright star crept over the rim and shone in the marine-blue sky as harbinger to the impending illumination of the world.

A sudden insight hit me as if I had been struck by lightning: I was pregnant, in spite of all our precautions! For a while I lay motionless. To have a fifth child was small fry in this culture, but with an inflation rate of 86 percent it was not an easy acquisition.

When I told Manfred, he turned pale. "I'm sorry. I thought I'd been careful enough. Anyway, I have to take the blame for this."

"No. We both are in this together."

When I told Lilo we would have another baby, she looked horrified. "One more?" I didn't know how to justify it or how to console her.

At that moment I promised myself that this would be my last child, no matter what.

The hot summer months waned, and one morning Rosa didn't come to work. Neither did she appear during the next days. I missed her as if she'd been my relative.

On my own now, I experienced how difficult it was to attend to a baby, expect another, buy vegetables and meat at the

Vega, the huge outdoor market across town, cook for six and attend concerts, read books and write reviews. It would have been a mess, if Lilo hadn't helped out.

Through María, who still washed ours and other people's clothes, I heard about a maid who lived nearby and was looking for a new job. When she knocked on my door and I opened it, I thought the blond-tinted, well-dressed lady with heavy makeup was a peddler of cosmetics.

"My name is Inez," she said, her head erect. "I understand you're looking for a helper."

I hid my surprise and asked her to come in. As she looked around our small house I had the uncomfortable feeling it wouldn't be good enough for her. Yet she accepted the position. Not only had she nothing of Rosa's warmth and grand-motherliness, she even appeared cold and cynical. I also wondered how she could afford her good clothes.

Absorbed in these thoughts, I entered a bus to the CONDOR to hand in my book reviews. The only free seat was one next to a priest. A harmless male — I wouldn't have to worry about any advances.

After a few minutes the truth burst upon me that I'd been wrong. The priest was sneaking his hand around my sleeveless arm. I jerked it away, got up and remained standing until my bus stop came.

Annoyed I stormed into Paschko's office and handed him my book reviews.

"You look pretty upset," the Chief Editor said.

"Imagine, a priest in the bus was fondling my arm!"

Paschko smiled. "It's spring! If I were a priest I'd fondle your arm too!" Used to his off-color jokes, I just shrugged. "Why," he continued. "Love-making is the most important occupation in Santiago and men can't get enough of it. Have you seen how many brothels Santiago has?"

"No."

Paschko laughed. "Many wives work there on and off to supplement their meager allowance for clothes. There's this joke that a man, going to a brothel, finds his own wife there as a call girl..." He roared with laughter.

I shook my head. "The church has so much influence. How come it doesn't interfere?"

"The brothel is considered to be an educational institution. The father takes his son to the best-known brothel for education...."

"You're kidding," I said and stepped to the door.

"I'm not." Pleased with having shocked me, he waved me goodbye. "Next time I'll tell you about the brothels for women!" Finally I fled the scene.

In June the first cold days arrived with rain and mud, and the little kerosene stove came back into favor. We had long, flat electrical radiators below the windows, but electricity was rationed, and if the meter reader discovered an overuse he simply would cut off the electricity.

On August 1, 1955, I went to a concert I had to review. Halfway through the concert I felt my first labor contraction. I endured the pain until the end of the music and then went straight to Señora Ida's hospital. Writing the concert review between labor pains, I had just finished when Irmgard was born.

Cut off from the outer world and its challenges, I was overwhelmed by joy to have this baby girl in my arms. Her hair was reddish-blond, her blue-green eyes a bit slanted, which lent her tiny face an exotic touch. My last one, my baby forever! I instantly bonded with her and refused to think of a time when she no longer would be with me.

Manfred came for a visit, bringing me a huge bunch of red roses. He kissed me and then took Irmgard in his arms and cradled her.

"How are the children?" I asked him.

"Fine. They all send you hugs and kisses." He looked at the sleeping woman in the other bed. "How's your roommate?"

"Cora's very nice. One of those Chileans who adore Germans. She had a miscarriage."

Later, when Cora woke up, I asked her how she felt.

"Better," she said. "Next time I hope to keep my baby."
She was sunny and serene and had a nice, soft soprano voice.
She often sang for me from her bed and let me guess which
classical or pop song it was.

One morning her husband Ramón sneaked in at a no-visitor
time, told her something that left her in tears and quickly
disappeared.

"What's the matter, Cora?" I asked.

"We have to move from the place we're staying in," she
said, still sobbing. "And this just four weeks before we move to
the south. I don't know where we can stay for such a short
time."

I thought of our unused maid chamber. "If you don't mind
staying in a small room for four weeks, stay with us."

Seldom had I seen such a fast change from misery to
happiness. "Oh really, Eva? ¡Un millón de gracias!"

"There's only one small bed in that room."

"We always sleep in one. We both are thin."

Manfred was a bit skeptical when I told him, but he finally
gave in. "If it's only for four weeks...."

He took Irmgard and me home while Cora had to stay in the
hospital for two more days.

My three girls were very proud of their new sister, as every
newborn child in Chile was considered to be an asset, if not a
gift beyond measure. They also were the guarantors against the
parents' old age.

My dear neighbor Alicia, herself a mother of three sons,
became Irmgard's godmother, a fact that further cemented our
friendship.

A few days later Cora and Ramón moved into the tiny
maid's quarters.

Notwithstanding Irmgard's immeasurable value, she brought
on a problem, which I hadn't anticipated. Her diapers would dry
neither outside in the rain nor indoors, where they hung from

chairs around the kerosene stove.

Manfred turned on the electrical heaters. "That's what we got them for." Hung up on the flat radiators, the diapers dried in no time.

The next day I went outside. Our garden was so rain-soaked it resembled a rice field. I checked the electricity meter. Due to the drying of the diapers, in one day we had overdrawn our ration.

"Now they're going to cut the power," I said. "From now on we'll sit in the dark and won't be able to cook!"

"Don't worry about it, señora," Inez said. "All you have to do is call on a guy who fixes the meter. Everybody uses him."

"I don't understand."

"Let me get him for you."

Two days later Inez brought a corpulent, middle-aged man to our house. He muttered under his alcoholic breath something like "fixing the meter for you." I nodded and he staggered to the meter.

"You have to give him some money, señora," Inez said. "About two hundred pesos." The price for a bottle of wine.

Minutes later he knocked at the door. "I fixed it." I gave him two hundred pesos. "For a refreshment," he mumbled.

When he was gone I ran to the meter. Indeed, he had turned the fingers back to almost zero. I saw him wobble from one house to the other, obviously doing the same trick.

I laughed in my sleeve. We had outfoxed the authorities who did nothing to develop Chile's rich resources to provide us with enough electricity. I stared at María's shack and her clandestine cable running from the powerline. We all were victims of an inefficient government. So I continued to use "the fixer."

When the winter rains stopped and the spring sun dried up the land and air, we finally could dry clothes outside, and "the fixer" was no longer needed.

There was no opportunity either. "That guy is in jail now," Alicia told me. "We all used him. He was a meter reader for the electrical company in another district. He knew when the reading was scheduled in our neighborhood and always came a day before that. They finally caught him."

The "fixer" was out of circulation, and then another helper disappeared from our life. Inez stayed away one day and never came back. After school Lilo helped me, but it wasn't enough. In my distress I again asked María for help, and one day later I hired a dirty, fourteen-year-old orphan, named Mercedes, whose widowed father had just hanged himself. I put her in the bathtub and gave her fresh clothes.

"I love children," she told me. "And I like working for a rich family."

Rich or not, Manfred built a shelter for Mercedes, between the kitchen wall and stone fence with planks, cardboard and thatch. He bought a used bed, put it on the earthen floor and told Mercedes this was her own place.

"Rich people are the nicest people in the world," she said as she occupied her own "room."

Strangely enough, run-away Inez still lived in the neighborhood. I saw her once and she said she no longer had time to work in homes. I heard she had advanced to the position of prostitute, but I never checked that out, and with a friendly live-in maid I certainly had cut the better deal.

I dearly needed Mercedes' help for the preparations for Little Bear's first communion. "Can I invite Josef-Stalin?" Little Bear asked.

For a moment the Soviet dictator came to mind, but then I knew she meant her best friend, María's eight-year-old son José-Stalin across the street, who, in admiration for the Soviet leader, had been named after him. Little José-Stalin possessed his mother's sweet nature, had wide-spaced, dark eyes and an unforgettable lop-sided grin.

Manfred laughed out loud. "Inviting a communist to a first communion?"

"José-Stalin doesn't know what a first communion is," I said. "And Little Bear doesn't know what communism is. Why not invite him?" So sweet little Josef-Stalin was invited to our garden party and with him a few of our friends.

"We're also celebrating the fall of Perón in Argentina," Manfred announced at the party. "Today he was overthrown by the military. At least Evita didn't have to see that."

"Hurrah!" the guests called out in chorus.

At the party the Palmas had invited us to spend a day with them at Viña del Mar's beach. We gladly accepted.

The day was warm and clear. With child-like delight we swam in the cold Pacific ocean, sunbathed on the white beach and built sandcastles. We thoroughly enjoyed the day and only regretted that we had left our camera at home.

I had told Mercedes we'd be back in the late evening, but we returned before dusk. We entered the house, and as we didn't see Mercedes, Manfred knocked on the kitchen door to her shack.

No answer. He opened the door and we walked in. Mercedes sat on her bed, obviously embarrassed. Was it possible that the 14-year-old girl had a man in her bed? But her bed was flat.

Manfred made one step forward. "Who's hiding under your bed?" Bending down, he called out, "Get out of there!"

Now I saw it myself. A pair of high-heeled shoes stuck out. Manfred pulled on them and — Inez came out.

She jumped to her feet, smoothed out her silky dress. "I was so scared that I went into hiding."

"Get out of here!" Manfred said, barely controlling his voice. Inez disappeared like fog in the sun.

"What was she doing here?" Manfred asked Mercedes.

"Visiting."

"I forbid you ever to let this woman in again!" he said in a loud voice. We left the shack. What a homecoming!

On the way to the bedroom Manfred stopped. "I don't like

the whole thing," he said. "I wonder if that Inez hasn't stolen something."

I shrugged. "What could she have taken?"

"My camera." He opened the drawer, where he had left it. The camera was missing. "As I suspected!"

Knowing how much Manfred loved his Agfa camera I went over to Alicia the next day to ask for advice.

"There's only one way to get the camera back," Alicia said. "Go to the police, talk to the detective and promise him five thousand pesos. But only when he brings back the camera."

Five thousand pesos! Manfred could buy a suit for that! "How ridiculous! Isn't it his duty to catch thieves?"

Alicia looked calmly into my eyes. "How long have you lived in South America? Are you still so naive?"

I told Manfred later.

"I hate these bribes and I don't want to be part of such a thing," he said. "I'd rather be without the camera. Unfortunately it has exposed film in it. With the shots from Little Bear's first communion."

Still, I thought I should try. The next day, before I picked up Little Bear and Renate from school, I went to the police station of our district and asked for the detective for thefts. A handsome young man in an elegant gray suit and dark tie slightly bowed to me. *"A sus órdenes, Señora,* at your disposal," he said with a charming smile.

I told him about the theft and our suspicion and gave him Inez' name and address.

"Sorry, but chances of getting your camera back are close to zero." There was regret in his voice.

"I'll pay you five thousand pesos if you bring me the camera."

"Momentito, por favor, a little moment, please." He quietly slipped out of the room.

After about two minutes he came back. "We'll do something about it," he said. "Could you be here on Thursday evening at seven?"

On Thursday night at seven I entered the waiting room at the police station. A dozen shabbily-dressed men sat on the wall benches. I had to stand. I felt weak and sick, but the men didn't exactly look as if they'd jump up for a woman who looked dead tired.

Two minutes later, Inez in an elegant white flowery summer dress and with freshly-coiffed, blond-tinted hair stalked into the room. Inez.

Instantly, three men jumped up to offer her a seat. She sat down in triumph and ignored me. Luckily one of the men was called in and I could sit down.

Ten minutes after seven our detective appeared, looked around, raised his hand briefly to acknowledge me and called Inez in, who, head erect, strode through the door with him.

At 7:30 our detective came in for me. "She's already admitted she stole your iron. You didn't mention it."

"I hadn't noticed."

"She makes good money. She's working the streets now." He looked at the wall clock. "We'll get her to tell about the camera before eight." He left.

How did they time that? I asked myself. I waited.

At 7:45 the detective came back, a slip in his hand. "She's taken your Agfa camera to a pawn shop. This is the slip. She got ten pesos for it."

The price of a loaf of bread! I thought.

"I myself have to get the camera from the pawn shop," he added. "Will you be at home tomorrow morning?"

"Of course."

At that moment, the door opened and a battered woman staggered out, her face beaten green and blue, her hair a scrambled mess. I recognized Inez by her white, flowery dress which was now wrinkled and appeared burnt in certain places. She stumbled past me without seeing me. In a flash I realized she had been tortured, just as I had seen it done in the desert. Seeing this battered woman, I realized I had paid five thousand pesos to have a woman tortured, whether I'd intended it or not.

In a flash I remembered what Carlos Gómez had told me in the Atacama Desert, "In Santiago they beat them with rubber truncheons and apply electric shocks to their tongues and genitals to get them to sign confessions...." Now I'd seen the results for myself.

When the detective brought the camera the next day and I paid him the five thousand pesos, I felt like the chief priest who paid Judas Iscariot.

15. WOMEN'S PLIGHT

The CONDOR was Chile's first newspaper to announce:
MOZART'S 200th BIRTHDAY
EL MERCURIO, Santiago's biggest daily, picked it up, and
the tabloids followed, except those reporting only the murders of
the day.

"There will be hundreds of celebrations in Santiago," von
Plate said. "Be prepared for a lot of work. Write a few articles
on Mozart for us. Some facts. Some anecdotes."

Interviewed at several radio stations, I also had to give talks
on Mozart at bookstores, schools and clubs. "Frau Krutein is
serving Chile as Mozart's ambassador," Paschko told staff and
visitors of the CONDOR.

Enthusiastically I threw myself into studying for the
requested speeches and articles.

"How do you like doing research on Mozart?" Already in
bed, Manfred pretended he hadn't noticed my new obsession.

I joined him. "I'd love to do this forever."

"Is there anything I can help you with? You read so late at
night! You'll overtire yourself."

I turned and flung my arms around him. "You are the most
incredible husband I've ever seen! Most men want their wives to
be their slaves. But you even want to help me with my outside
work. You are a rare treasure!" I buried my head on his chest.
He kissed the top of my head. "You know I always felt men and
women have the same rights."

I held him tight. "Where in the world would I ever find
anyone like you?" That night our union was filled with
tenderness and gratitude for being together in the turbulence of
life.

149

Two Chileans were now living with us, and we could freely observe their relationship. Perky Cora and haggard Ramón assured us that they felt at home in their tiny room and single bed. They played cards in bed until late in the morning, and sometimes, when they heard me going around whistling, they called me in to wish me a good morning.

"Señora Eva, you'll think we are professional gamblers," Ramón said.

"We just love playing cards," Cora said.

"Don't you have to go to work?" I asked. I knew that at least Cora had a job at the Social Security office.

"We open at 1:30. There's still time," Cora said. No word from Ramón. He usually left the house with her, but I assumed he had no job.

"Are you sure," I asked her later, "the bed isn't too small for the two of you?"

She smiled. "It's perfect for the 'daily relations.'"

I remembered that when I saw bruises on Cora's face one morning and concluded that their "daily relations" had become a bit too passionate.

Then I forgot about it until one morning I realized she wore a long-sleeved sweater, although a hot sun already blazed in the morning sky. "It's going to be hot today."

She didn't meet my eyes. "I think I'm catching a cold."

Still I didn't suspect anything until I saw blood on her throat, a spot she probably hadn't seen in the mirror. "Cora, what is this?"

She broke into tears. "He beat me."

"Did you have an argument?"

She sobbed. "He beats me every day."

"Whaaat? But why?"

She blew her nose and wiped away her tears. "If I say one word he doesn't agree with, he beats me." She pushed her sleeve up. Her arm had blue and green bruises.

"Oh, Cora, how can I help you?"

"You can't. It's just part of married life. You see, Eva, your husband is German. The Germans treat their wives differently. Chilean husbands expect obedience and subordination from their wives."

What about my own daughters and their future? I asked myself. I told Manfred about my concerns.

"Chileans are very nice to deal with," he said. "But if our girls marry one of them, they could fall into the same trap and be without their rights. Unless the laws change in favor of women's rights. But until then...."

"How come men are so dominant here in the first place?"

"Blame the Spaniards who brought that attitude along four hundred years ago."

"And before that, where did the Spaniards get it from?"

"Maybe from the Arabs, their oppressors for centuries."

I sighed. "What can we do about it now?"

"We'll find a way when the time comes."

"The time is already here," I said. "Lilo is a teen-ager. She's blond, blue-eyed, pretty and outgoing. Chilean men will go crazy for her. She's also intelligent, but how many men care about that?"

Even with brown hair and eyes one of my girls was desired. One evening I stepped out to the long driveway to see if the blossoms of the four-o'clocks had already opened for their nightly splendor. Long before I could see them I smelled their sweet scent. In the light of the streetlamps I recognized the red, star-like blooms. Their aroma and the calls of the crickets made me feel that there was no place on earth as pleasant as this half-forgotten country at the end of the earth.

It was almost 9:00 p.m., the time when Renate, now age nine, was supposed to come home from her girl friend's two blocks away. I walked to the gate to look if I could see her. The dark street was empty and quiet as usual. And there she was coming — but not alone. A man was walking with her, a young policeman who had his arm around her shoulder. He stopped shortly before our house, kissed her forehead and left.

I unlocked the gate. "Who in the world was that?"

"He saw me walk alone and asked if he could go with me," she said innocently. "He said it was dangerous for little girls to be alone on the street."

Now it was I who put an arm around her shoulder as we strolled toward the house. "He was right. But next time I'll walk you home."

Meantime, the schedule of operas was established and the opera house called me to coach three Mozart operas. The rehearsals began after the evening performances, shortly before midnight, and ran into the early morning hours.

"See how long you can do this," Manfred said.

"It's not forever. Just these three operas."

We began with "The Abduction from the Seraglio." On an upright piano, barely in tune, I played Mozart's glorious music one night after the other, and its magic swept me to heights most humans don't even know exist.

As for the opera plot, brutalities were carried out by Arab men against women in the same manner they were happening under our roof. I was afraid that one day Manfred and I might be forced to take a stand.

The day came sooner than I expected. One Sunday morning we heard piercing cries that even penetrated into our bedroom. We jumped up, threw our morning robes on and rushed to Cora's and Ramón's door.

Slaps on naked flesh, Ramón's curses, Cora's cries: "Manfredo! Eva! Help me!"

When Manfred opened the door I witnessed how a woman was degraded by her own man. Ramón, pajama-clad, had his back to us, slapping Cora's bloody face. Poor Cora, in her nightgown, knelt on the bed, her black hair disheveled, her nose bleeding, her eyes puffed and red from crying.

Manfred grabbed Ramón's arm. "Stop that, man! Stop beating her and get out of my house!"

When Ramón turned around there was no hatred but shock and despair on his face. In obvious shame Cora wrapped a blanket around herself.

"Pack your things and leave my house," Manfred said to the wife-beater in a controlled voice.

Confused, I asked, "Can I help you, Cora?"

Still wrapped in her blanket, she kept her eyes cast down and shook her head.

"Get out, man!" Manfred's voice rose in anger. We left the room.

"I thought these things happened only in operas and movies," I said.

"You can see, your operas are written from life."

"Ramón looked shocked and desperate when we came in," I said. "He apparently lets out his own frustrations on Cora."

In the late afternoon Cora, well-dressed, her facial bruises partially covered with makeup, came to us in the living room, her suitcase in hand.

"I want to say goodbye and apologize for what happened," she said.

Manfred got up and gently touched her arm. "It wasn't your fault and I meant only he should leave."

"I know," she said. "But I'm his wife and I have to follow him."

Frustrated, Manfred made a helpless gesture. "Do you still want to stay with this slave driver? He was going to kill you!"

A sad smile showed on her face. "You are German, Manfredo, you don't understand. A Chilean wife follows her husband, no matter what." She stood in the doorway. "Goodbye! Thank you for letting us stay for so long."

I got up to hug her. "I'm sorry you're leaving. Where will you go?"

"I don't know," she said in a helpless voice. "Ramón has no job. He was talking of going to the South. The government gives land away to people who build streets and lay water pipes for agriculture."

That wife-beater, who didn't even pick up his dropped fork but let his wife do it for him — that guy should work on construction in the rainy South? I walked her to the garden door.

She took a last long look at the alpenglow of the mountain wall behind our fence. Yet even as we watched, the glories of the scene passed away, the sun sank beneath the horizon, and the Andes stood out, pale and phantomlike, in the deepening twilight.

Seeing this same type of scene repeated on stage, I continued with my various musical duties.

"I think it's time for the Mozart year to come to an end," Manfred said.

"In a few weeks it will be over," I said.

Yet before that our life changed dramatically.

16. GETTING ON

In February 1957 Manfred hit the jackpot. He was hired by Braden Copper Company, a subsidiary of the North American Kennecott Co., as initiator of quality control and liaison between the respective departments of the mining corporation.

"Imagine, to start quality control from scratch," Manfred said. "A gigantic task! Not only will I order a lot of new equipment from the United States, but I also have to persuade the workers to change their work habits."

"How are you going to manage that? Chileans are very conservative."

"You know my strength is my imagination."

"And your nature rejects all manner of convention."

Best of all, his salary was to be paid in U.S. dollars, which would take us out of the flood of the rampant inflation of the Chilean currency. I felt undeservedly showered with good things by a cornucopia that drew its riches from the United States.

In our euphoria we were ignoring the price we all had to pay for our good fortune: Manfred had to live in Rancagua, a town fifty miles south of the capital, while the children and I stayed in Santiago because of their German school.

"Rancagua is a sleepy, colonial rural town," Manfred told me on a weekend. "I sleep there, but I work a lot of time at El Teniente. That's the world's largest underground copper mine at 7,000 feet altitude."

"So you work not only with Chileans but with Americans as well?"

He nodded. "But the relationship between the two nationalities isn't easy. The Chileans feel exploited by the Americans. Strikes are imminent."

"Remember the graffiti 'Yankees go home?'"

"Of course. I constantly have to mediate."

"You are a born diplomat," I said. "If there's anyone in the world that can do it, it's you."

"Thanks. But initiating quality control will be a hassle." He took a long draw from his cigarette. "In the United States quality is a matter of course."

"But the U.S. doesn't need you. Chile does."

"Time will tell if Chile will ever thank me for that."

One day good, old Rosa came back. I didn't ask her where she'd been. Coincidentally, days later Mercedes' grandmother took the fifteen-year-old girl away and Rosa became the one and only one, spreading her warmth and kindness over our entire family again.

One weekend, Manfred's Rancagua colleague Federico Chávez dropped in on us. His chubby figure looked funny and very simpatico and his full-moon face radiated with joy when he greeted us. "A pleasure to see our U-boat captain and his charming wife!"

Manfred placed a wine bottle and glasses on the table.

"I thought Manfredo was now a mining engineer," I said.

"To us he's still a U-boat captain. He often wears turtle-necks like the skippers in the movies. Besides, he's a good story teller and keeps us spellbound with his U-boat patrol stories. Señora Eva, you've got a very interesting husband."

"I know he's a good catch."

Federico's gray eyebrows arched. "Want to hear news? The Soviets have launched the first artificial satellite. They call it Sputnik. It's orbiting the earth every ninety minutes."

"This is incredible!" I burst out. "The Soviets did it? Not the Americans? What a setback for Wernher von Braun!"

"Your son's godfather, isn't he?" Federico asked. "But wait! I know the Americans. They'll pick up the challenge, catch up and surpass the Soviets. You'll see."

Manfred said, "If the Americans want to catch up with the Russians, they'll have to make an enormous effort."

"Exactly," Federico said. "They'll need more scientists and engineers than they have now. I'm toying with the idea of going to the States to work there."

I glanced at the jolly man. "You would leave your wonderful country, Don Federico?"

"To work for progress, surely!" He raised his glass to Manfred for cheers.

Uneasy, I looked to Manfred for help. He didn't respond to Federico's gesture. Staring at the table, he said, "There must be a lot going on in America now."

Fear of losing Manfred to America seized me. The easiest way to shoo it off was to change the subject. "How is Señora Elena?"

Federico, picking up the ball, began to tell us at length about his wife and her illnesses. The American lure was banned, at least temporarily.

As if to catch up with developing technology Manfred bought a 1941 Studebaker. It cut in half his commuting time in the bus, which was always filled with country people and their chickens and baby pigs.

"Are we now rich, Mami?" Little Bear asked.

"No. We just are car owners now."

The Studebaker itself shed its old parts on the road right after our purchase: first a right wheel rolled away like a die, a week later a left one. Only the Latin ability to react in a flash prevented the drivers behind us from rear-ending the Studebaker. Each time we collected the wheel with fatalistic stoicism and had it fastened anew.

In quiet moments, however, the poverty I'd seen during my six years in South America imposed itself on my consciousness. I had to fight the thought I was taking something from the poor majority, for whom I wanted to work. I couldn't discuss this

with Manfred, who was happy to be able to provide a more
comfortable life for his family again. So I pushed the warning
thoughts to the backburner.

Also, I had to turn my attention to the Toros' New Year's
Eve party. They only gave one fiesta per year, but that one was
huge. It was an opportunity to meet people.

I bought a long, black taffeta dress with a V-neckline so low
it was almost indecent. Manfred, wearing his black, tailored suit,
which he had brought from Germany, looked like a Hollywood
star.

The long day's heat was gone and a refreshing coolness
hung in the air. When we arrived at the Toros' house around ten
in the evening, gay music and laughter poured from the open
windows.

Inside, many guests in elegant attire had already gathered
and were in a festive mood, thanks to the unlimited drinks
offered by the hired butlers. The ladies wore long black evening
gowns, fine jewelry and heavy perfumes.

"But nobody else can wear a neckline like you," Manfred
whispered in my ear. "I'm proud of you."

The continuous radio music lent gaiety to the crowd. Gloria
had all the rooms on the ground floor decorated with flowers,
paper streamers and Japanese lanterns. Cigar and cigarette smoke
drifted through the rooms and out the open windows, constantly
replaced by more. A maid and two butlers served tiny caviar
sandwiches, local wine and Pisco sour, the Chilean vodka.

The Toros appeared to be a harmonious couple again. They
introduced us to people we had never met, but we also saw many
we hadn't seen for a while. Miguel and Lonny Fuentes were
there too.

"Good to see you again," Miguel said in a low voice. As we
shook hands our eyes locked for a split second longer than
politeness demanded, reminding me of the days of his love affair
with Dolores. His deep-set eyes filled with melancholy as we
politely hugged and kissed.

Lonny, who months ago had taken back her radio show from me, was radiant. Her blue gown with chiffon wings hugged her curvaceous figure. I wondered if she had forgiven Miguel his summer affair with Dolores.

In the far corner of the room stood a priest, who wore his long, black cassock and the round, white collar even here at the New Year's party. He balanced a wine glass in the palm of his hand, and his feet whipped back and forth to the music.

"Every family needs a priest as a show piece," Manfred said under his breath. "But I didn't expect that from the Toros."

"Why do priests wear a cassock wherever they go?"

"Protection from women."

"In Germany they don't wear it."

"Here the women are much more dangerous."

Our gossip was interrupted by Ricardo. "Come meet Gloria's brother Victor. A very radical Jesuit, who stands up for the rights of the poor. He just arrived from Brazil."

Not the Toros' show piece, but Gloria's look-alike-brother — the same features, the brown, curly hair over the slightly curved forehead and the vivid hazel eyes. Slim like his sister, he probably was in his forties.

"Victor speaks German, Spanish and Portuguese fluently," Ricardo said. "The latter from his years in the Brazilian Amazonas area."

We shook hands with the unusual priest. Urgent questions came to mind, but before I could ask them a young, bespectacled, distinguished-looking gentleman joined us.

"Dr. Fernando Moenckeberg," Ricardo said. "My colleague specializes in malnutrition and mentally handicapped babies," Ricardo said. "He's a pioneer in the field."

"How great is the need for this in Chile?" I asked.

Moenckeberg looked at me as if surprised by my ignorance. "Señora, two-thirds of our children are undernourished and therefore mentally stunted to some degree." He adjusted his glasses. "It's not a popular fact, since it mainly occurs among the poor people."

Here was someone actively involved with the disadvantaged! "Where do you work? I want to know more about it."

Through his glasses he stared down at me without a smile. "You just have to ask Señora Gloria."

"Dinner is ready!" Gloria's voice sounded over the din of voices and music. "Please be seated."

"Can I talk to you later?" I asked Moenckeberg.

"Certainly."

There was a rush to the ashtrays to extinguish all cigars and cigarettes, the guests stepped into the dining room and I lost sight of Dr. Moenckeberg.

Six tables of eight were elegantly set, with fine china and crystal glasses of different sizes. To find one's own name card, the guests rushed around calling out names of people each knew. As in Europe, married couples sat separated. My table partner was a gray-haired, corpulent gentleman. Jesús Ramírez, said his name card.

Soft background music sounded from the radio. While the butlers served wine and creamed turtle soup I found out about my neighbors to the right. I heard Don Jesús address the thick-set man on my right as "Senator." The statesman's hair, devilish eyebrows and enormous mustache matched in pitch-black color. His overlong nose pointed aggressively at anyone who addressed him, when he immediately jumped into politics. This was no surprise in Ricardo's house; he liked to invite interesting debaters and sometimes even questionable characters.

The senator talked loudly, and his black, fiery eyes took in every detail. He kept his audience entranced. "We need a change!" he announced. "President Ibáñez is weak, ineffectual and senile. We have to work to get a capable, energetic man for our next president, Jorge Alessandri! He will revolutionize the economy!"

Gray-haired Don Jesús raised his voice. "For 140 years we've had a democracy, and we're proud of it. To change things here would take a revolution, and that kind of thing doesn't happen in this country."

The howling of sirens disrupted the conversation. "Fire alarm!" I cried and wondered why no one paid any attention. The sirens came closer. "My God, there's a fire in the neighborhood!" I said.

Don Jesús turned his old, dignified face to me. "How long have you lived in Chile, señora? Don't you know that many owners set fire to their houses before the new year? To collect insurance money! This one is late." He looked at my V-neckline. "By the way, I love your dress."

Since empty glasses were incessantly refilled, many guests were already tipsy and their voices became louder.

Father Victor who had abstained from the wine raised his voice. "It's against God's will to let one class concentrate all the power and wealth and deny poor people education and the raw basics of life."

"Victor is on the side of the poor," Gloria called over to me. "We need him here badly." She looked at the clock on the wall. Only two minutes were left of the old year. "Champagne! Let's celebrate the new 1958!" she called out.

A current of electricity swept through the room while the three servants distributed the champagne. When the grandfather clock began its twelve strokes, the crowd set up great shouts of *"¡Felicidades!"* Glasses clinked together, arms were thrown around shoulders and kisses were planted. Manfred hugged Gloria. Lonny Fuentes held a handsome man other than her husband in her arms. A man I didn't know kissed my cheek noisily. I saw Miguel standing in a corner by himself and on the other side of the room sat Father Victor alone.

My eyes searched in vain for Dr. Moenckeberg. I asked Gloria where he was.

"He's been called to the hospital. An emergency case."

The music picked up again and the dancing resumed. Manfred rushed to me, grabbed my arm, and we joined the others for a wild cha-cha-cha. When the music changed to a rumba, the dancing pairs separated and joined other partners. Miguel Fuentes was my next one.

"How are you?" I asked him, looking in his melancholy eyes, hoping to read his feelings.

He looked away. "As usual."

"What's the matter, Miguel?"

"Lonny's taking her revenge. She's got a lover."

"Tit for tat."

"But there's a difference from a man having a mistress and his wife having a lover. Besides, she's doing it in public. Look at her." He pointed in Lonny's direction. She danced cheek-to-cheek with the handsome man whom she'd kissed at the turn of the year.

I asked: "Have you heard from Dolores?"

"No. Not since she left Chile."

"She has a little boy, called Michael."

A small gleam shone in his eyes. "German for Miguel."

The smoking had resumed after dinner, and now the air got thicker and hotter. We were dancing the mambo when a paper lantern caught fire. Those who saw it shouted for help while the others kept dancing.

"Hey! Ricardo hasn't paid his insurance premium!" one guest shouted. "He's setting his house on fire!" One of the butlers had just opened a champagne bottle and now rushed to the fire and poured the bubbling content over the paper moon.

"That means good luck for the New Year!" Manfred shouted. *"¡Feliz año nuevo!"* A happy chorus echoed.

"¡Atención!" Gloria shouted several times. "Now comes the game. Every man chooses a partner and dances with her with only an apple between their foreheads. No other touch is allowed. Like this." She grabbed a red apple and placed it between Ricardo's and her forehead. They swayed back and forth, and their foreheads held the apple — until it finally fell down. "The couple, who can hold the apple the longest, wins," Gloria said.

She distributed twenty-four red apples to the men. One was left; it should have been her brother's, but he had retired to a quiet room to read his daily breviary.

On Gloria's signal each man rushed to the woman of his choice. To my surprise five men dashed toward me. Three men pulled my right hand and two my left. The winner for my hand was the senator, who pulled the most. As we placed the apple between our foreheads, I saw his greedy eyes engulf my cleavage.

We lost our apple earlier than the others. The winners were Lonny and her new lover, and they received a lot of cheers.

"I may have lost tonight," the senator said to the crowd. "But I certainly had the best view!"

Since it was three in the morning and we all had had too many drinks, I took the remark as a compliment.

Many guests were about to leave. I regretted that I hadn't been able to talk to Father Victor.

When we thanked our hosts for the wonderful evening, Gloria said to me under her breath: "Come see me tomorrow afternoon. I want to show you something. Wear simple clothes." As others took our place, I just waved to her and nodded.

What in the world was she going to show me?

17. SUFFERING

Instead of sleeping in on New Year's Day, I went to Vitacura in my oldest dress and sandals and bursting with curiosity. Located at the edge of the capital and only recently developed, this part of Santiago had many new homes like that of the Toros. The mountains seemed farther removed from civilization and uncultivated fields were dotted with shacks. The day was hot and dust hung in the air. I rang the door bell.

Inside, the house was cool and shady. A jar with papaya juice stood on the table. Parched, I drank a full glass.

Gloria had an old, dark dress on and was packing several bags. "The leftovers from last night."

"What a party!" I said. "So many interesting people! Your brother. Dr. Moenckeberg."

"Moenckeberg is studying the effect of malnutrition on children. Of course, on poor children. The rich ones get enough milk."

"What do the poor mothers give their children?"

"They roast flour and mix it with water."

"Oh my God! How can the children survive?"

"Some grow up crippled or retarded. Moenckeberg prepares statistics for the government. A tedious process." She'd finished her packing. We grabbed the stuffed bags and left the house.

"Where are we going?" I asked.

"You always wanted to see a *población,* a slum area. I'll take you to one today."

"That's where you take the food?"

She nodded. "My good old maid Filomena got sick and went home to her *población.* She is so good with the children and I want her to come back as soon as possible."

"Are you happy to have your brother with you?"

"Very much so. He asked for an assignment in Chile." After a pause she added, "I need him."

"Oh?"

"I've made peace with Ricardo — which means I'm expecting my twelfth child."

"That's the result of your peace making?"

"I hadn't meant it that way. But that's why I'm glad I can talk to my brother about it."

In the heat of New Year's Day we walked toward the mountains, approaching the shantytown settlement.

"The people who live here have no water, no electricity, no toilets," Gloria said. "It's a disgrace for the whole country."

"Doesn't the church help the poor?"

"The official church deals only with rich people. A few priests have organized groups that feed the poor, give them medical help and teach them to read and write."

"And your brother is one of them."

"He and other Jesuits. The Pope condemns them, though."

We had arrived and entered the *población,* walking on a narrow dirt road. On both sides stood miserable huts of wooden boards, nailed together with cardboard. Clothes were hanging from a rope hung between roofs. Women of every age stood in front of their shacks, their skin dry and cracked, some pregnant, many of them barefoot and dressed in faded rags.

At least a dozen children of all sizes and ages appeared. The youngest were naked. Other faces peered from doorways, too timid to come out. A few children ran and hid behind the women. It was a world of deprivation and penury in which the only consolation was solidarity -- similar to the shacks in the Atacama Desert.

"I don't see any men," I said. "Where are they?"

"At work or drunk. Today's a holiday, so they're probably drunk. Or asleep." She turned to a young pregnant woman, who held a toddler with a runny nose in her arms. "Where does Filomena Rodriguez live?"

The woman pointed to a neighbor's shack. We walked over to the windowless hut.

"Let me go in alone," Gloria said. "It's dark inside anyway." Gloria grabbed all the bags and went in through the open door, which served also as a window.

I looked around. A rotten smell rose from piles of garbage in which miserable dogs were digging. A little boy squatted on the ground and defecated. No one chased him away. The women in the doorways stared at me. I wondered what they could be thinking. In their eyes I was probably rich and living off the money that could rescue them from their misery. Hell, no! I wasn't rich and I wasn't on the side of the rich! What was I then? A spectator who'd come to experience the horror of watching these poor wretches? No, and a thousand times, No!

Gloria came out of the shack, a great deal paler than before. "Let's go," she said, folding her empty bags. "Filomena is better. She'll come back to us in a few days."

The sinking sun was dyeing the sky blood-red and, although the heat had lessened, I felt a fire in me. "You are one of those who help the priests with the poor?"

"Yes."

"I want to be one too." I felt unburdened. We were already near her house. "Tell me where and how to get started," I said.

"Come to my house tomorrow. In the morning."

My opportunity came the next day. At the boundary between two worlds stood a wooden hut, small and unpretentious like a border-guard station on a country road. The two worlds were those of the rich and the poor. On the wall toward the rich world rebels had smeared the name —

A L L E N D E

The rich just ignored the hut. Yet the guards in this hut were the life-savers of the undernourished children.

When Gloria and I entered the hovel, a petite, black-haired woman weighed a screaming baby girl on a pan scale. She read the figure, measured the baby's height and gave both figures to a white-uniformed woman, who jotted them down in two notebooks.

I couldn't take my eyes from this lady in the doctor's coat. Short, in her forties, her smooth, black hair framed her exotic face. Her gray eyes under expressively-curved black eyebrows radiated intelligence.

"Dr. Ana Araya," Gloria said under her breath. "She's collecting data for Moenckeberg's statistics on the malnourished babies."

The nurse returned the baby to her poorly-clad mother, who wrapped it up in fresh diapers. "She gained 250 grams," the nurse said.

The mother received two cartons of milk from Dr. Araya, said, *"Gracias, doctora,"* and left, making room for the next mother and baby.

The doctora glanced at us. *"Buenos días,* Gloria. Did you bring a new volunteer?"

"Sí. Eva Krutein, a mother of five."

"Mucho gusto," the doctora said, short for 'nice meeting you.' "Gloria, you can take over for me now. Here are the last figures."

Gloria took the notebook and approached the pan scale.

Dr. Araya turned her penetrating eyes on me. "Do you have any background in medicine?"

"I know how to give shots."

She wrote quick notes on the back of her notebook. "What's your accent?"

"German."

"Good stock. Are you a nurse?"

"No. A pianist."

She looked up. "Oh, I've seen your pictures in the papers. Where did you learn to give shots?"

"In the Atacama Desert."

"So you've seen the most remote misery of our country." I nodded. "You may find the *población's* misery even more wretched, although it's just inches away from the rich families."

She slid her notebook into the wide pocket of her uniform. "We need a lot of helpers here. Even more so at the hospital." She turned to Gloria. "Tell Eva what to do." She waved her hand at us and said, *"Hasta luego,* goodbye."

The petite woman, who had done the weighing, left, and I, excited with anticipation, took over for her. The next mother removed the clothes and diapers of her baby girl and handed her to me. The baby was just a little bit of skin stretched over a tiny skeleton. I put her on the pan scale. She didn't move. She didn't even cry. She just lay there.

Some were worse than others. But each time I put a fragile baby on the pan scale, I felt as though I had a new child, and the more undernourished it was the more I felt drawn to it. I had reached my ultimate goal to work for the poor.

Although this milk distribution center was open daily, I worked there only once a week to balance my life with my family and my reviewing of concerts and books for the CONDOR. After April, when the cows' lactation period ended, the center was open only one day a week — not because of a lack of volunteers but for a lack of powdered milk.

"Where does the powdered milk come from?" I asked Gloria, on our way home.

"Dr. Moenckeberg approached UNICEF, and from there came the first powdered milk and also the first manufacturing plant to produce it. Also the United States helps through CARE. But there's no end to the needs of the poor."

"Can't they stop having so many babies?"

"No. Because they don't know how. It's been a woman's fate for centuries to surrender to her husband's sexual wishes and to have as many children as possible. Lots of the children die early anyway because of lack of milk."

One day, in a sudden outburst of spontaneous, violent protest, the poor of the *poblaciones* organized themselves and marched to the center of Santiago, shouting and pillaging. But no one listened to their message, and the police drove them back into their misery. The poor people's outcry was snuffed out and quickly forgotten.

The suffering didn't change, but there was weight gain in the babies who were brought to our center regularly. One rainy day, when Gloria had brought in more volunteers, Dr. Araya walked in for a quick check. Afterward she approached me. "I need volunteers for an outpatients' hospital in a *población* in Carascal. Would you come with me?"

"Of course! Carascal is even easier to reach from my home than this place." I found Gloria and told her.

"Just go!" she said. "We have enough volunteers now."

I kissed her. Together with the *doctora* I climbed into her beaten-up Citronetta and we drove away.

The rain fell relentlessly on mountains, streets and people and, worst, penetrated the miserable shacks of the poor. Entering the run-down *población,* the Citronetta dug its tires into the mud of the lane between the thirty or forty huts. The engine's revved-up noise made some of the occupants stagger outside to find out what was going on. I saw their faces, red from alcohol yet somehow hopeful that a car's appearance could bring a change to their hopeless lives.

As the Citronetta stuck in the mud, the men rushed to help us. With teamwork, some pushed, others pulled the small car to a higher place. The *doctora* and I climbed out into the rain.

"Muchas gracias, caballeros," she thanked them, grabbed her medical bag and asked me to help her carry a huge package.

"Food supplies from the United States," she said. "Powdered milk and cheddar cheese. They also sent penicillin this time."

The men helped us carry the large package to the "hospital." It was a shack, a bit larger than the others, and even had a window. Several adults sat on wooden benches, waiting for the *doctora.* An empty table in the middle of the room was to be used for examinations and surgery. We placed both bags on the floor.

Before the first patient could get up there was a commotion at the open door. Two men carried in another. They laid the rain-dripping patient on the naked table.

"He just collapsed," one carrier reported.

"Open his shirt," Dr. Araya said. And to me over her shoulder, "Get the stethoscope out."

She examined the pale, emaciated man. His abdomen was bloated, his eyes sunken. "Severe malnutrition," she said. "He needs to be hospitalized. Call the ambulance." The man was carefully put on the wooden floor where he remained unconscious.

I swallowed hard. I had known hunger too, but only as an outgrowth of a lost war. Who was the enemy here?

Disciplined, one patient after another sat or lay down on the table. The *doctora* diagnosed and provided them with medicine, while I handed out food from the big package — too much at a time, in my eagerness to reduce suffering.

One woman with black and blue bruises on her face, one eye swollen shut and an open wound on her arm, softly cried when the *doctora* examined her.

"Who beat you up?" the doctor asked.

"My husband," the woman sobbed.

"Why did he beat you?"

"He's always drunk and beats me."

"Do you ever defend yourself?"

"No. How could I? He's so much stronger."

I clutched my hand at my mouth to keep myself from shouting in revolt against her macho and all the others.

With a big sigh, Dr. Araya dressed and bandaged the woman's wounds and released her into her life of subsistence.

A young girl with a slightly swollen belly was next.
After a quick exam, the *doctora* asked, "How old are you, my dear?"

"Twelve."

"You are pregnant." There was no reaction on the girl's pale face. "Who made you the baby?" the doctor asked.

The girl shrugged. "My dad, or my brothers."

"All sleep together in the same shack," Ana Araya said to me. "Give her double rations."

With tears in my eyes I gave her food and the doctor released her with a soft pat to her face.

Meanwhile, the unconscious man on the floor still lay unconscious; I was careful not to trample on him.

All emergency cases were handled immediately. We heard the cries of a baby before the mother even appeared at the door. The child's tiny face was bloody and bruised. "My husband was drunk and threw her at the wall," the mother said. "He's mad because it's a girl and not a boy."

Rage filled me. Against men, against all societies with male domination, against governments and religions which supported this view. Mechanically, I assisted Dr. Araya and handed out food supplies to the patients. I prayed the drunk machos in the huts wouldn't devour the food all by themselves.

The last wretched creature was a heavily-bleeding woman who was helped in by two others. With trembling hands and clenching my teeth, I handed all the gauze available to the doctor to stop the hemorrhage.

"A self-induced abortion," Dr. Araya said to me, giving her a shot for the bleeding. "I don't know if I can save her. It's gone too far."

For a moment I leaned against the wall, feeling worn out and helpless. In the distance I heard a horn's "Da-hee-da-hee-da-hee," getting louder. It stopped in front of our "hospital."

Three orderlies rushed in. Dr. Araya pointed to both the malnourished man on the floor and the dying woman on the table. "You've got two," she said to the orderlies.

After both were carried out to the ambulance, our job was over for the day. We stepped out of the shack. The rain had stopped. Exhausted, we climbed into the Citronetta and sat there, wordless, staring at strewn garbage, a dead dog and empty liquor bottles, all half-buried under the mud.

The *doctora* finally spoke. "We fight uphill against poverty.

You and I are just two volunteers. We need hundreds. Theoretically, we've got free medical care for any Chilean who needs it, but not enough doctors."

"Is there any hope it will get better?"

"Only if our efforts are translated into political power. But it's a long way off. Abortion and divorce are illegal, but the women haven't rebelled yet."

"Being so much at men's mercy, how can they stand it?"

"By identifying with the Virgin's suffering." She sighed. "The rich can get everything with their money. Six years ago women got their voting rights. Most were satisfied and stopped working in politics."

"Doesn't the church guide the women?"

"The church is an exclusive male club."

The sun had broken through. I yearned for a long walk in the fresh air. "If you could take me to the Mapocho River, I can catch the trolley."

"Shall I see you next Monday?" she asked.

I assured her she would. Relieved, I strolled into the sunshine.

Yet later, when I stepped out of the bus I saw gloomy clouds hanging around the mountains.

18. THE ABYSS

Gloom hung heavily even on Vista Hermosa street. Near my house, neighbors had left a bucket outside containing raw intestines, removed from some animals to be cooked. Several stray dogs, emaciated and hungry, had knocked down the bucket and fought ferociously for the revolting leftovers. I became nauseated, hurried the last few steps to my house and threw up in the bathroom.

Afterward, as I washed my pale face and studied my wide-open eyes in the mirror, I knew — I was pregnant again. Our careful precautions hadn't worked.

For a while I stared at myself. Again I heard Lilo's horrified voice a year ago, "One more?" and I recalled my silent promise never to provoke that question again.

The answer was abortion — a cardinal sin by church command and illegal by state law. All the cases I knew paraded before my mind, being performed out of despair and without evoking the law. A woman's problem — so who cared?

There was no doubt in my mind that I would have to do it. But whom to approach? All day long and the next I racked my brains until it hit me — I would consult Señora Ida, the petite midwife, who had helped Wernher and Irmgard come into the world. Now I would ask her to do the opposite.

A day later, Ida's pretty face radiated when she saw me. "Señora Eva! What can I do for you?"

"I'm pregnant again. I need an abortion."

Her smile vanished. She looked away for a few moments, then studied me closely. "How many children do you have?"

"Five. I can't have more."

She seemed to consider. "Let me check you first." In her office she confirmed my pregnancy. "Are you really sure you don't want another child?"

"I am sure."

"Come see me on Monday morning. At eleven. A surgeon will be on duty then. Don't eat breakfast."

I felt very much alone, but I also realized I'd always been on my own in difficult ventures — the flight from the Russians and now preparations for killing my tiny baby. I disagreed with the common opinion that no soul was present until four months after conception. To me, body and soul were one entity, and life started at the instant of conception. I clearly saw I was going to murder my sixth child, but I also knew that under no circumstances would I ever have one more baby.

With a great deal of determination, I pushed all moral worries away and concentrated on the arrangements I had to make. To involve Manfred was out of the question. He was wrapped up in his work and helpless with medical decisions anyway. But Alicia, Irmgard's godmother, lived across the street and was one I could trust to keep my secret.

I decided to walk to her house. She and her maid were cooking ahead, preparing a fiesta for her husband's colleagues. Julio, her curly-haired six-year-old son, hung around the kitchen in hopes of a handout.

I sat down on a kitchen chair. "I'm going to have surgery tomorrow. Do you have time to pick me up from the hospital in the early afternoon?"

She agreed promptly and didn't ask any questions. I appreciated her tactfulness. I told her the time and place.

Monday morning I ate no breakfast, as instructed. At 11:00 sharp at the hospital, I asked for Señora Ida. In white coat and cap, smiling as usual, she just said, "Follow me," and led me through the busy corridors.

A young nurse joined us. Together we entered the operating room. As I inhaled the strong smell of disinfectant and saw the gynecological table and the instruments, I suddenly felt choked by an irrational fear I might be too late. I rushed to the table.

"Take off your panties, Señora Eva," I heard Señora Ida's amiable voice.

I obeyed and, otherwise fully dressed, swung myself onto the operating table. My arm was readied for the injection. The last thing I saw was a bucket next to the table.

Hovering between sleep and nausea, I saw a huge round clock on the wall. It said 11:45. But I was not in a room. I was still lying on a gurney, covered with a bedsheet. Warmth spread between my legs. Blood? Where was I? Becoming more and more aware, I realized my gurney stood at the end of a corridor, put away, forgotten. Voices spoke in the distance and I hoped one would come closer and speak to me. But no one came. The huge fingers of the clock moved to 12:00, then 12:30 and finally to 1:00. Had Alicia forgotten to pick me up? Had everyone forgotten about me? No wonder, I thought, I'm a murderer, I belong in jail.

Just ten minutes after one o'clock, I heard foot steps approach. Suddenly Alicia's friendly face bent over me. "There you are! I was looking for you for half an hour!"

An elderly nurse was with her. "Can you get up?" She removed the bedsheet. She stopped, shocked. "Holy Mary! What a mess!"

I raised myself on my elbows. I was swimming in blood.
"They haven't put gauze on you!" Now I knew what had felt so warm between my legs.

"Lie down again!" the nurse said. "I'll get you some bandages."

Alicia stared at me and shook her head. "You could have bled to death! I'm only grateful I finally found you. I asked at the reception desk, but they couldn't find your name. We looked for you everywhere."

Now would have been the time to tell her why I was here, but I didn't, and she didn't ask.

The nurse returned with a lot of gauze which she placed on me. With her help I stepped from the gurney.

I teetered like a drunk. Alicia and the nurse supported me to the door of the hospital, and from there I walked, arm-in-arm with Alicia, to her Chevrolet.

She drove me home and I went right to bed, yearning to escape from my guilt feelings into sleep.

To recuperate physically from the ordeal was a minor event compared to the impending confession I had to undergo. Kneeling in the confessional, I told the parish priest about the abortion.

"You dare to tell me this in such a calm manner?" He shouted so loud I feared my fellow confessors would hear it. "You are a murderess! You have committed one of the greatest crimes on God's earth! For such a huge crime I don't even have the authority to absolve you. You have to confess before a bishop!"

Thrown out of the confessional, I felt like a worm, crushed underfoot. I stumbled out of the church and wondered how I would find the bishop. Eventually I located him at the Cathedral downtown.

At last I knelt and confessed to the bishop. To my surprise he was kind and forgiving. "Say ten 'Hail Marys' and five 'Our Fathers,'" he said and absolved me quickly. It sounded as if abortion confessions were routine to him. The thought that I was just one of so many sinners relieved me somewhat. Moreover, I buried my feelings of guilt and shame deep in my subconsciousness.

However, I felt a strong desire to be close to Manfred. Unfortunately, I had him with me only for short weekends. Even before the abortion our separate lives had begun to bring tension between us. There was no time for communication and I felt lonely.

In one of our rare, uninterrupted hours on the terrace, with a glass of cool Chilean wine and in front of the great Andes, I asked, "When are you taking a vacation, Manfred?"

He took a sip and put his glass down. "Now is not the right time for me." He paused. "I'm working on a transfer so we can live together again."

I abruptly turned to him. "Is that true? There is a possibility you're going to work in Santiago?"

He raised his hand. "Santiago or else. I said I'm working on it, but it may take a while." He pulled out a pack of cigarettes.

Just the idea of having a normal family life lifted my spirits. "I can wait." Two words were buzzing in my head. "What did you mean by 'or else'?"

He lit a cigarette as if to highlight his answer. "The United States."

His words, though spoken softly, sounded to me as shrill as an air-raid siren. They made me belligerent. "Have you been thinking of this for a while?"

"Yes, I have."

I pushed my glass away. "Let me tell you, I feel very little enthusiasm for going to the United States. We now live in a fascinating country. It's beautiful, people are warm and helpful, and I've become involved."

For a minute he kept silent. "It all depends on the bosses. And on luck."

Had he heard me at all? I wondered in dismay. Not knowing how to make him listen, I shrugged my shoulders, got up and went into the house.

19. AT THE CROSSROADS

The wall calendar said September, 1958, and spring was near. I happily returned the stinking kerosene stove to the junkroom, where Rosa ironed, listened to radio soap operas or told the children scary ghost stories.

Over the next weeks Santiago veiled itself with the splendor of subtropical blossoms. The scent of jasmine and honeysuckle penetrated mansions and shacks alike, and the world seemed to be on its way to better times.

Even the church renewed itself. In Rome John XXIII was elected to the papacy, and he began major transformations in social matters.

"He's the first pope to arouse sympathy for the poor people in the world," said Father Victor, Gloria's Jesuit brother.

"He's a Marxist who will destroy the dignity of the Holy Church," the Catholic hierarchy grumbled. I only hoped the time had come to relieve the poor from their suffering.

And it had. John XXIII firmly placed the church on a new path. He called attention to the existence of the oppressed poor and emphasized the human right to a decent standard of living, education and political participation. The new Liberation Theology blew through the Church and its organizations like a fresh wind.

"Liberation from what?" I asked Father Victor.

"Hunger, illiteracy and ignorance," he said.

Indeed, soon literacy courses were announced in the slum areas, and I was asked to teach. For a while I swayed between my work with Dr. Araya, which was going into its second year, and this new challenge, until I decided to discuss it with Gloria and went to her house.

She was pale and her shoulders slumped. With concern I asked her how she felt. Two sharp wrinkles appeared between her thin, dark eyebrows. "Horrible," she said.

"What's the matter, Gloria?"

She gestured to the sofa and plunged on an armchair. "Big things are happening. You know the new pope has eased the church's stand on birth control. My brother Victor had a long talk with me. He was shocked to see me expecting my twelfth baby." She paused, shifting uncomfortably in her chair. "He said how selfish Ricardo was to keep me pregnant all the time without asking me if I wanted a baby or not. I'm pretty exhausted."

"I can see that. You've never looked paler."

"Victor said the church now allows family planning — according to the couple's responsibility. I told Ricardo. He said, 'NO! Either we go on as before or we'll have separate bedrooms.'"

The macho's unfettered seminal power! "What did you say?"

"I said, 'Separate bedrooms, then!'" Her voice trembled with rage. "So I moved my bed out and put it in the guest room." She sat there, erect and decisive. "You won't believe how relieved I am not to have more babies after this."

"I do believe you. I'm so glad you made the decision. Now it's a new life for you." A disturbing thought came to mind. "How does this affect you financially?"

She shrugged. "We'll see. He never gave me more than the minimum for the household anyway. I always managed by sewing for others."

"I never knew that."

"There was little reason to tell anybody. Now I can sew again."

I got up and hugged her. "If you ever need any help, let me know, will you?"

"I will," she said, with a trace of a smile.

Stirred by Gloria's lot, I made it to the walk-in clinic. Only then did I realize I had forgotten to discuss my own problems with Gloria.

However, when I saw Dr. Araya hauling several packages from her Citronetta, I knew I would stay with her instead of switching to literacy teaching.

"More food?" I asked, picking up the remainders.

"Not enough. We need a lot more for feeding school children. We need school supplies for the workshops, sewing machines for teaching women to sew and so much more."

Today was injection day for polio. While I gave shots to the children, thoughts milled around my mind.

"We'll get what we want," I said to the *doctora* later. "Times change. Even the church has changed."

"But some parents think children are a good investment for their old age and reject family planning."

Controversies notwithstanding, I felt that Chile was awakening from its medieval fetters and I was privileged to play a role in it, no matter how tiny. In high spirits I looked forward to the future.

Particularly the presidential election turned out to be a real fight between conservatives and liberals. As long lines inched into the voting locales, enthusiastic voters drove through Santiago's streets, stretching out a hand toward oncoming cars with one raised finger or two, three, four or all five, indicating the candidate they preferred. We were not Chilean citizens yet, but we enjoyed the amusing show which gave us a clue to who would win.

Indeed, Jorge Alessandri won, but Salvador Allende fell just short of victory. Undaunted, Allende continued to proclaim his well-known slogan:

I'LL MAKE IT NEXT TIME !

Meantime, Manfred's transfer to Santiago was still pending. After all, nothing good was ever done in a hurry and I could wait. I waited week after week. Until one day Manfred sent a note, saying he was coming home with news.

Anticipating the good tidings I prepared myself for them, wore my best dress, fixed an exquisite meal with good wine and caviar and even prepared to surprise Manfred with his favorite pieces by Bach on the piano. I placed candles on the table and was ready to sing to the whole world that my man was finally coming home to stay with me forever.

In the evening I heard his car stopping in front of the house and shortly after, he stormed in as usual, handsome like a Greek god, his hair wind-blown and a big smile on his face. A moment later I was in his arms.

"Congratulations!" I said. "You made it!"

He released me from his arms. "You don't know what I have to tell you."

Lighting the candles, I asked, "Can I guess?" I looked at his lively face, softly lit by candlelight. To my surprise I saw an expression in his features I had never seen before.

He kissed my cheek. "Let's sit down."

We both sat at the dining table, opposite each other. "I won't work in Santiago," he said. "But I won't stay in Rancagua either." Perplexed, I stared at him. "We are going to move to the United States of America," he said.

I sat as if paralyzed. The room closed in on me. I felt like an insect, caught in a spider's web. Anguish rose up to my throat. "I'll never leave Chile as long as I live!" My throat choked.

Soothingly he touched my hand. I withdrew it from him. "Let me tell you why I made the decision, Ev. You know that I always wanted to go to the United States. I have never given up that goal. Working for Braden Copper was the first step."

I wanted to cover my ears with my hands, but my arms felt heavy as lead.

"And now a great opportunity presents itself," Manfred continued. "With the Russian Sputnik in the sky, the Americans were awakened to the challenge of beating the Soviets. Now they're searching for scientists and engineers to build up their technology."

What on earth did I have to do with Sputnik? Why was I listening to this?

"Since America needs more technical personnel," he

continued, "Congress has changed the laws. I can apply for immigration."

My eyes squinted when I stared at him as if he were my enemy. "You know I love Chile. It has accepted me and my music and I'm devoted to improving the life of the poor. I belong here. And it's the children's home."

He got up from the table and walked to the window. "But I am not happy. Rancagua was nothing but a golden cage for me. The Chileans are the nicest people in the world, but their conservative attitude just doesn't allow change. There's no outlet here for my ideas."

At last I exploded. "You only think of yourself and your idiotic idea to go to America! To hell with that!" I got up, grabbed the candles and threw them in the corner. In the sudden darkness I heard his steps toward the light switch. A moment later the cold ceiling light illuminated his red, angry face.

He brusquely grabbed the edge of the table as if he was about to turn it over. "No, I'm not only thinking of myself. I'm also thinking of our girls. I don't want them to marry anyone under a law that takes all rights from them. Confrontations happen in the best marriages — we are having one right now. But if they are allowed to sink into subservience, with absolutely no rights — I don't want my daughters to suffer from that!"

Loosing control over myself totally, I shouted, "You go alone! I stay in Chile!" I kicked my chair to the side, ran to the door, flung it open and slammed it behind me with the biggest bang I could muster. I ran into the bedroom, threw myself on the bed and cried out my desperation.

20. ¡ADIOS!

Manfred's decision shook the family to its foundations. Lilo, sixteen, and Little Bear, twelve, were startled for a moment. Then Lilo said with determination, "I don't want to leave all my friends here. I'm not going."

"Me neither," Little Bear and Renate said.

So I began to make plans for the future. The children and I would stay here while Manfred lived and worked in the United States. It also dawned on me that the enormous distance could eventually destroy our marriage.

On the other hand, if we followed him to the United States, my life elixir, Chile, would be removed and I would certainly deteriorate. Chile or Manfred — I had to choose.

Maybe I could persuade him to stay in Chile? I could also move to Rancagua and send the three older children to boarding schools in Santiago! I suggested this possibility to him on the next weekend.

"It would be cruel to the children," he said. "Put that out of your mind."

In my distress I turned my heavy guns on him. "The USA is constantly at war. In Chile there's peace. Do you want to expose us all to war?"

"The USA manages to keep its wars outside its territory."

Beaten, I raised myself one last time. "Maybe you won't get a visa?"

"I've talked to the American ambassador. With the change of immigration laws, it won't be a problem."

He had it all figured out — as usual when he put his mind to something. I was crushed. All that was left for me was to let him go and live without him. I shuddered.

183

I now began to see my daily environment and its demands and beauties in an entirely new light. We would have to move to a smaller house. I alone would be responsible for the children. My work would go on, and Manfred would send me dollar checks for our living expenses. Or would he? We had to discuss these details next time.

The day before Manfred was due to come home, a gray, rainy day, I went to see Gloria to ask her for advice on my new situation and found her in her living room in a conversation with her look-alike-brother.

"Victor has opened a foundation for mothers and children," she said after we'd greeted each other.

Glad to put off the pending discussion of my own problem I turned to him. "Where, Father?"

"In Carascal. On the other side of the Mapocho River," he said. "Near the clinic where you work for Dr. Araya."

"Congratulations! What does your foundation offer?"

Staring intensely at me, he said, "Everything the mothers and children need. Education, food and clothing. In that order."

"It has been sporadically offered here and there, but this will be the center of it all," Gloria said.

"The basis of it are the donations from other countries," he said. "I'm already getting shipments from Germany. If you have time, come see me at my office." He smiled. "Maybe you'd like to work with us."

The focus now on me, I told them about my decision.

Gloria exploded. "Are you out of your mind? A woman without a husband in a country that doesn't protect its women? Why do you think I'm staying in Ricardo's house, although I'd rather be on my own?"

She didn't agree with me, just discarded my plans! "I thought you of all people would understand!"

"And I thought you'd been long enough in Chile to know that you would be scorned and jeered if you stayed alone."

"At last I've found a niche in this country and now you are

trying to destroy all my plans!" I shouted. Tears of self-pity welled up.

Then I heard Father Victor's voice, penetrating my despair. "I think Gloria is right. And I want to tell you something." I stared at his face. His features distorted by my tears. "We need you in the United States," he said.

I thought I had misunderstood him. "'We?'"

"First of all, your husband needs you. Second, we who work for the poor need you. We'd lose you as a volunteer, but you could help us much better from the States. You could be a liaison to American charities."

I listened.

"Americans are very generous and cooperative. They are masters in fund-raising and in collecting huge amounts of things needed in other countries. With your dedication to the poor you could become an ambassador for Chile. And I'll bet you'd be an excellent one."

I wiped off my tears and, chin in hand, glanced out the window. The rain had stopped. The drops on the tree leaves reflected the sunshine and sparkled. I listened to the scenario the priest created.

"As I have received goods from Germany, you could send the same and much more to us from the United States. I already have connections with freighters able to ship merchandise from the United States to Chile free of charge. Go to America and get us help."

I put my arm down and looked at his eyes — Gloria's penetrating eyes. "I've never dreamed about such things," I said. "And I still don't see how I could do it."

"Start out with your parish, then go higher."

His game plan hadn't shaken my decision to stay in Chile but at least I conceived it as a friendly offer. "Your trust in my abilities is an honor to me, Father. But it disregards my love for Chile."

The priest focused on me like an opponent. "And you disregard your love for your husband. Have you pushed that into the background?"

He must have seen my checkmate because he said softly, "Think about it, Eva. Your situation is not an easy one. Take your time for a decision."

I went home, collapsed on my bed and fell asleep immediately.

For an entire week I dragged along, not realizing what process was going on in me. Mechanically I did my chores, talked to whomever was around but felt utterly removed from my surroundings.

The morning of Manfred's next homecoming I stepped out into the front-yard, automatically removed the gate lock and opened the portal for his car. Sauntering through the carport, on which already hung tiny grapes, I stared at the persimmon tree, whose branches grew over the balcony and soon would bear heavy fruits of sunset color. I'd miss them!

With a shock I understood that something in me had made a decision. I would follow Manfred to the United States of America! My love for him had triumphed over my love for Chile.

I knew my turnaround had not come from my mind, but my heart. How could I ever have doubted my love for Manfred? To weigh my love for him against my love for Chile had been an illusion. Father Victor had shown me how to combine both. I could be with Manfred and still work for Chile. It sounded so simple now, but how forces in me could have been working in secret was beyond me.

I told Manfred when he arrived home.

He took me in his arms and held me tight. "I'll do what I can to replace Chile for you and the children. I promise you won't regret your decision."

I leaned my head on his chest and closed my eyes.

"Not only can you work for Chile in America, but you'll also find good music and many new fields," he said and I felt the vibrations of his voice in his chest. "And the women up there have a much higher status than anywhere else in the world."

His prophetic words made me feel reborn. I clasped my arms around his neck and held him tight. Committed and full of hope. From then on all arrows pointed to the positive. The children sensed my attitude and began to look forward to the new land.

"In America all chewing gum is free!" Little Bear announced. Together we opened the atlas. The immensity of that country amazed me. "Forty-eight states!"

"Actually fifty," Manfred said. "Alaska and Hawaii just joined the Union. Which one do you prefer?"

I shrugged.

"What are your requirements?" he asked again.

"A good climate and an opera house."

"New York has the famous Met, but the weather is terrible." His finger moved to the West Coast. "California has the best climate. Like central Chile."

"San Francisco has an opera house."

"Let's move to San Francisco then," he said. It was as simple as that.

California! Exotic, glamorous, eccentric! How would the children feel there? Impossible to tell. The sixties had just begun and life was changing everywhere in the world.

For Manfred and me there came a time of wandering from one farewell party to the other in Santiago and Rancagua. The company didn't want to let him go and neither did his colleagues nor our friends. Because of the Chileans' love for verbal expression, at least five to eight speeches were given at every dinner party.

"One more party and I'll collapse," I said to Manfred.

At least he was still with me! I knew I could follow him to the United States only after he had sent a copy of his prospective work contract to the American embassy in Santiago.

The day came when Alicia drove us in her new large Chevrolet to Los Cerrillos Airport, where we had arrived nine years ago. At least two dozen friends had gathered to see him off.

"The billeting officer is leaving," Vera Hermann, our travel agent, said.

I kissed Manfred, not knowing when I would see him again. He boarded the propeller plane that took him over the snow-capped Andes to Buenos Aires and then to the United States of America.

Condemned to wait for a notice about his first job and a copy of his working contract, I began to dissolve our household and sell as much as possible.

Two weeks later we received Manfred's long-awaited letter from San Francisco.

> "Hurrah! I got a job as a design engineer with Utah Construction and Mining Company in Palo Alto, a suburb of San Francisco. I'm enclosing a copy of my contract. Take this to the American Embassy and apply for visas. Make reservations for your flights, give all the crap in the house away, bring only personal items. Hurry up! It's great here and I'm waiting for you!"

"Hurrah!" I repeated.

An hour later I entered the American Embassy and applied for visas. "Sorry, the German quota is closed," the immigration officer, a cold, lanky man, said. "You may call from time to time to see if the regulations have changed."

To him I was just a number, not a human being. I left the embassy.

I checked with the embassy every week. The answer was always: "No change."

After two months of fruitless inquiring, the cold, lanky immigration officer declared, "We can give visas to four of you, but not to the rest."

"I don't understand."

"You and your oldest daughter were born in Danzig, the former Free State. Under American law the two of you still have this citizenship. The Danzig quota is open. Your two youngest ones were born in Chile and have free entry into the USA. But for your two German-born children, we cannot issue visas since the German quota is closed."

I decided to make an extra effort to shake up the American bureaucracy, and so I wrote to America's President Eisenhower for help.

A few days later I woke at dawn. The wall clock read exactly six. The children were still asleep.

Suddenly the ceiling lamp swung back and forth and a noise like a passing freight train filled the air.

Earthquake! I jumped from my bed, woke up Lilo, Little Bear and Renate, and pulled Wernher and Irmgard from their beds. "Earthquake! Get out of the house!" I shouted.

Glasses fell to the cement floor of the kitchen, ringing like a thousand high-pitched bells. The walls moaned and creaked like wood in a fire, and heavy things fell in all rooms.

We made it to the garden, although it was difficult to keep our footing on the rocking floor. The children clung to me, crying and whimpering. "It will be over in a second," I said.

Once outside, I saw the house sway during the shocks and the persimmon tree shook as though to get rid of its last fruits. We all were in our pajamas and stood in the cataclysm like pillars of salt.

Only after the tremor ended did I realize it had lasted longer than any earthquake I'd ever experienced.

The children finally released their grip on my pajamas. But the ground trembled again, for a shorter time than the first, but no less frightful. We waited it out, prayed, crossed ourselves and gnashed our teeth.

When the earth calmed down, we went inside and turned the radio on.

".... the epicenter is 270 miles south of Santiago, in Concepción. The strength of the earthquake has reached nine on the Richter scale. But the aftershocks go on. In addition there has been a seaquake and tidal waves. Huge areas are devastated. Villages are inundated. Entire islands near the coast have disappeared."

The calendar showed May 21, 1960, and the newspapers marked it as Chile's darkest day, not knowing the worst would come the next day. Two earthquakes, ten on the Richter scale, destroyed the seaport of Valdivia in the south of Chile. From a population of 70,000, three thousand were killed.

Of all the countries sending help, the United States produced the greatest impact ever in Chile. Their assistance was immediate, generous and decisive.

"You've sent people, not just supplies," the Chileans repeatedly said to the Americans.

They were amazed to see black and white medical troops working side by side. Chilean taxi drivers, storekeepers, and shoeshine boys refused to let the Americans pay for anything. As one group of American helpers was leaving in the wee hours of the morning, kitchen men in the local hotel insisted on getting up to cook breakfast for the Americans housed there. The hotel rejected any payment. At the airport thousands of Chileans saw them off.

I wrote to Manfred:

>"I'm glad to see the conciliation between the two countries. It brings them closer, and the step from Santiago to San Francisco for us now seems easier."

We were still cleaning up the damages, when I got a note from the American embassy to appear at the office. I went to the immigration officer's desk.

"We received a copy of your letter to President Eisenhower and got new orders," he said.

I had won the battle! The three-month wait was over. Coolly and automatically the American issued the visas.

In August, 1960, at Santiago's Los Cerrillos Airport, our friends swamped us with farewell gifts. Hugging and kissing went on and on. Not only my close friends Gloria, Alicia and Ana Araya but also many strangers had assembled.

Father Victor appeared with photographers, giving me an illusion of fame and worthiness. "Our ambassador of the poor is leaving for the United States," he declared.

With tears rolling down, we stepped on the plane, left Latin charm and chaos behind us and faced that mysterious, uncertain thing we call our future.

During the flight along the Pacific Coast I saw Chile's daylight fade away, and when the blood-red sun sank into the Pacific I felt I had left my heart in the wonderful country that had been home and a haven for me.

BOOK TWO

21. THE VOLCANO EXPLODES

After being away from Chile for ten years, we were shaken up by the news that in September, 1970, the Chileans had voted for the socialist candidate, Salvador Allende. His own prophecy, that he would make it next time, had come true. Barely receiving a meager majority of votes, he still advanced to the country's presidency. The rich boiled with rage and the poor rejoiced. Yet the large middle class radically split the nation into two enemy forces.

Now living in Los Angeles, California, Manfred was working on a secret mission for the U.S. government and I pursued my Master's degree in music. For detailed news we depended on letters from our Chilean friends. The first one came from Ana Araya.

"....You won't believe peoples' state of mind on election day. People from the *poblaciones* were euphoric. They marched singing through the streets, danced, shouted, hugged each other, laughed. They thought their salvation had come. Indeed, they now have privileges and jobs. Houses made of brick are built for them, and their children get free breakfasts and lunches at school.

"In comparison, the rich were scared to death. In their hysteria they stormed the banks, sent their money overseas or fled the country.

"Unfortunately, we, the middle class, experienced something the country had never seen before. The nation had split into two irreconcilable groups — those for Allende and those against him. The split went right through families — as in ours — and created an atmosphere of fear and distrust. Can you imagine this happening here, in Chile?

"As for myself, I hope the new government will accomplish what the last one didn't. We are still doing what we did when you were my assistant. A physician himself, President Allende is very open to our nutrition programs, which we consider the salvation of the Chilean children. Imagine, all children get a half liter of milk every day! They no longer die of malnutrition...."

I let the letter sink to my lap. My thoughts flew to the turmoil in Chile. The volcano had exploded. How much I yearned to be there! All the energies we had put into the salvation of the children had now borne fruit.

Following Father Victor's advice I had started out with our parish and then gone higher to persuade CARE directors to mail educational tools, food and clothes to Chile.

We soon received a letter from Gloria Toro, written in her characteristic terse style.

"....With just a meager majority Allende became president. Months ago Ricardo had moved to live and work in the *población*. As a reward for Ricardo's political support Allende appointed him Undersecretary of Health. Ricardo works with him in the presidential palace now! Needless to say, I did not vote for Allende."

The word "not" was underlined three times.

"Pancholo, your Little Bear's favorite friend, teaches literacy and crafts to the poor — in Allende's camp. All the others, married and with children, are against Allende.

"The rich people and many of the middle class (like myself) are fighting also against Allende. Imagine, a communist as our president! I understand that your government too tries everything to make Allende fail. I hope it will succeed...."

I sighed. Dear old friend Gloria, angry as ever, she and Ricardo politically opposite each other! Yet both were my friends and I wished I could be with them.

Manfred received a letter from Enrique Palma.

"....soon the country will be in chaos, and what we have avoided so far must come: a revolution.

"Marlene and I don't want to be trapped and might leave for the United States before the storm breaks loose. We hope to see you in the near future...."

I hope to see all of you soon, I thought time and again.

Gradually, it became obvious that Chile's political and economic situation was in a decline. Up to my ears with teaching at the university, I allowed myself only to read the headlines in the newspaper.

CHILE CONGRESS VOTES TO RESTRICT ALLENDE SOCIALISM GOAL

CHILE STRIKES PARALYZE TRAINS AND BUSES

US BANK DENIES CREDIT TO CHILE

TRUCKERS' STRIKE CAUSES VIOLENCE IN CHILE

"We left just in time," Manfred said.

"I worry not only about my friends, but Chile itself," I said. With effort I suppressed these feelings. Then Manfred brought more news home.

"I got a phone call from Enrique Palma. He's left Chile to escape the turmoil. Marlena will follow once he gets a job here. I invited him for dinner tonight."

And then here was Enrique, tall and robust as ever, smelling of English cologne, handsome with his black hair and elegant mustache, his brown eyes radiating long-missed Latin warmth. We hugged for a long time.

During dinner we listened to his account. "Lots of workers thought, with Allende as president, all things would turn around in their favor. They could hardly wait. Imagine what happened to Marlena one day before the election. She cashed a check at

the bank and walked out to the parking lot. The moment she got
her car keys from her handbag, a man appeared from nowhere
and took the keys from her. He said, 'From tomorrow on I own
this car and you work.'"

"Incredible!" I said. "And then?"

"Marlena screamed for help. People near her made the man
give the keys back."

"Did they catch him?" Manfred asked.

"Wait! The police happened to see the brawling and ran to the
group. The man did not run away, but argued that from now on
they, the poor, would own cars and the rich would have to
work. Marlena drove away as fast as she could."

"I can't believe people could be so stupid," I said. "Maybe it
was only an isolated case?"

"Not at all," Enrique said, lighting a cigarette. I'd never seen
him so agitated. "Now listen to this," he said. "Also the evening
before the election Marlena and I sat in the living room,
watching television when the door bell rang. Our maid had the
day off, so I went to open the door. It was our gardener, smiling
as if he had won the jackpot. Before I could ask what he wanted,
he rushed in, went to the living room and looked around. I asked
him, 'What's the matter with you?'

"He said, 'I want to see my house. Tomorrow Allende will
win and your house will be mine.'" Enrique forcefully blew out
the smoke.

"You must be kidding!" I said.

"I'm not. Similar stories happened to many of our friends.
You can see what people make of half-digested political ideas."

"Is Allende doing something to set people straight?" Manfred
asked.

"The Allende government has no chance to survive," Enrique
said. "As you know, most Chileans are conservative and despise
communism. It's said that the CIA and the Brazilian government
are shoveling millions of dollars to Chile to persuade them to
stay on strike."

"How in the world do people manage?" I asked.

"Marlena and others stand in food lines for hours, while the poor people get the food distributed in the factories. Imagine, one day the housewives took to the streets shouting and beating their empty pots and pans. They even sang:

        'Allende, son of a bitch —
        he's going to fall in a ditch.'"

"What a spectacle!" I said.

"Our civilized country has come to that."

"What happened to the American copper mines?" Manfred asked.

"They are all nationalized, and Kennecott and Anaconda are the losers. Like the farm owners. The farm workers just took over their bosses' huge haciendas."

Manfred shook his head and sighed. "How bad must it be, when people leave their own country."

"It's a nightmare down there, Manfredo." His voice became more agitated. "Production has stopped, there's nothing to buy, Chile is just one huge line. The shop owners hoard everything. Crime has risen and family members fight each other...."

"Is there any hope it will get better?" I asked.

He shook his head. "It can't get worse than it is. Allende's government failed from ignorance and inefficiency. Sooner or later Allende will quit."

We talked all evening, and I wept for Chile in its hopeless crisis — and for the final collapse of the peaceful times. Or had they been peaceful at all? I remembered the widespread misery and the tortures. Surely, they hadn't affected me directly, but I had always felt so close to the suffering as if it had been my own. Now I had to hear about events in Chile second-hand. Having Enrique with us was a consolation.

Manfred was able to arrange a job at his company for Enrique — unfortunately not in Los Angeles, but at the firm's headquarters in Houston, Texas.

As soon as Marlena arrived in Houston, she called us. "It's hell in Chile! All truckers are on strike. Not a crumb of food is coming into Santiago! The chaos is indescribable. If no rescue comes, the population will starve to death. People are shooting each other because of different opinions. Many are fleeing the country. Since I had a flight reservation for so long, I was able to escape."

For a moment the thought came to mind that we had left Germany in time, before the anticipated Russian invasion of Western Europe, and we had now escaped the chaos in Chile. But the Russians had not invaded and I hoped things would smooth out in Chile as well.

This time my hopes fell short of reality. On September 11, 1973, the military and police forces exercised a *coup d'etat*, in which Allende was shot to death. A military junta under the leadership of General Augusto Pinochet took over the government and converted the 165-year-old democracy into a dictatorship.

NEWSWEEK described how Chileans lived in cold terror.

SLAUGHTERHOUSE IN SANTIAGO!

"Midnight knocks on the door...headless corpses in the Mapocho River...police machine gun ten defenseless high school boys in the back... physical torture on arrested people has become a daily business."

Chile had exploded like a volcano! The gypsy warned me twenty years ago, *"¡Chile está perdido!"* Helplessly we watched the news about the junta's violent takeover and its persecution of Allende's activists and sympathizers. Newspapers vividly described how they were arrested, tortured and killed. The gypsy's warning on our first day in Chile echoed in my mind. In my sleepless nights I worried about our friends.

"What do you think happened to Ricardo, Ana and all the others?" I asked Manfred.

"We won't know until we talk to an eyewitness."

"That could take years!"

"I don't think it will take that long."

He was right. Pinochet created a new class of citizens — exiles. And one day we met two of them, Sergio and Gabriela Gutierrez, both teachers. At a South American concert we happened to sit next to a young couple and heard them speak Spanish with the familiar Chilean accent. We addressed them with a Chilean greeting, and they were happy to talk to sympathetic souls. We invited them to our home.

I took in their long-missed, dark Latin features. Their talk and behavior were heartwarming. While we ate cazuela, steak and drank Chilean wine, Sergio told us about his ordeal.

"As a member of the Socialist party I knew they would come and arrest me one day." He paused. "It happened two weeks after the coup. Army soldiers dragged me and many others from our homes to the National Soccer Stadium and held us prisoners. First, we were three thousand people. Five days later we were eight thousand."

"How terrible!" I whispered.

"About three hundred soldiers guarded us. Heavily armed. From time to time they beat us with the butts of their rifles. Loudspeakers constantly droned messages like 'You damned communists are murderers, rotten dogs!' Many prisoners became hysterical and screamed. Floodlights were on us day and night. We were forbidden to speak to each other."

He swallowed hard. "Then came the individual questioning. First a barber came, shaved off one side of my head and left the other half with hair."

I closed my eyes, ashamed of the humiliation.

"Then a plain-clothes man asked me questions and two policemen stood by for the beatings. I described my political activities. I had delivered pamphlets, and here and there given a speech. For each answer I got a blow in the face." He drank half his glass of wine, obviously to resist being overwhelmed by his horrible memory.

"What did they ask you?" I asked.

"They asked, 'Who else worked with you? Their names and addresses! Do you know anybody with arms?' When I remained silent, the beating resumed. They finally broke my jaw so I couldn't speak any more."

"Are you okay now?" I asked.

He nodded and finished his wine. His head erect, his eyes looked into the distance of the room and the past. "At last I was sentenced to five years in a special torture place." He placed his elbow on the table and buried his face in his hand. "Every day... I was blindfolded... stripped naked... strapped on a table...." Tears ran down his fingers. "Then... they applied electrical shocks... to my tongue... and my genitals. I screeeeamed...." He stretched the syllable, then choked, unable to continue.

Gabriela put her arm around his shoulders and let him cry.

"I shouldn't have asked him," I said to Gabriela.

She shook her head. "He had to tell his story. It's the only way to get rid of the pain of the memory." She put a handkerchief in his hand. He straightened up, wiped his tears and sighed deeply.

"During all this time I had no idea where Sergio was," Gabriela said in a matter-of-fact voice, and I understood she was trying to bring the story down to an easier level.

"Like all the other wives, I went from one jail to the other and always heard: 'He's not here.' Finally when there were no longer enough jails to hold the thousands of men, they shipped the milder cases to internal exile."

"What in the world is that?" Manfred asked.

"They sent prisoners to remote areas of the country from where there was no escape. Sergio was sent to Taltal, a village in the northern desert, and I was allowed to go with him. The police in Taltal alternately set him free on probation or jailed him on a whim. When he was free, he had to report to the police five times a day. When he was in jail, he was tortured."

I looked at Sergio. Rings heavy under his dark eyes, he stared at the table's edge as if looking at the abyss which he had confronted all those years.

"How could you stand it, Gabriela?" I asked.

"I was working on my PhD dissertation and commuted to the

University in Antofagasta off and on. So most of the time I was near Sergio. To encourage him. To console him."

"Were you the only prisoner in Taltal?" I asked Sergio.

He sighed and blinked as if to clear his mind. "No. There were several of us. And Taltal wasn't the only place with exiles. The island of Dawson in the Strait of Magellan was another place. Many died there of exposure and starvation. In Taltal, I was lucky."

"How many were exiled in total?" Manfred asked.

"Tens of thousands. Maybe a hundred thousand."

"God of Mercy!" I shouted.

"A very simple method to get rid of adversaries," Sergio said with a bitter smile.

Gabriela took over. "Only a fraction of the exiles were sent to remote places in Chile itself. The majority were expelled to foreign countries."

I served ice cream, covered with Kahlua. Nothing was good enough for them, who had gone through hell.

"How did you guys get to America?" Manfred asked, refilling the wine glasses.

"From the beginning of the dictatorship the church had been on our side," Gabriela said. "Cardinal Silva particularly took a firm stand against the exploitation of prisoners. He founded an organization that made contact with European countries and the United States, asking them to accept exiles from Chile. I applied for Sergio and myself."

A touch of a smile appeared on her face. "You won't believe it, Manfredo, but I even had a choice! I chose the United States because of its close proximity to Chile. After three years of Sergio's imprisonment, he was driven into exile abroad...." She tried to control herself, her voice choking. "He was absolutely forbidden to return." She began to cry. "Exile is terribly degrading...."

I got up and held her close to me. For a while no one spoke. Sergio pulled her out of her mood. He reached across the table and touched her hand. "Nothing lasts forever. Neither does the dictatorship. One day we'll return."

I looked at him in admiration. The hellish experiences hadn't destroyed him. He was hopeful, waiting for the liquidation of the brutal government.

Still disturbed by Sergio's and Gabriela's ordeal, we were condemned to read in the newspaper how the Nixon Administration had authorized the spending of eight million dollars on covert actions in Chile during Allende's presidency, seriously disrupting the country's economy. They had financed striking labor unions, slanderous articles in newspapers, leaflets, scare-and-spoil campaigns, purchases of radio stations and newspapers and coup plotters.

"Our government has done that?" I asked in shock.

Manfred kept reading aloud, "Also, the White House and the State Department have misled the public and the Congress about the extent of the U.S. involvement in the internal affairs of Chile...."

"Nixon, Kissinger and the CIA," I said. "We didn't know about it and were lied to."

"Sounds familiar, doesn't it?"

I nodded. "Nazi Germany and the extermination camps. It means we are responsible for what our government does."

"You mean collective guilt?" Manfred said. "I reject that."

"I don't. Because we support the government with money, votes and apathy. We didn't move a finger, when the CIA bribed the truckers."

"We didn't know about it," Manfred said brusquely.

"We didn't know about the Nazi mass killings either. But I still feel responsible for them."

For a while we were silent. My thoughts went down across the equator to the country where so many of my dear friends lived. And slowly but steadily the certainty spread out in me that I had to go to Chile myself and find out what had happened to my friends.

22. DICTATORSHIP

In 1978, Manfred and I took a LAN flight to Santiago, where it landed at the new, modern Pudahuel airport.

I felt excited after our eighteen-year absence. I knew my peaceful, sleepy Chile no longer existed. Would I still love it? Our experience with Germany's Nazi period told me that established dictatorships were not visible in the streets. So we were curious to compare Pinochet's Chile with Hitler's Germany.

When we exited customs, we found dear old Alicia Hurtado waiting for us. Her hair had turned gray, but joy radiated from her still expressive face. With outstretched hands she greeted us. "Welcome back!" Her gray eyes shone. We hugged and kissed.

Alicia's 32-year-old Chevy was still running. We climbed in, Manfred in the back and I next to Alicia.

As we drove, I took in the looks of my beloved city. "Look, Santiago is more beautiful than ever!" I said. "It's swept and washed. No graffiti on the walls. The grass on the plazas is green. Nowhere a sign of a police state."

"Neither was there one in Nazi Germany," Manfred said. "It sure does look healthy and happy. What's the population of Santiago now?" he asked Alicia.

"Five million. And we now have everything we need and don't need. Luxuries are imported by the tons."

"Who can afford them?"

"More people than ever."

"It looks like Pinochet has pulled the country out from chaos and backwardness."

"And order has returned. We no longer have strikes."

"No street crimes either?" I asked, trying to hide my sarcasm.

203

"We had strict curfews for years and still have them on and off. Not tonight, though. It's Saturday."

"How do you feel about the curfew?" I asked.

She smiled. "Lots of wives praise it. Philandering husbands can't stay out half the night with excuses of late work. Believe me, the curfew has done more for men's fidelity than all the years of preaching and yelling. For the first time families spend evenings together at home. Isn't that something?"

"What do you do about your guests when curfew comes?" Manfred asked.

"Another blessing — guests no longer stay until dawn."

"And all this in the name of the security of the country."

Alicia smiled politely.

When we stopped at red lights I stared with surprise at the people on the street. "Look how they walk, Manfred! No slow shuffling anymore. They all seem to be in a hurry."

"They all work now," Alicia said.

"But they are as elegant as ever," Manfred marvelled.

Driving through residential areas, I realized I missed something on the streets, but I didn't know what. Suddenly it came to me. "Where are all the stray dogs? I see full garbage cans but no scavenging dogs."

"They're all gone," Alicia said.

"How did that happen?"

"One day the government announced in the media that pets should be kept in the house for a week because poisoned meat would be strewn out in the streets to kill all strays. It worked." The notorious efficiency of the dictatorship — like in old Nazi Germany!

Alicia changed the subject. "Too bad you can stay only for a week. Our house is almost empty since all three boys have moved out. Tonight you'll relax, I hope. What about tomorrow?"

"I want to see the Toros. They seldom write letters. I hardly know how they are."

"You know that Dr. Toro disappeared, don't you?"

"He did whaaat?"

"He's missing. So many are. And also...but Gloria herself will tell you all about it."

Worried and agitated, I rushed to the Toros' well-known chalet, knowing that I would now get to see the other side of the dictatorship. I was alone. Manfred had gone to visit one of his former colleagues.

Gloria had changed. Dressed in black, dark rings under her eyes, the two vertical dashes between her brows deepened. We hugged for a long time, then sat down in the living room with a view to the front yard, where dark-red roses were in full bloom.

Gloria reclined on the sofa as though seeking support. "You are coming from a different world. It will be difficult for you to understand what happened to us here in the last years." She paused. "You may not know. Ricardo disappeared."

"My God, how did that happen?" I still expected to hear a runaway story. In the United States husbands also "disappeared," when they didn't want to pay any alimony.

"He was Undersecretary of Health under Allende. He stayed with Allende while the palace was bombed. Allende died there. I never heard from Ricardo again."

"Didn't you try to locate him?"

"Of course. All families of *desaparecidos*, disappeared ones, try that. The church is on our side. Cardinal Silva stands up for human rights. We can always count on his help. But the junta disposes of dead bodies in secret ways. So there's no trace left."

"Do you think he is dead?"

"We have to tell ourselves that he's dead. I often said that no one disappeared in this country. Now I'm one of those who are searching for their men. You may remember he and I had separate bedrooms, but he's still the father of my children."

"Of course. How are the children?"

She swallowed. With visible difficulty she said, "I lost Pancholo."

A mother losing her son! Pancholo, Little Bear's favorite

friend, dead!

Gloria began to cry. I rushed over to her, grabbed a napkin from the table, sat down at her side and held her hand. "Oh, my God! How did it happen?"

She wiped her tears with the napkin and composed herself. But the corners of her mouth sank. "Pancholo was very active during the Allende time. He taught literacy and crafts to the poor. That alone was enough for the junta to punish him. But he had even moved out of here to live in a *población* to be with the poor people."

Elbow on the sofa's arm rest, head in hand, Gloria spoke with a low and passionless voice. "Then came the coup. Ricardo disappeared. I was terribly afraid of what could happen to Pancholo. I went to the *población* to persuade him to come home or at least hide somewhere else. But the junta had already raided the entire *población,* killed many and arrested others."

"But, why? Why?"

She looked up as if I had asked a stupid question. "They were labeled communists. Pronto. It usually meant instant death."

All that I had read before appeared now as naked truth before my eyes.

"Pancholo and many others had been taken away. I looked for him, went from one jail to the other, from one morgue to the other. Always the same answer: 'He's not in our cardex file.' I think I had gone to ten different detention quarters, but there was no sign of Pancholo."

She stopped and, fearing the worst, I clung to the edge of the sofa.

Her voice became a whisper. "Then one morning his body lay in front of our doorsteps." Tears ran down her cheeks. She fumbled for the napkin.

Her head sank and she said, sobbing so I could hardly understand her, "He was mutilated. His eyes put out and his testicles cut off." She slumped in her seat.

Though I couldn't hold my tears, I took her in my arms and let her cry on my shoulder. After a while she freed herself from my embrace, dried her tears and leaned back in her armchair.

I closed my eyes in terror. What I just heard was beyond any understanding. Who was I to have escaped this hell? None of us spoke. There was no hope or consolation. Only pain and despair.

"We buried him," Gloria said at last. "The entire family attended. Except Ricardo, of course."

While I helped Gloria make tea, we both tried to find our way back to everyday life by talking about tasks of immediate needs. We washed vegetables and peeled potatoes, and it hardly came to mind that the amounts were way too big for a lunch for two.

Suddenly I saw two matrons in simple street clothes enter the front yard. "More visitors?" I asked Gloria.

"They're housewives from the neighborhood." She got up to greet them. Soon four more women walked in.

"We're cooking meals for the school children," Gloria explained. "They get half a liter of milk at school, but this will be the only meal to carry them through the day."

I followed the women into the back yard. Everyone had brought some rice, oil, onions or meat — whatever they could afford on their meager budgets.

Gloria herself returned to her old, strong self. Her posture erect, she was in command of herself. "This food is supplemented by my brother Victor's foundation. By the way, he's very grateful for all the food that comes from the United States. He knows you were instrumental in shipping much of it. But, excuse me, we have to get started." She turned around to direct her helpers.

The women began to cook the children's lunch in a huge cauldron in the back yard. Tables and long benches were carried out and set up for fifty children.

About one o'clock four dozen children, from six to eight years old, marched in, all black-haired and swarthy, in worn-out clothes, still a bit shy and hesitant. Yet in no time they lined up for buns and cazuela, the favorite soup of the old days, which they devoured with lightning speed. Their mood and liveliness improved visibly and after the second helping, they kidded and laughed like other children around the world.

After the mass feeding the children went back to school and we cleaned up the back yard.

"Do you do this every day?" I asked Gloria.

"Of course. Many others do it too."

"Do you get paid for this?"

"What do you mean 'get paid'? To see children eat, isn't that enough?"

My dear friend Gloria was back to her old fighting spirit. In a way, she hadn't changed. As ever, she stood up for those who were in need, and by doing this, she drove her own misery into a corner.

We had only a few more days in Santiago and I didn't allow myself to be disgruntled while visiting other friends. Since Manfred wanted to see his friends and I mine, we kept doing our visits separately.

On my way to Ana Araya's home in the foothills of the Andes, I wondered in what condition I would find her. Everyone seemed to have had unusual, if not horrible experiences.

I found Ana on crutches, but her exotic face lit up with a huge smile. She still wore her smooth hair cut short, but it was now gray instead of black. Yet her eyes radiated joy and warmth. "Eva! How wonderful to see you again!"

I rushed to her and hugged her carefully so as not to disturb her physical balance. "What happened, Ana? Why the crutches?"

"I broke my hip. Very simple. I was stupid enough to hold out against the mob. I fell and broke my hip."

"What mob?"

"Come, sit down. Let's have a cup of tea. Everything feels better then."

We sat down at a small table and the maid brought tea and cake. "I see maids are still in use here, in spite of the revolution," I said. "In the United States we don't have that luxury."

"The maids are better paid now, live with their families in the *poblaciones* and work only five days a week. But before you talk about yourself and your family I have to tell you that the chamber group you initiated is still going strong."

"The MÚSICA?"

"Exactly. And it has multiplied itself. There are at least fifteen such groups." She smiled. "Now about yourself."

"I teach piano. Manfred works in ocean thermal energy. Lilo and Little Bear are married and each has two children. Renate got her Bachelor's degree in Spanish and German and Wernher and Irmgard are in college. Now it's your turn. Tell me how you broke your hip. Are you still in pain?"

"Once in a while. It happened when I went with my husband to our hacienda. One day, without warning, workers stormed the farm for a take-over."

"What did they want to take?"

"Our hacienda!"

"I don't understand."

"It was an outgrowth of misunderstood socialist ideas. Many workers thought after Allende's victory they all would be lottery winners. They 'took over' many haciendas. Ours was one of the last ones. When they approached our house I blocked the door with my body, but they trampled it down and I fell and broke my hip."

"Ana! You should be the last one to be treated this way. Your dedication in helping the poor and their children! Doesn't that count for anything?"

"Ah, no one thinks of individuals during such an onslaught. Nevertheless, when the coup happened I was in the hospital — as a patient! That was my luck. Everyone who had worked for the poor was considered to be a communist and marked for punishment."

"Damn!"

"Dr. Moenckeberg was already so famous with his nutrition program that the junta didn't dare touch him. He was able to protect me. The church too helped political prisoners and the thousands of unemployed."

"Why was there such mass unemployment after the coup?"

Ana smoothed her short, gray hair. "The government imported merchandise from other countries in huge amounts. Our factories couldn't keep up with the quality. They closed down and laid off their workers by the thousands."

"And other thousands were jailed. What about the 'disappeared' ones? Why can't they be found?"

"Unidentified bodies were taken from factories by the truckload directly to the crematorium. Others were thrown into the Mapocho River, sometimes with their heads cut off. Life is cheap in Chile nowadays."

"Oh, my God! What happened to my gentle Chile, where supposedly a revolution could never happen?"

"That certainly was an illusion. Chile is no longer innocent."

"How do the people cope with all this?"

"Many stay aloof. Like sleepwalkers. They prefer not to know about anything. At the height of the violence bodies from the nightly killings were left next to the curb. People on their way to buy bread next morning would glance at them out of the corners of their eyes and continue on their way."

I pictured many of our friends having done exactly that.

"Nobody trusts anybody," Ana continued. "I told you in my letter, the splits go right through the families." She paused for a moment. "I'm ashamed of my country. There's no freedom anymore and hatred demoralizes our people."

"It's not your fault, Ana."

"But I still feel responsible. I'm part of this nation. Atrocities happen here everyday and I let them happen."

"Ana! What could you do? If you revolted you would be shot and it wouldn't have helped anyone!"

Ana kept silent.

"I understand your feelings, Ana. Under Hitler's dictatorship we also let hatred and violence grow without fighting it — out of fear of being put into concentration camps ourselves. And in the States we don't move a finger to stop the CIA from its subversive activities out of fear of losing our jobs."

Ana herself came to our rescue. "One of life's dilemmas. We have to cope with it." An ironic smile appeared on her face. "And all this in contrast to the luxuries in the stores."

"At first sight a traveler thinks this country overflows with wealth and order," I said.

"The government actually got big loans from the United States. In the last two years, the loans were tied to demands for human rights. Prisoners were released and sent into exile."

"We've met some in California."

Ana poured more tea. "Let me tell you something positive for a change. Since thousands of husbands are unemployed, jailed or missing, our women took over! They moved out of their homes, their traditional territory, to bring in money. And I predict that this will continue."

"So machismo is dead?"

"Absolutely not. Neither was it under Allende. But there's family planning now! All of us physicians who work with Moenckeberg approached Cardinal Silva to allow the use of the birth control pill."

"That's unheard of! A cardinal allows birth control pills? Next thing you'll tell me he even distributes them!"

She smiled. "Not quite. This is the way he expressed it: 'Every confessor has to entrust the decision over the number of children to the married couple.'"

"What a far-seeing view coming from a cardinal!"

"It's not he alone, Eva. In the United States most Catholic couples have no more than two or three children. I can't imagine that praying alone stops babies from coming."

I laughed. "Certainly not the praying. Rather fear of the cost of raising children."

Ana couldn't hear enough of my impressions of life in the United States and we spent hours comparing the two different cultures.

The conversations with Ana and many others in Santiago

brought me to a better understanding of Chile's recent past and its present, and on the four-and-a-half-hour flight to Easter Island I had ample time to absorb it all.

Easter Island is geographically and culturally as far away from Chile as Hawaii is from California. It seemed to be a little paradise, a remnant of the relatively peaceful 50's in Chile.

Since the population spoke Polynesian, we were glad that young Eduardo, our guide, spoke Spanish. We enjoyed his guidance through the remnants of the ancient culture with the famous 70-foot-high stone colossi.

On our last day Manfred and I sat with our tall, dark-haired guide under shady palm trees, warding off the incessant flies. Eduardo had been so knowledgeable and patient with us, we had become good friends. At last I asked him, "Why do you, a well-educated young man, live here on Easter Island?"

He picked up a blade of grass and studied it. "Because the government exiled me to this place."

"Eduardo, you an exile?" I looked around. "But what an outstanding place to be banned to!"

"At least it's 2,400 miles out of harm's way," he said with a bitter smile. "But I'll tell you why I'm here. I worked for Allende's campaign, and when he became president he appointed me Undersecretary of Agriculture because of my PhD in this field. Then came the coup. People like me were invariably shot to death." He ran a nervous hand through his hair. "But my family were strong supporters of Pinochet. And in consideration of them I was exiled to this place."

"You were pretty young to be an undersecretary in the president's palace," Manfred said. "A friend of ours became the Undersecretary of Health under Allende, but he was at least twenty years older than you."

Surprised, Eduardo looked up from the blade of grass. "You mean Ricardo Toro? He was your friend?"

I was startled. "Do you know what happened to him? His wife told us he 'disappeared.'"

"He was shot to death before my eyes."

"Where then did they leave his body?" Manfred asked.

Eduardo shrugged. "Cremated or drowned or buried in a mass grave... But I saw him dead."

Gloria was left in doubt about Ricardo's existence for five years, while we on Easter Island heard about his death by accident!

We immediately changed our travel plans. Instead of connecting in Santiago to a flight home, we decided to stop over to tell Gloria what we had heard. Only then could we go home to California. I did not know how long I would resist Chile's lure in the future.

23. VIOLENCE

Eight years later, in December 1986, we returned to Chile again — just three months after an assassination attempt on President Pinochet. On our first morning, Manfred and I took off from Alicia's house and went to the new Metro station. The subway platforms were super-shiny, reflecting the lights and signs. I was as proud of the gleaming subway as if it were my own. With a muted roar, the trains came in every three minutes. Santiago has more earthquakes than Southern California," I said. "But we haven't managed to build a subway, not even for crowded Los Angeles."

"Because nobody is after us with a whip," Manfred said. Inside, the ride was almost noiseless.

I inspected the passengers around me. "The women are still well-groomed and elegant," I said to Manfred in a low voice.

"But they don't flirt anymore," Manfred said. "Look, they wear tailored suits and carry briefcases and probably go to work. What a change!"

"Another change: the men don't offer their seats to the women. Where has the proverbial Latin *caballero* gone?"

At *Universidad de Chile* station we left the subway. Up on the busy thoroughfare, the Alameda, I stared at Santiago's new appearance. Near the familiar 400-year-old San Francisco church stood new, ultra-modern highrise buildings, designed in the bold style of Frank Lloyd Wright. Sun and trees reflected in the one-way glass paneling.

"It's amazing how well they blend the contrast between old and new," I said. "I have to admit I'm overwhelmed by Santiago's new face. The Metro. The streets spotlessly clean and orderly."

"Pinochet's achievements."

"That's one side of the coin," I said.

Then my first shock hit me. In front of a public building stood two soldiers with submachine guns at the ready. Huge posters on the corners carried the demands:

TURN IN EVERY COMMUNIST!
INFORM ON ANY POSSESSION OF ARMS!

"That's the reverse side of the dictatorship," I said. "The police state is now visible in the streets." Policemen in twos and threes walked the Alameda at a slow pace, focusing on oncoming faces with precision.

"It's ridiculous to put a show on like this!" Manfred said. "What in the world has Chile come to?" He abruptly pointed into the crowd of people. "Look who's there! John from the airplane!"

I recognized the amiable, jolly Chilean-American who had entertained us on the plane from Los Angeles with his great sense of humor. He told us how impatient he was to see Chile again after eighteen years. Now here he stood with a camera, taking shots of the bustling street life.

We shook hands and hugged. Wide-eyed, he rejoiced seeing his hometown again, rejuvenated and impressive as it was, with all the street vendors, who put their merchandise on a cloth on the ground — toys, combs, saints' images and playing-cards. Shoeshine boys crouched before customers, newspaper boys called out headlines and vendors sold ice cream cones.

While we strolled along the Alameda together, John cheerfully clicked his small pocket camera.

Across the street stood one of the imposing, modern buildings with two military guards, submachine guns at the ready. "Hey, that's a new building!" John said, taking a shot.

Seconds later two policemen popped up out of the blue sky and handcuffed John. "You are under arrest."

"For what?" John cried.

"For photographing the Ministry of Defense, commie."

"I'm not a communist!"

"That's what you all say."

An armored patrol car stopped in front of us. The policemen pushed John into it, and the vehicle drove away.

"We're back in Nazi Germany," Manfred said.

"What can we do now?"

"Nothing. As we could do nothing in Germany when things like this happened. John should have known that taking pictures of official buildings is prohibited."

"Can't we do anything to help him?" I asked.

"Not if we don't want to be arrested as well."

At lunch we discussed the incident with Alicia and her white-haired husband, Jaime.

"Since the assassination attempt on Pinochet in March, we are in a state of emergency," Jaime said, his soft brown eyes sober behind his framed glasses. "Because the terrorists attack so suddenly, soldiers have to be prepared to fight back within seconds. Besides, we have curfew from two to five every morning."

"Back to medieval times," I said. "How can you stand this?"

Jaime shrugged. "One gets used to it, Eva. We don't get involved in anything political and keep a low profile." He cleared his throat. "We should not forget, what Salvador Allende gave Chile was nightmare and chaos. We actually welcomed the junta's takeover, because it rid us of the communists and promised to bring law and order to the country."

"But how many atrocities have happened!" I snapped. "Have you forgotten Carmen Quintana, the girl that the soldiers doused with kerosene, set on fire and left her to die?"

Jaime wiped his mouth with his napkin as though to rid himself of guilt. "Eva, under every strong regime sadists come to power. This is not the first time."

His argument hit my conscience and muted me.

I thought of his words when I woke up in the middle of the night, as I sometimes did. Usually I turned around and fell asleep again, but tonight I felt like "exploring" the curfew from

Alicia's back yard, here in our old suburb of La Reina.

Stepping out into the darkness, I was wrapped in the perfumes of the garden — roses, jasmine and the overpowering "four-o'clocks", which opened and emitted their sweet scent only at night. The moonless sky, partially covered by the silhouettes of trees and the Andes, was studded with stars. No noise disturbed the peace and quiet of the night. Not even a bird sang, and my ears relaxed in the wonderful absence of sound. It was later I realized the stillness was achieved by the enforcement of the curfew and its subsequent threat and punishment.

I wanted to experience La Reina during the day also, but, sadly, missed two of my dearest friends. Gloria was in Germany and Ana was in the United States.

As I strolled nostalgically through our old neighborhood in the foothills of the Andes, a petite, well-dressed woman approached me. At first I thought my memories had conjured up a ghost. But it turned out to be Cora, who, thirty years ago, was beaten so terribly by her husband, Ramón, in our house.

I didn't believe my eyes. We hugged and kissed. "Cora, what a surprise! How are you doing?"

She looked radiant. The years of our separation shrank to nothing as she bubbled over with excitement. "I got an annulment of my marriage with Ramón long ago," Cora explained. "Then I married a nice man. He was thirty years older. He died last year and left me a bungalow. It's around the corner, Eva. Please come in, even if it's only for a minute."

I couldn't resist her amiability and followed her to the bungalow. With pride she showed me around until we climbed upstairs and entered her bedroom. On the wall opposite her single bed hung a larger-than-life poster of the dictator, Augusto Pinochet. Erect, in general's uniform, with folded arms, grim mouth and gray mustache, he resembled his own idol, Hitler. Only the swastika was missing.

"Isn't he wonderful?" Cora asked. "Did you see how much Chile has changed? The new buildings, the Metro? The disciplined driving? The great Pan American Highway, 3,800 miles from north to south?"

"Yes, I've seen it," I managed to say.

"Our president is a great man and I love him. You shouldn't believe what your American newspapers say. They just tell lies about him."

"But it's a well-known fact that he let people be tortured and killed!"

"Can you show me any?" she asked.

"I have talked to people who were tortured."

She shrugged. "Those were communists. They deserved it."

How far apart had our worlds become!

"Your journalists are all leftists," she said lightly. "They only write bad things about him." She stepped over to the monster's image and kissed his mustache. Then she turned to me. "I love him," she said, and her voice trembled with sensual pleasure. "He got rid of communism. Eva, he is the greatest man that ever lived." Suddenly she giggled and said to me with mock-confidentiality, "I could crawl in his bed the minute he snapped his fingers."

I felt sorry for her, an obvious victim of machismo. She'd staggered from a sadist to a father figure to another sadist, inferior forever.

"It's sticky in here," Cora said and stepped over to the window and opened it. "Wow! Look at the sunset!"

I stepped nearer to the window. An apparition of three purple suns, on top of each other, swam between pink stripes of clouds. Silently we stood spellbound. No camera at hand, I knew the mirage would last only seconds. After a moment the illusion dissolved into dark-red cloud layers.

"Those sunsets exist only in Chile," Cora said.

For fear of hearing that Pinochet was making them, I pretended to be in a hurry and said goodbye to her.

On this spot and within minutes, I had experienced Chile's extremes — the excess of a delusion and the wonder of a mirage. Later I told Manfred about it.

"Same old Cora," he said. "Unfortunately she isn't the only one to worship that brute. Half the population doesn't want to know the truth about the atrocities. How many of our old friends here do you think are devoted to Pinochet?" Without waiting for me to answer, he said on. "About fifty percent."

"And we are tossed from one extreme to the other. That's Chile."

"It's us, too," he said. "We keep our friends no matter how far their opinions deviate from ours."

Since stimulating friends couldn't be taken to California and books could, we went to check out several bookstores. All were stocked with all kinds of literature in Spanish, English, French and German. Only books about the Allende time were missing. We decided on a few picture books of Chile as presents for our children and friends at home.

From outside came a faint sound, like people singing. As we walked toward the tree-studded Plaza de Armas, the city's center, the singing became louder. As we arrived at a busy intersection, all buses and private cars had stopped out of respect for a group of women on the street. Clad in simple summer dresses, they shouted and clapped in rhythm, *"¡Justicia y libertad! ¡Justicia y libertad!* Justice and liberty!"

A minute later all vehicles began to honk their horns in solidarity: The police were coming!

The women immediately threw a bunch of fliers into the air and disappeared into the crowd of onlookers.

I quickly picked up a flyer before the police could confiscate it. It read:

>"Truth and justice for the disappeared.
>Punishment for the guilty.
>Truth and justice for the executed.
>Punishment for the guilty."

These were the desperate wives and mothers of "disappeared" ones, risking their lives for these demonstrations. While some people said hundreds had vanished, others said thousands, but the pain caused by the wound of a disappearance could not be measured in numbers.

In silence we walked a few blocks to F.L., the foundry where Manfred had worked thirty-four years ago. Time seemed to have been suspended, for the engineers and many workers were still there, looking older, but they recognized their former superior with joy.

Even Jorge was there, the good-natured independent trucker of the days of old, still working for the foundry. Manfred invited him to the cafeteria for a beer.

"We have to thank you for our survival," Jorge said. "If you hadn't sent us so much money, we might not have survived."

Manfred looked puzzled. "I've never sent money to Chile. Please explain."

Jorge smiled. "By 'you,' I actually meant your CIA."

I winced. Seeing Manfred's face becoming tense, I feared he would blow up into Jorge's face.

"I was a union leader in Allende's time," Jorge continued. "To tumble him, the only way for us truckers was to strike. But we had no money. Then the CIA gave us more money than we ever needed. We stayed on strike, food wasn't delivered anymore, and finally Allende shot himself."

I was going to say that Allende's death was still a mystery but thought it wiser to end the discussion and go home.

As we left the foundry, Manfred said, rage in his voice, "That was the last thing I expected. To be identified with the CIA."

"I too felt angry." With a bitter smile I added, "And we don't even protest."

"Think what happens when one does. Remember Orlando Letelier?"

I remembered the former Chilean ambassador to the U.S. "Of course."

"When he protested against the torturing, the junta reached him even in Washington, D.C.," Manfred said.

"... and put a bomb under his car and killed him," I added.

"Just leave me out of the dirty politics," he said.

I only hoped our next visit would be more pleasant. Alicia's son, Julio, had invited us to see his company in the afternoon and later to dinner at his house. We'd known him long ago as a curly-haired child with a sweet tooth and loved him dearly.

We went to catch a bus to his company. Through the windows we saw truckloads of soldiers speeding by, always aiming, fingers crooked on triggers. Filled with sadness and disgust, but still without fear — because the survival of one dictatorship had dulled us — we took in the show of the dictator's fear of assassination.

Once at Julio's work place, we found him still curly-haired, but now he was an unkempt, ingenious bachelor with a PhD in computer science and co-owner of a computer company with 130 employees.

Julio took us to a cold room where about thirty computers whirred and vibrated. "They're doing work for the government. Figuring out taxes and statistics."

"I'm very impressed," Manfred said. "I've never seen so many computers in one place."

"I brought them from the United States and offered the program to the government."

"Chile has become as modern as California."

Julio adjusted the air-conditioner. "Pinochet pulled Chile from its medieval fetters. He has to get the credit for our upbeat economy."

Shocked, I stared at our liberal friend. "You are saying that?"

"Every coin has two sides. True, Pinochet cried 'Wolf!' at every so-called communist and allowed thousands of his adversaries to be tortured and killed. But he pulled the country out of chaos and backwardness and joined the U.S. and its capitalism."

"For what price!"

"No matter. In the end only the winner counts. Chile now runs busily after money and luxury." He stepped to the door. "Tonight I want you to meet my partner, Gustavo. Can you be be at my house for dinner at nine?"

"Of course, thanks. And you have two different sides also."

"I'm just a pragmatist."

We had to fight the rumbling of our stomachs, until we entered Julio's two-story house in the suburbs, where he, his German shepherd, Max, and his partner, Gustavo, lived.

For privacy, Julio had given his maid the evening off and served the prepared Chilean delicacies himself in the spacious kitchen: the hearty *cazuela* soup, *humitas* made from mashed corn and boiled in the corn husks, *empanadas*, turnovers with cheese or meat and for dessert, *chirimoya alegre,* Chile's most delicate fruit swimming in fresh orange juice -- all washed down with Chilean wines until Manfred, Gustavo and I simply begged for water.

Gustavo was a handsome man in his thirties, ash-blond and blue-eyed. "I was very much devoted to General Pinochet," he told us. "I worked for the government in a very trusted position for years." He didn't specify. "One day an old friend from college came to me. His brother, active in middle-left politics, had disappeared. He asked if I could discover his whereabouts. I told him, 'Under this regime no one disappears.'

"I used my position to get access to secret files and found out the brother was in jail. He was in a special jail for political prisoners." He paused for a moment. "When I arrived there, I heard the sound of beatings and cries for help. Then I saw the torture myself."

For a moment I covered my ears with my hands.

"My friend's brother was dead," Gustavo said. "He was tortured to death. I told my friend and then I left the government. Now I'm working against this murderous regime."

I sighed. "What's the point in this endless torturing?"

"To get information on so-called communists. That's all."

I moaned. Chile with its long history of non-war and a reputation of gentleness had developed into a nation of hatred and violence!

Suddenly, the lights went out. "Goddammit, they've done it

again," Julio shouted, got up and brought candles.

"Who's done what again?" Manfred asked.

"Active communists who keep pressure on the government," Julio answered. "They occasionally blow up oil pipelines or bridges. Or they topple electric transmission towers like tonight."

"Or the government itself did it," Gustavo said. "To create a reason to blame the communists and to arrest more people."

By candlelight and good wine we gradually relaxed. When Julio began to speak in a low voice about Chile's training-sailing ship, ESMERALDA, it sounded as if he were divulging a secret. I was all ears again.

"The ESMERALDA was used for transporting political prisoners. Out in the Pacific, the prisoners were all shot. Before the bodies were thrown overboard, the agents slit the bellies open so the bodies would not float to the surface."

"Julio!" I cried. "This is more than I can bear! Who told you that? You weren't on the ship yourself, were you?"

"No. My brother, Manuel, was. He's a witness. And it's better never to talk about it."

We sat in silence.

Eventually, electricity returned. The warm lights illuminated the cozy living room and helped us to readjust to the consoling presence of our friends.

At midnight we drove back to Alicia's to spend our last night before traveling to the bottom of the world, Antarctica.

Early in the morning we flew to Chile's extreme south. In Punta Arenas we boarded an expedition ship through the Strait of Magellan. Far away from all atrocities, we were ready to enjoy the frozen continent.

"Antarctica is the size of the United States and Europe combined," the ship's geologist told us. "There are more than sixty research stations of different countries in Antarctica. Chile has the largest. To protect it, the government keeps soldiers in its sector."

"I only hope we won't have to face submachine guns down

here," I said to Manfred. "You never know. Pinochet himself went to Antarctica last year."

"Looking for communists?"

"He probably feared even the penguins were indoctrinated."

The ship remained anchored far from the coast while we were transferred to shore in motor boats through a labyrinth of icebergs to the frozen grounds of Antarctica. Soon we were surrounded by sleepy elephant seals and thousands of lively penguins, with screeching predatory skuas circling above us.

To give us relief from the 30-degree temperature the Chilean scientists invited us for tea and cake in their prefabricated steel lab, which housed the fifteen scientists.

"We are five hundred people here," a biologist told us. "We have a school with two teachers and a hospital with a doctor. Also we have the first Antarctica-born baby!" He radiated with pride. "We are all one big family."

After short lectures the biologist led us out into the cold wind. When two wrapped-up children tramped by, I let the travel group go on while I stopped to talk to the children.

"¡Hola!" I said to them, seeing by then that they were a girl of about twelve, and a boy, probably not older than eight. "¿Cómo están? How are you?"

"Bien," the girl said.

I turned to the little boy who seemed a bit shy. "How's the winter here?"

"Cold," he said, giving me a cute, lop-sided smile. A memory began to stir in me. Where had I seen this lop-sided smile before? Those dark, wide-set eyes, that strand of black hair falling on his forehead... Nonsense! I scolded myself. Just a fancy.

A huge tank-like caterpillar tractor with the driver on top rolled straight toward us. "Let's get out of the way," I said to the children, pulling them to the side.

Yet the caterpillar stopped right in front of us. "¡Papi!" the children screamed, jumping up and down.

Their father! I looked at the driver and saw the same wide-set eyes and special grin like his son's. My blurred memory struggled for recognition.

The driver jumped down from his monstrous vehicle. "Do you want a ride, José?" he asked his son.

At that moment the memory took shape. "José-Stalin?" I asked, incredulous.

Terror in his face, he looked at me.

"José," I said, "don't you remember me from Vista Hermosa Street? Your mother's name is María. She used to wash my clothes. We were good friends." Wordless and resigned, he took his eyes from me. "Remember my daughter, Little Bear? You always played together."

He turned to me. More than before he resembled the cute little boy of thirty-three years ago, only he was a man in his forties now, hand-in-hand with his look-alike son. "Señora, I don't use that second part of my name anymore. José is enough."

I nodded. "I understand. But tell me, how did you get to Antarctica? And how is your mother?"

"My mother died years ago. She worked too much. She gave us all the food and ate too little. One morning we found her dead in her bed. She died in her sleep."

"She surely deserved such an easy death. She was a wonderful mother."

"How's Little Bear?" José asked.

"She's married and has two daughters."

Manfred called behind me, "Ev! Where have you got to? The scientist is showing us his greenhouse."

The children pushed each other to be first to get on the caterpillar.

"I'll be there in a minute!" I called back.

Manfred acknowledged with a hand gesture and returned to the group.

José seemed to understand the situation. "I'll make it short. After my mother died, the soldiers came for my father and took him away. I've never seen him again. They took me and my brothers to a ship. We sailed to Punta Arenas."

Above us the cries of predatory birds pierced the air.

"We all were supposed to be communists. Especially I with my double name. The soldiers made fun of me, calling me 'Uncle Stalin.' They beat me more than the others."

A gust of wind chilled me.

"One day they hit me on the head. I collapsed and they shoved me in a corner and threw a roll of rope on me. When I came to, I crawled out. All the prisoners were gone. The crew had changed. They were soldiers going to Antarctica. They put me in a uniform and took me to this place. Now we work here. On furlough in Santiago, I married a woman with this girl here. And now we have this boy."

In spite of ice and wind I felt like hugging him, but I just smiled. "I'm happy for you, José. Thank you for telling me your story. I'll tell Little Bear."

"Muchos saludos," he said and lifted his son up on the caterpillar. "You'll be next," he said to his step-daughter, who patiently walked alongside the rolling caterpillar, resigned to being number two.

For a while I followed them with my eyes, happy about the outcome of José's ordeal. It was almost midnight. The wind had ceased, and the sun shone brightly on the many different creatures of this continent — the innocent animals and the humans, burdened with pain and guilt.

I turned to join Manfred and our group. Tomorrow we'd fly home, and I wondered if I'd ever see Chile again.

24. PEACE

In 1989, Chile voted grandfatherly Patricio Aylwyn into the presidency, who returned the country to a democracy. Three years later I was about to finish writing this book but still had questions for which I couldn't find answers in California. So I decided to fly to Chile again.

Carefully choosing the right month for my trip, I settled for March. I figured, with the summer heat over and the families returned from their vacation, I'd be able to find them all together in the capital. Besides, the air would be clean, the temperature comfortable and the rainy season wouldn't have started yet.

Manfred was busy writing his spy novel, and so I alone boarded good old LAN CHILE in California's spring and fourteen hours later I got out into Chile's fall season.

Arriving at Pudahuel Airport in Santiago with a cool mind, determined to use my two weeks in Chile as efficiently as possible, I was overwhelmed by all the love my friends bestowed on me.

Alicia Hurtado picked me up and we hugged for a long time. Her husband had died three years before. Now eighty-one, white-haired but radiant as ever, she offered me the same well-known Chilean hospitality I had experienced through the decades.

"I have a whole list of people who want to see you," Alicia said. "They left their phone numbers and confirmed dates."

"Oh, yes. I'd written to them for interviews."

"Who'll be first?"

"Gloria Toro."

I walked along Gloria's street, whose maple trees had grown to a dome. Unfortunately, they blocked the view to the mountains I hadn't seen for so long.

I noticed many cars parked on both sides of the street. Someone probably had a party going.

An old woman opened the gate for me and said, *"Buenos días,* Señora Eva." When she saw my surprise, she added, "Remember me? I'm Filomena."

The Toros' maid from forty years ago, the same Gloria and I had visited in her *población* when she was ill! "How are you, Filomena? Do you still live with Señora Gloria?"

"Oh, no! I live with my family in the *población.* We have brick houses now. I just come to help the señora when she has company."

We walked toward the house. "How are your children?" I asked.

"They all have gone to school and learned something. We are not poor anymore."

"I'm happy for you, Filomena."

She ushered me into the house, which I remembered so well. Fourteen years ago Gloria had been cooking lunch here in a huge cauldron for poor children.

Now I stared with curiosity at another huge crowd in the back yard. More than a dozen healthy, happy children were rolling in the grass or romping in a swimming pool that hadn't been there fourteen years ago. Foolishly, I tried to tell who was who from my memory when I realized I was looking at the next generation, which I hadn't met yet. I scanned the groups of adults, sitting on small tables, scattered throughout the greenery, chatting, laughing, eating and drinking. The mixed aroma of dishes penetrated my nose.

"¡Hola, Eva!" Gloria's high-pitched voice called from behind me. I turned and we hugged for a long time. A reunion, shared memories, camaraderie.

Then we looked at each other, both seventy-one. "You haven't changed," she said. "Except for a few more pounds."

"You haven't changed either. You look energetic. The old fighter."

"Believe me, I need my energy to hold my twenty-three grandchildren in line. They and their parents are all here so you can visit with them."

I kissed her cheek. "Thanks. How wonderful!"

So I was looking at ten of Gloria's twelve children. Pancholo was dead, and her twelfth baby had died right after birth. "I remember all of them. But except for the oldest ones, they won't recognize me."

"Never mind. Get yourself something to eat and drink and join whatever group you wish."

The large dining room table groaned under the weight of Gloria's culinary goodies. I took samples of the various salads, avocados rolled in ham slices, grilled salmon, birds stuffed with truffles, glazed fruits, papayas, coconuts, pineapples and various cakes and cookies, and iced coffee, topped with whipped cream. With my loaded plate I stepped into the eucalyptus-scented back yard and sat down at a table under bunches of ripe grapes that hung from a trellis.

The group briefly interrupted their heated discussion to introduce themselves as four Toro "children" and their spouses. "We're discussing the Rettig report," Gloria's fiery lawyer son, Pablo, explained to me. "The recently published report on the activities of Pinochet's secret police. Now we are enjoying freedom of information. Sorry, the report says, and lists only a little over 2,000 people murdered or 'disappeared.' The other hundreds of thousands are not counted, including our father and our brother."

"Why aren't they counted?" I asked.

"The commission was told to deal only with the identifiable cases. But at any rate, the publication has led to the reconciliation of the divided nation."

"Is Pinochet going to be punished now?" I asked.

"There's a problem!" said Monica, Gloria's daughter with a page-boy haircut. "In 1978, when he was still in power,

Pinochet released an amnesty, erasing all committed crimes. And the constitution, written under his government, permits him to stay on as army commander until 1997."

A medley of voices arose, which made everything unintelligible to me. I tried to say something, but my voice drowned in the torrent of words.

"Silence!" Monica shouted. "Let Eva say something!"

"How are you folks going to resolve the situation?" I asked. "Put the thugs to trial or what?"

Pablo clenched his fists. "Hang them all!"

"No, we cannot," Monica said. "It's a dilemma for our democratic government. If our government prosecutes military men for crimes committed while in power, it risks an uproar from the armed forces, as happened in Argentina."

"And if it does not prosecute them?" I asked.

"Then this would send a signal to authoritarians the world over — that democratic governments don't have the courage to punish officials who commit atrocities under the cover of national security." She looked at me. "Pinochet had learned from Richard Nixon. Nixon managed to get a pardon and Pinochet released an amnesty."

"Hey, Monica! You should become a politician. You already talk like one," Pablo kidded her.

"If I become one, the first bill I'll submit will be to have you appointed as my personal counselor," Monica said. Everyone clapped.

"Joking apart," I said, "many things seem to have improved here. Or have they?"

"We're happy now," Monica said. She counted on her fingers. "No malnourished children. School system as good as in Europe and free. Illiteracy down to four percent. All workers health-insured. Isn't that progress?"

"I never expected anything less from Chile," I said. "Did you also abolish poverty?"

"No, but it's reduced considerably."

"Are you happy with the democracy now?"

"We are no longer afraid," Monica said.

"That's not true!" her sister Cecilia almost shouted. "Crimes have increased so much we need two attack dogs instead of one to protect the house!"

"She's right," her husband Manolo said. "The police have lost control. That's the bad side of democracy."

I got up with him to refill our plates and glasses. At the buffet, Gloria's oldest daughter, Ilona, the beauty queen of the family, spoke to me. "Eva, please come and sit with us."

"I'd be happy to."

Ilona introduced her siblings and their spouses as I sat down. I was curious what the theme at this table might be. The Toros' tradition of discussing issues passionately had survived a generation. Ricardo's spirit was among us.

"Women's status?" one of the dark-haired young men asked. "You gals already have so many privileges! What else do you want?"

"We want rights, not privileges," Ilona said.

"I heard you've had family planning for years," I said.

Ilona lit a cigarette. "That's true. You can see the results. My parents had twelve children, but each of us has only two."

I looked at the romping children in the swimming pool. "Is abortion still illegal?"

"Oh, yes."

"Divorce?"

"Also. But we manage to get around the laws. Through annulments."

Two children came to our table, crying and accusing each other for having started a fight. The appropriate parents wiped the children's tears, calmed them down and kissed them. The children stopped crying. "Can we watch *tele?*"

Sighing from the depths of her heart, the mother took them into the room with the television set. The children here weren't too different from those in California.

I turned back to the group. "Divorce camouflaged by annulment sounds easy."

"But there's a catch," Ilona said. "Do you know that husbands own everything and wives nothing?"

I thought of Gloria's plight thirty-six years ago. "That hasn't changed in all those years?"

"Not at all. Let Pedro and Regina tell you what they had to go through."

"Both sides have to sign a resignation before the annulment can get processed," Pedro said. "When I went to my ex-wife to ask for her signature, she got on her high horse and said: 'I'll sign only if you give me the house, the car and the children.' No doubt, this was her only chance in life. I had no choice and gave her what she wanted."

Regina's face showed a bitter smile. "When I went to my ex-husband for the signature, he signed and shouted: 'You'll get nothing from me. Get out of here!'"

"It looks like men still have all the rights. Are you going to do something about it?" I asked, looking from one to the other. The four men kept silent. Three wives, except Ilona, shrugged.

"You work, you make money," I said to the women. "Why can't you get equal rights?"

"Do American women have equal rights?" Ilona asked.

"Not quite. But we definitely have more rights than you do. And we're constantly fighting for it."

Two vertical lines appeared on Ilona's brow — her mother's notorious anger-wrinkles. "The laws will never change unless more women get into politics."

Tumult and boo-calls from the men arose. "Women don't belong in politics!"

"Stay home!"

"Become teachers, but not politicians!" I thought I was back in California.

Gloria's voice broke up the tumult. *"¡Atención!"* Clapping her hands, she tried to get attention from the crowd. "A new guest has arrived."

All heads turned toward the veranda door. A priest, Gloria's look-alike, stepped into the garden. Her brother, Victor! The founder of the Center for Mothers and Children, the public representative of welfare, Gloria's savior from run-away pregnancies, the man who had alleviated my transition from Chile to America. Slim as before, but now slightly stooped with white curly hair, he raised his hand to stop the applause. I noticed a photographer with his long-lens equipment aiming at the crowd.

"Dear folks," Father Victor said in his sonorous voice. "We all have the pleasure to greet a woman whose love for our country was exceptional and never ceased to burn even in the northern hemisphere."

When I saw his eyes focussing on me I winced.

"Señora Eva," he continued, "In the thirty-two years of your life in the United States you have became a source of goods which, particularly during the years of agony, were highly appreciated. You helped educate, feed and clothe thousands of mothers and children in need. In gratitude for your graciousness and in the name of our Foundation I have the honor to present you with a plaque and a musical souvenir of Chile."

He approached me. Overwhelmed, I got up and met him. He handed me two small, flat items. One was a thank-you plaque with the inscription: "GRACIAS A EVA KRUTEIN." I unwrapped the other: a compact disc with songs of the Aymará, the Indians of northern Chile, our erstwhile neighbors.

I offered my hand to Father Victor — no hugs with a priest — and thanked him.

Seeing the photographer constantly clicking his camera, I knew it was time for a short reception speech. I turned around to Gloria's huge family. "Dear friends, including Father Victor as a family member. I am deeply moved by being honored for something that was a labor of love for me, because my heart was still here in Chile. My biggest help were the directions you gave me thirty-two years ago, Father: 'Start out with your parish, then go higher.' I tried in my little way to help, but it was American generosity which provided the numerous gifts and I just became instrumental in pushing the shipments to your

Foundation, Father. Thank you for your great deeds."

Tumultuous applause rose from the crowd, the photographer kept shooting until Father Victor shook my hand again and then mingled with his numerous family members.

It was high time for me to go. In the turmoil it was easy to say my thanks and my goodbye to Gloria.

"Knowing you, I'd say you'll be back again," she said.

"If Manfredo were here I'd never leave!"

I was happy for her. After the many tragedies in her life she seemed to have arrived at a point from which she could look around with joy and satisfaction. This knowledge made the going away easier for me. After all, I still had a lot of things to do.

The following days were filled with research at the National Library and interviews with directors of various social and cultural institutions for a deeper understanding of Chile's contemporary life.

The eloquent director of the Women's National Service, a charming petite woman, told me, "It's not the laws that have to change, but the women's attitude as mothers. They have to raise both genders equally, not prefer their sons, and they have to provide equal education for their daughters."

"How will you achieve that?"

"Education is the key. Our service provides free workshops for women, where they can learn what they have missed. The poverty level is considerably reduced now."

"Who are those who are still very poor?"

"The unskilled ones. Again, education is the key."

"So you mainly teach school subjects?"

"We do teach the three R's, but we also teach them, for example, how to react when beaten by their husbands, where to go for protection. If the case is brought before a judge, the husband is sentenced to 100 or more days in jail."

This sounded naive to me, but for centuries-long-suppressed wives it could mean revelation and salvation.

Rushing from one appointment to the other, I was well aware of Santiago's appearance — its new, futuristic-styled buildings, stuffed shops and the elegant dress code of the people in the malls. And miracle of miracles — everyone was on time! Without question, Chile's economy had progressed to the point of being equal with California.

Yet there was one setback that made my visit incomplete. Only five years ago, I had stood in admiration before the colorful light shows on the Andes, created by the setting sun. Now I was choked by a noxious gray smog, caused by the city's 400,000 cars and buses. Driving with leaded gas and without catalytic exhaust filters, they spread an acid odor, so that often I used my handkerchief as a gas mask.

The mountains we used to see even from downtown remained invisible. I hoped to have a good view from a higher place. I called Ana Araya and invited her for tea at the *Giratorio,* a high tower with a revolving restaurant, from which we should have a splendid view over Santiago and the mountains.

I chose a table at the window. But the view presented only a blue haze with a fuzzy contour of the Andes. Their luminosity was snuffed out. Gone, gone forever.

I looked around. What a surprise! Almost all the well-dressed women at the tables smoked, but the majority of men did not! Ana would have to explain this to me.

Minutes later she entered the restaurant, still using a cane. I got up and we hugged and kissed each other with affection. It felt good to look at her intelligent face with those warm, gray eyes. "Does your hip still hurt after so many years?" I asked.

"It's now turned into a severe arthritis. But let's not talk about that. How are you?"

"Wonderful. Lilo's daughter has a little boy, and now I'm a great-grandmother." We sat down and ordered tea.

"Now tell me, what are your impressions of modern Santiago?" Ana asked.

"I haven't seen one drunkard on the street."

"Most have another addiction now. Television. On the other side, the idiot box keeps the men at home with their families."

"A triple hurrah to progress!" I said sarcastically. "Something else I haven't seen — homeless people."

"Not even the poorest family will let anybody sleep on the streets. Even non-relatives are taken in. The close-knit family has kept its spirit of solidarity."

"I take off my hat to you Chileans."

"Thanks. In this regard we deserve it. But not in others. Look at the air."

The slowly revolving floor had turned to where downtown would have been seen had the smog not blanketed the city with a dark-gray layer of soot.

Ana became agitated. "It's not air anymore, it's poisonous slime! You won't believe the respiratory illnesses we've got. The contamination is killing children and old people."

"It sounds like Los Angeles."

"We're copying your good and your bad things."

"What are the good ones?"

"Democracy, of course. Freedom of expression."

"Congrats again."

Ana gave a small gesture of acceptance. "You and I were always concerned with the status of women. Now we can see some progress."

"Tell me. It's still close to my heart."

For a moment Ana looked out the window into the filthy air. "Women work and make money. They no longer put up with all their husbands' demands. In turn, men are less polite than before. Tit for tat."

I looked around. "I see all women smoke. Is that a sign of emancipation? And why don't most men smoke?"

"Yes, it is a symbol of freedom for women. Meanwhile men have learned that smoking is bad for their health."

"Then they are still one step ahead of the women?"

She nodded.

The waiter brought tea and a selection of cakes on a platter.

Each of us chose a piece.

"There seems to be no trace of the mass executions and tortures," I said. "I wonder how the gentle Chileans could ever do that."

"You must understand it was mainly soldiers that did the mass killings. And soldiers are trained to obey blindly and kill under orders."

"A strong analysis!"

"Just simplified. In contrast, torturers are selected because they are known to enjoy being cruel. They are sadists for whom torturing is a sexual turn-on. When their victims writhe with pain, they may get an orgasm."

I was aghast. "Ana! My God! I've never heard of anything like that!"

A bitter smile showed in Ana's face. "You wanted the truth, you got it. You see, we doctors had to heal the victims and come to terms with the tormentors. Now the whole nation has to deal with it, after the report on the activities of Pinochet's secret police came out."

"I've heard about it."

"It's passionately discussed everywhere." The waiter refilled our teacups and offered more cake. Ana declined.

"Diets seem to be known here too," I said.

"It's a fad like in America."

Outside twilight had darkened, and in the restaurant lights were turned on.

"By the way, how does birth control work?" I asked. "The pope is so much against it."

"But our local priests are not."

"This is such an important development. How did it come about?"

Ana leaned forward as if for emphasis. "When the pill arrived on the scene, women grabbed them like life-savers. The Cardinal and the priests simply couldn't stop the pill. Of course, with sexual freedom came AIDS."

"Is AIDS as bad here as it is in the United States?"

"Percentage-wise, I think it's lower here. We use a broader approach to education in sexual matters than you do in America."

"Like what?"

"I'll show you. Let's pay for the tea and leave."

We then took the elevator down directly into a subway station — the Metro, Santiago's piece of jewelry.

Piped-in music played the end of Mozart's "Little Night Music" and then the beginning of Beethoven's Seventh Symphony. Holy Chile, this was more than luxury!

"Look at the wall over there," Ana said.

Three huge well-lit boards struck my eyes. One advertised a shampoo, the other welcomed Plácido Domingo to Chile. The third, the largest one, captured my complete attention. Divided in three columns, it warned of SIDA, Aids, explaining

1) What AIDS is,

2) What NOT to do,

3) How to do it RIGHT.

No one waiting for the trains could escape the signs.

"I'm impressed," I said. "No way could we advertise it that blatantly in America."

"Do you want more sex education? Let's go up to the street again."

Night had fallen and the multi-colored neon lights of a movie theater lit up the streets.

"Let's go in there," Ana said. "If just for a few minutes. If we're lucky I can show you something you don't have in the United States."

I trusted her. Seats were reserved and could be chosen as for a concert hall, but I didn't think Ana wanted to show me that.

We were seated when advertising began — previews of American gangster movies, advertisements of Coca-Cola and deodorants. But then a woman's head was shown on the left and a man's on the right, with a printed conversation:

The woman: "I'm unable to have an orgasm because you

ejaculate too fast."

The man: "What can I do about it?"

The woman: "Try Adolin pills. They will retard your ejaculation, until I have my orgasm."

Then the pillbox was shown.

"Well, what do you think?" Ana asked.

"My sex education is now complete."

Laughing, we left the theater. I had no more questions about women's status.

Ana and I had to part then. We were sad, not knowing when we would see each other again. I watched her stop a taxi and disappear. As if for consolation I gazed in the direction of the mountains. Long ago, the snow on top had shimmered even on moonless nights. Now the view was gone. Like Ana.

When I arrived at Alicia's, curly-haired Julio was there with his handsome friend, Gustavo, who, on our last visit to Chile, had told us the terrible story about the jails under Pinochet.

"How do you like Santiago now?" Julio asked.

"I've been here a month but haven't seen the Andes! Where have they gone?" I asked.

"I'll show them to you," Julio said without hesitation. "Let's go to the mountains on Saturday. You shouldn't leave Chile without seeing and touching them again."

I counted the days. Then, on Saturday, Julio and Gustavo came to pick me up.

"Take your swimsuit along," Gustavo said.

I took it, muttering, "I thought we were going to the mountains."

Alicia, at eighty-one, preferred to stay home. "Julio drives up hill and down dale. That's too much for me."

Julio brought one of his three dogs along — Max, a beautiful German shepherd. Max was a wild and loving dog, who knocked down every unsuspecting person and after that licked his victim back to life. Playfully, I began to romp with Max in the Toyota until Julio threatened to throw us out. "Both.

The dog and the great-grandmother."

Max and I promised to behave, and Julio drove on, steadily uphill. The paved, winding road ran along the Maipo River past vineyards and orchards toward Argentina.

After an hour the pavement ended and we faced a bar across the road. At the door of a guard house stood an officer, visibly happy to be pulled out of his boredom.

"We're only five miles from Argentina," Julio said. He had to show his driver's license, the officer jotted down the license plate number and then pulled up the bar for us. As the car rumbled with difficulty onto rocks and loose gravel I thought my inner organs would be torn from their places. Finally, Julio stopped.

Here at 15,000 feet we had arrived at a steep hill, sloping down in natural terraces. On each of them was a small, hot sulfur pool, from which water ran down in rivulets to the next lower level, gradually cooling off. Snow, which the sun couldn't melt in the thin air, lay around the pools in patches.

We left Max in the shadow of the car and approached the lowest terrace. Julio and Gustavo were already in their swim trunks. But for me, there was no shack, no bush to hide for changing clothes.

"We'll hold out this towel before you," Julio offered.

"Okay. But don't look!"

"What for? We are gay," Julio said.

"Oh! Then there's no problem."

Despite my light-hearted answer I was still surprised by Julio's casual statement. Why had I never thought of that? In any case, he was my dear friend, almost a son, and he would always mean the same to me.

Panting in the thin air, we climbed up a few steps to the lowest bubbling pool. The water was about ninety-five degrees. Cradled on all sides by the majestic Andes, I deeply inhaled the sulfurous vapor, which supposedly had healing power.

"Were you surprised when I told you we were gay?" Julio asked.

"A little. I had never thought about it. I usually don't care who goes to bed with whom."

"We've been together for six years. During the dictatorship we couldn't talk about it. We would have been arrested. Now we have freedom of expression."

"Viva democracy!"

"Let's get in the snow," Gustavo said.

While my heated body cooled down in the snow, I looked at the majestic spectacle of the Andes, snaking toward infinity: purple peaks, white-crowned volcanoes, ravines and gorges whose sheer, icy walls would melt in summertime. Grateful for being in such beauty I remembered the old saying that God had stored all the beauty left over from Creation and given it to Chile. I'd love this country in eternity.

Gustavo intruded in my rapture. "Shall we try the next level now?" We ascended to the higher, hotter level, where the sulphur vapors were denser.

"Ouch!" I yelled. "It's almost 120 degrees!"

"Not quite," Julio said. "Get in slowly."

Already intoxicated by the mountain air, I felt the hot water adding even more to my exhilaration. Yet I felt heated to the point of boiling. "Let's cool off in the snow."

The three of us climbed out of the sulfuric water and laid down in the largest snow patch.

Tomorrow I would fly home to California. I had caught the past and carried it into the present. In many ways, Chile and California now were so much alike that they appeared to be physically close as well. I felt I could walk over in a single step.

As I rolled to and fro in the snow, I realized that this country was no longer in extreme agony and didn't need me any more. When I left Chile more than thirty years ago, my heart had remained there and only my body moved to California. Now I could take my heart into the northern world — with Chile forever enclosed in it.

MORE WOMEN'S WRITING
FROM AMADOR PUBLISHERS

EVA'S WAR:
A TRUE STORY OF SURVIVAL
by Eva Krutein

ISBN: 0-938513-09-5 [Trade $17]
ISBN: 0-938513-08-7 [Paper $9]
260 pp.

This gripping story of flight, refugees, privation, defeat, moral quandaries, growth and finally healing is strangely moving and compelling. It becomes a powerful anti-war statement from a woman's perspective. One year is recounted, beginning in January, 1945. Danzig, a Free City between the Great Wars, was seized by Hitler in 1939, and threatened by Soviet troops as Eva flees with her daughter.

They say that history is written by the winners, yet this bit of history comes from that nation which lost the war. Now that that nation is recovered and reunited, this sort of remembering is all the more important. And Eva Krutein is no loser. She and her family emigrated to Chile, and then to California, where they now live. She is an accomplished musician and writer.

"A marvelously moving and often humorous real-life story... sad revelations, painful memories, excruciating experiences are tempered by compassion, love and a powerful, contagious optimism. Music permeates this tale." Alfred-Maurice de Zayas, JD, PhD, Senior Legal Officer, The United Nations, Geneva, Switzerland

"Her novel-like presentation makes for exciting reading. The story of German refugees has not been well covered, so this should find a place in academic and public libraries."
-- THE LIBRARY JOURNAL

"An excellent, provocative and important book."   -- Laurel Speer, poet and critic

"Eva's account is one of fervent desire for peace in a setting of chaos, deprivation and horror... Yet EVA'S WAR is not exclusively about grief and guilt. It is about forgiveness, trust, accomplishment and love of life."
-- Thora Guinn, ALBUQUERQUE PEACE CENTER NEWS

THE TIME DANCER:
A NOVEL OF GYPSY MAGIC
by Zelda Leah Gatuskin

ISBN: 0-938513-12-5 [245 pp. Paper $10]
A romantic tale of time travel, mistaken identities and parallel worlds. Can one really navigate the sea of time? When George Drumm falls in love with the Gypsy Esmarelda, he must learn the secrets of the Spiral Map of Time, or lose her to the future. But the Gypsy is on her own quest. The two leapfrog across the Spiral in search of lost cats, missing satchels and each other, and in the process share glimpses of their magical universe with the residents of the dusty town of Caliente, in the Alternate World.

Novelist and mixed media artist, Zelda Leah Gatuskin, resides in Albuquerque, NM. THE TIME DANCER draws on her work with mandalas and symbols as well as her study of ethnic dance.

"A twisted, clever, spellbinding tale for the 1990's. Gatuskin creates a vivid and bizarre universe, certain to satisfy the appetite of enthusiasts of such authors as Lewis Carroll and J.R.R.Tolkein."
-- Michael Bush, Associate Artistic Director
MANHATTAN THEATRE CLUB, New York City

"Gatuskin weaves a delightfully magical story, which tricked me into thinking she was from another time, or maybe a Gypsy in a past life. I'll never look at my cats the same again."
-- Lisa Law, author, photographer, producer, director
FLASHING ON THE SIXTIES

"THE TIME DANCER is a delightful story -- full of quest, high spirits, memorable characters and thought-provoking ideas. Gatuskin takes an intricate premise, time travel and makes it clear, believable and focused."
-- Suzanne K. Pitré, playwright and author

"I am intrigued. I find particularly fascinating her use of certain shapes to travel time since these shapes are the foundation of this deeply spiritual dance form. As a teacher of Belly Dance and its esoteric significance, I would highly recommend that my students read this magical tale."
-- Swari Hhan, author
BEYOND THE EROTICISM OF BELLY DANCE
BELLY DANCE AS SACRED DANCE

HUNGER IN THE FIRST PERSON SINGULAR
STORIES OF DESIRE AND POWER
Michelle Miller
ISBN: 0-938513-15-X [170 pp. $9.00]

A ghost town hermit desiring renewed human contact begins a journal to record her four years in isolation. A man (her animus?) appears, leaving mysterious and puzzling clues to his presence, and initiating a strange courtship which compels the woman into a profound and bewildering journey of mind, body and spirit.

Subterranean encounters between the sexes move across contemporary American city and desert landscapes.

Michelle Miller is a writer and editor, and an award-winning playwright. She lives in Albuquerque, New Mexico.

WINNER! Zia Award [BEST BOOK by a New Mexico woman writer, 1992]   -- NEW MEXICO PRESS WOMEN

"Michelle Miller goes where woman has not gone before. She has the guts and the imagination to ask our most dangerous questions. Read her -- you won't ever feel as alone again."
-- Sharon Niederman, Arts Editor
THE SANTA FE REPORTER

"Miller's narrator speaks spontaneously in a range of emotions we can feel, hear and experience -- anger, loneliness, humor, longing. Miller crafts a seemingly fantastic experience into one of startling reality, one that dares us to look at our real hungers as women in a world that so readily accepts masks. In these stories, which all deal with some aspect of our instinctual urges, the reader has the opportunity to experience a similar hunger, a "hunger for anything that might happen between people without masks or ritual or fear."
-- BELLES LETTRES

"This is a power piece that goes straight for your emotional and sexual jugular. Miller is an emerging major talent who has here penned that combination of biography, short story and novel all into one trip that examines desire and the need for power. Male and female and place come together. -- BOOK TALK, New Mexico Book League

"Michelle Miller is a high risk writer. She is an experimentalist of the Joyce Carol Oates school, who gambles and gambles big... And when her risks do pay off, they pay big... The personal element given to the story by this confessional diary approach makes it interactive in the strongest sense, trapping the reader in a net of interest.
Eva von Kesselhausen, SMALL PRESS REVIEW

A WORLD FOR THE MEEK
A FANTASY NOVEL
by H. G. Z. Willson
ISBN: 0-938513-01-X [192 pp. $9]

A post-blast life-affirming fantasy, in which the lone survivor finds a baby in the kiva, rears him, loses him, goes Zen-crazy walking from Duke City to the Gulf of California, where he survives a very long time, and finds love and meaning among the dolphins and the octopi. When the dolphins find our Noah, they think they've found a fossil.

This fantasy novel is more in the tradition of *Gulliver's Travels* and *Robinson Crusoe* than the modern interplanetary invasion and star war craze. Here sensuality and curiosity have replaced violence and acquisitiveness. Willson is also the author of *This'll Kill Ya,* a modern anti-censorship fantasy romp.

"Magically written, and full of wisdom." -- BOOKS OF THE SOUTHWEST

"...a magical flower of fantasy...eerie...transcendent. As we contemplate the very real prospect of a devastating near future, Willson's daring meditation through the destruction and out the other end is a wonderful affirmation. It is also an unusual and delightfully rendered story." -- SMALL PRESS REVIEW

"...very readable...really entering a world where the ego is transcended." -- Northrup Frye, author & critic, UNIVERSITY OF TORONTO

"This wistful and eloquent book rivals Miller's CANTICLE FOR LEIBOWITZ. The devastated southwest landscape, and his subsequent idyll on the shores of the Pacific, are both compelling and vivid. This is speculative science fiction at its most tender and hopeful -- and fun to read, too." -- Gene H. Bell-Villada, author & critic, WILLIAMS COLLEGE

"Willson combines mythic material from several traditions: the Biblical Apocalypse, Native American wisdom, and flashes of Zen Buddhism." -- THE BLOOMSBURY REVIEW

"...original and fascinating, surprising and uplifting at once...an exercise in modern mythology, creating something grounded in our world and yet speaking to our problems on a more symbolic level...a good tale about the art of living." -- FACT SHEET FIVE